Mura Dehn

Mura Dehn

*Champion of Black Social Dance and
the Traditional Jazz Dance Company*

Kim Chandler Vaccaro

methuen | drama
LONDON · NEW YORK · OXFORD · NEW DELHI · SYDNEY

METHUEN DRAMA
Bloomsbury Publishing Plc, 50 Bedford Square, London, WC1B 3DP, UK
Bloomsbury Publishing Inc, 1359 Broadway, New York, NY 10018, USA
Bloomsbury Publishing Ireland, 29 Earlsfort Terrace, Dublin 2, D02 AY28, Ireland

BLOOMSBURY, METHUEN DRAMA and the Methuen Drama logo are trademarks of Bloomsbury Publishing Plc

First published in Great Britain 2026

Copyright © Kim Chandler Vaccaro, 2026

Kim Chandler Vaccaro has asserted her right under the Copyright, Designs and Patents Act, 1988, to be identified as Author of this work.

For legal purposes the Note from the Author on p. viii constitute an extension of this copyright page.

Cover design: Ben Anslow
Cover image © New York Public Library

All rights reserved. No part of this publication may be: i) reproduced or transmitted in any form, electronic or mechanical, including photocopying, recording or by means of any information storage or retrieval system without prior permission in writing from the publishers; or ii) used or reproduced in any way for the training, development or operation of artificial intelligence (AI) technologies, including generative AI technologies. The rights holders expressly reserve this publication from the text and data mining exception as per Article 4(3) of the Digital Single Market Directive (EU) 2019/790.

Bloomsbury Publishing Plc does not have any control over, or responsibility for, any third-party websites referred to or in this book. All internet addresses given in this book were correct at the time of going to press. The author and publisher regret any inconvenience caused if addresses have changed or sites have ceased to exist, but can accept no responsibility for any such changes.

A catalogue record for this book is available from the British Library.

Library of Congress Control Number: 2025943292

ISBN: HB: 978-1-3504-2803-4
PB: 978-1-3504-2807-2
ePDF: 978-1-3504-2804-1
eBook: 978-1-3504-2805-8

Typeset by Deanta Global Publishing Services, Chennai, India
Printed and bound in Great Britain

For product safety related questions contact productsafety@bloomsbury.com.

To find out more about our authors and books visit www.bloomsbury.com and sign up for our newsletters.

Contents

A Note from the Author		viii
Introduction: Cakewalk Not Only Moved the Feet, It Moved the World		1
With Both a Spit and a Smile		4
1	Jazz Dance: The Soul Feeling of the Body	7
	The Essence of Cool	9
	Culture as Context	11
	A Living and Contemporary Folk Dance	13
	The Spirit of Swing	14
	The Partnership Was Absolute	15
	Codification and Hybrids	18
	Jazz Tap Dancing	19
2	The Realization of Maria Mura Tsiperovitsch	21
	Art as Direction for Living: Dalcroze, DelSarte, and Commedia Dell'arte	21
	Ellen Tels, the Duncan of Moscow	24
	Adolf Dehn	25
	Bohemian Paris	27
	Marriage Apart	32
	Family	35
3	The Dance Hall, the Dance Stage, and the Academy	39
	Stepping into Another World	40
	Dr. Jazz Cures All Ills	41
	Dancers and Teachers	44
	Early Concerts on New York Stages	48
	Dancing on the Left	52
	The Academy of Swing	56
4	Swingsters, Masters, and Champions	61
	The Dance Hall Takes the Stage	61
	The Masters of Jazz	63

5	Jazz Profound	73
	Ethnography, Inquiry, and Analysis	73
	Journey through the South	75
	Folk Arts as Creative Resistance: Black Awareness in Art	77
	Le Jazz Hot	82
6	*The Spirit Moves*: A Life's Mission	91
	An Epic of Negro Dance	91
	Black American Folk-social Dance 1920–80 on Film	96
	The Cast of *The Spirit Moves*	98
	Volume 1	98
	Volume 2	102
	Volume 2, Part II	105
	Volume 3	106
	Volume 4	106
7	*Rag to Rock*, Section I: The Program and Cast	113
	A Panorama of Company Names	113
	State-sponsored Engagements	115
	Jazz Comes Home	117
	The Program	120
	The Orchestra	122
	Dancers of the Theater	124
	Dancers of the Ballroom	128
7	*Rag to Rock*, Section II: The African Tour	137
	Morocco: Supporting the Mission's "Americana" Program Objectives	138
	Tunisia: Where the Fresh Air Is Mixed with the Smell of Jasmine	141
	Ethiopia: Attended by His Imperial Majesty Emperor Haile Selassie	143
	Somalia: Unselfconscious, Bawdy, Slapstick Humor	145
	Nigeria: Requests for Additional TV and Radio Exposure Too Numerous to Meet	146
	Guinea: A Marvelous Expression of a Dying Art	150
	Senegal and The Gambia: "We Had the Stars and The Moons In Our Eyes"	153
8	The Traditional Jazz Dance Company, 1969–74	157
	Boris	157
	Folder 242	159
	Rock 'n' Roll	168

9	Rhythm: A Driving Force	171
	Sculpted Verse	171
	Film Screenings and Festivals	174
	Herman Dutch Thomas	175
	Rhythm of Words	177
10	Lessons from the Academy	181
	Jazz Scholars, Fellows, and Aficionados	181
	Form, Function, and Characteristics: Resisting a Hierarchal Ladder	182
	A Knowing Body: American Is Part African	184
	Moved by the Spirit	185

Notes	187
Bibliography	225
Index of Mini-Bios	242
Index of Subjects	244

A Note from the Author

Dance is personal, and political. Why political? When Mura Dehn asked tap legend Baby Laurence this question in 1970, he answered: "Because in this society this is what you are involved with. You're involved with economy and politics and it is infiltrated in everything that you do." Reading this and many other interviews of Black dancers in her manuscript and archives deepened my understanding of the sociopolitical and dance milieu of the twentieth century. For that gift, Dehn's and all of the dancers' insights, I am deeply grateful. I am also indebted to my time at Temple University with Sarah Hilsendager, Edrie Ferdun, and Brenda Dixon Gottschild, who helped to open my eyes and change my perspective. My heartfelt thanks also to Allen Blitz for prompting me to agree to Bloomsbury's solicitation to write this book, and to Sally Sommer, Karen Hubbard, Wendy Perron, and Wayne Vaccaro for their encouragement. It could not have happened without the expert assistance of librarians Sarah Fisher (New York Public Library), Casiday Long (University of Arkansas), and Heather Dalal (Rider University), and conversations with Chenault Spence, Eiko, Mark Scherzer, Charles Reinhart, Pryor Dodge, Julie Fraad, David Butts Cairns, Robert White, Mark Kihara, Peter Loggins, and Sylvia Sykes, or my interview with Bob Boross, which was a catalyst for this undertaking. All of my work, research, reading, and writing throughout my entire teaching career was for my students' advantage, though I admit I was at times the foremost beneficiary. Likewise, while this project was for Mura, her dancers, jazz dance aficionados, and posterity, I am deeply moved and grateful for the experience.

Kim Chandler Vaccaro

Introduction

Cakewalk Not Only Moved the Feet, It Moved the World

In 1945 the editor's preface to an article by Mura Dehn in *Dance Magazine* stated: "The name of Mura Dehn may become as important to jazz in dancing as the names of Paul Whitman and Duke Ellington in music."[1] Thirty years later Jennifer Dunning penned, "For many dancegoers, Mura Dehn is known, a little vaguely, as a woman who had something to do with film and black dancers."[2] An extensive search in 2024 reveals her documentation and films are now widely consulted. Those acquainted with her film *The Spirit Moves*, subtitled: *A History of Black Social Dance on Film, 1900–1986*, recognize it as a historic contribution to the documentation of American dance. Her work is used by thousands of contemporary musicians, dancers and scholars, yet her fascinating life story is still unfamiliar. Dehn was independent and fervent, and immersed herself in Black social dance, visiting the Savoy Ballroom in Harlem habitually to experience the phenomenon firsthand. One of Mura's closest friends, Lillian Morrison, told me that when she asked if Mura had read Malcolm X's autobiography, she said, "Not only read it, I'm in it." Malcolm was a dancer and a Savoy aficionado before he was the Muslim minister el-Hajj Malik el-Shabazz. He wrote about an unnamed white woman who came to the ballroom almost every night but would only dance with Black men, and one of them, at times himself, would walk her to the subway.[3] Mura knew he was talking about her as she had danced and walked with him. She was tall, courageous and did what she wanted to do. Jazz became the driving force in her life, and she worked assiduously to document the dance she loved.

The first decades of the twentieth century felt a rhythmic phenomenon sweep the United States, creating new, unique dance and music arising from a distinct American experience. Jazz dance and music were popular/folk/vernacular forms, and continue today as cultural entities that communicate a story of American history. Mura Dehn, dancer, film maker and impresario, recognized the significance of the jazz dance idiom and spent her life researching and proclaiming its importance. She was inclined to view the dance poetically and metaphorically, yet still understood its relation to a new, widespread use and understanding of human movement that embraced both African and European aesthetics.[4] Hence, on the dance that developed at the beginning of jazz, which would become a global dance craze, she declared that "Cakewalk not only moved the feet, it moved the world."[5]

Cakewalk's roots may be traced to the early 1800s on plantations in the southern United States where enslaved Africans would mock the refined manners of slaveholders by imitating and embellishing their minuets and marches done at parties. The dances were adopted and transformed over a period of time, and evolved into contests where the finest strutters, with arched backs and high kicks, were awarded a prize, a cake, for the best "cuttin' of figgers."[6] Whites who either didn't know or didn't care about the derision in turn imitated the new form, a process of continuous interchange and evolution. Migrating from plantations through medicine and tent shows and competitions, cakewalk was later performed to the syncopated rhythms of ragtime in minstrelsy and vaudeville. It gained national popularity by the turn of the century, when Black entertainers Bert Williams and George Walker brought it to Broadway in 1898 for forty weeks. When their musical comedy *Dahomey* played London for seven months in 1903, cakewalk became an international vogue.[7] Dehn interviewed dancer Pepsi Bethel, who said:

> I feel the Cakewalk is the backbone of jazz because it's a dance that is clean and precise as ballet. I found also in the Cakewalk that it don't take a hundred steps to make Cakewalk. It only takes a few—the strut, the high kick, and the quality of the body, an arched back.[8]

In another interview in 1960, Mr. [Leigh] Whipper, President of The Negro Actors Guild, mentioned the *All-American Cakewalk Contest* in 1987 and said: "Cakewalk was the first dance originated by Negroes that was adopted by the white society."[9] Mura Dehn considered cakewalk to be a marker in American dance history. Created by enslaved Black people imitating and refashioning what they observed, it was a clear example of the exchange that took place between Africans, African Americans and the oppressive European Americans. A variation of the cakewalk was performed in every one of her retrospective concerts, and she coined the phrase as a way of encapsulating the process of what happens when cultures meet: the fusion of separate affinities into the creation of new art forms. She believed that African Americans, through jazz dance, changed the way the world experienced rhythm and the dancing body. Though largely marginalized by Eurocentric biases toward art and research, according to Dehn jazz dance was concurrently folk art and high art; it was layered with symbolism and meaning, and provided a forum for its participants to communicate emotions, social commentary, and political statement. Dehn understood this dance to be a mediator of the conditions and hardships acquired through generations of enslavement and racism in the United States, and boldly wrote about it, beginning in the 1930s, when few others were paying attention.

I investigated Mura Dehn's theories in 1994–6, especially on the dance form between the 1920s and 1940s, which she referred to as the "Golden" era of jazz and swing dance.[10] My culminating 1997 dissertation examined jazz dance as a cultural barometer and revealed the body and movement as pivotal in the shaping of history, consciousness and philosophies. As dissertations do, it was weighted with theory, especially pertaining to African and African American aesthetics articulated by Robert Farris Thompson, Brenda Dixon Gottschild, and Kariamu Asante, authors whose work influences contemporary Black performance theorists such as Thomas DeFrantz and Carl Paris. Though Dehn began writing forty years before these scholars, I clarified her work by aligning it with their canons (Thompson), principles (Gottschild), and senses (Asante), and they and their contemporary counterparts are mentioned herein where appropriate. Dehn's opus sits among those of her friends and mentors such as Zora Neale Hurston, Langston Hughes, and Marshall Stearns, all of whom contributed to our understanding of Black dance and arts in America. This current monograph, however, is primarily biographical. It's charge is to uncover what led a white, Russian, Jewish woman to an act of cultural preservation, and serves to credit, name and bring to the fore some of the artists who were the creators and originators of Black social dance during her lifetime. Dehn worked with hundreds of outstanding African American dancers and musicians over her career. Necessarily the scope of this project is limited, so it is focused on those who worked in her Academy of Swing, her film *The Spirit Moves* and her Traditional Jazz Dance Company that toured Africa in 1969. This book begins, then, with a tip of the hat to all of those still unnamed.

Eiko Yamada Otake, of the modern dance duo Eiko and Koma, was a close friend of Dehn who inherited the bulk of her materials and donated a large portion to the New York Public Library Dance Collection at Lincoln Center soon after Dehn's 1987 death, and additional items in 2017. The archive now contains twenty-six boxes of hundreds of articles, notebooks, photographs, documents, programs, manuscripts, and films. The latter, a six-hour exposé of Black social dance styles, including jazz, is considered her most important oeuvre, with literally tens of thousands of views online by early-jazz dance enthusiasts and historians. Those interested in the cakewalk, Lindy hop, swing, blues and bebop have found *The Spirit Moves* invaluable. Esteemed urban dance historian Sally Sommer wrote: "It is also one of our most important dance films, a unique visual record of vernacular jazz dancing, that exuberant heritage of movement that shaped the way we dance, on stage and off."[11] In a letter of support, Professor of Anthropology at Columbia University Alan Lomax penned:

> Americans, especially Black Americans, as well as everyone interested in the history of jazz dance and in Black creative history, owes [sic] a debt to Mura Dehn for the fine work she has done in documenting this tradition while it was at its peak of vigor and beauty. The films she is making will have a permanent place in the history of the American arts.[12]

With Both a Spit and a Smile

The formidable Mura Dehn was complicated and controversial, and led the late dance historian Terry Monaghan to quip she was sometimes mentioned with both a "spit and a smile."[13] While the vast majority of scholars, including Monaghan, give her enormous credit for what she accomplished, she isn't without criticisms for her rhetoric at times, or for phrases that are posthumously challenged as encouraging the Black narrative that shaped the last hundred years in the United States. Some question the legitimacy of a non-Black woman to document Black Dance. Who gets to write about Black dance is a question still grappled with today, especially in the aftermath of Black Lives Matter. The politics of belonging inside or outside a cultural milieu informs this investigation, as well as which narratives are dominant and oppressive, and which critiques are addressed. "Eurocentric" in this text refers to that line of thought which follows the lead of Western Europe and is still a prevalent ideology in the United States, as well as other places. I insist that racism exists, but there is only one human race. I use Black only as an adjective, and African American as a noun; inside quoted material of another scholar, I adhere to their descriptions, with no disrespect intended.

Mura Dehn's partial anonymity in dance scholarship, in a sense her marginalization from the academic arena, was caused by several factors and complicated by a strong personality and her seemingly myopic sense of determination. Dehn, believed many of her friends, could take rejection in a way others couldn't and did what she felt was right, regardless of the consequences. Studying the landscape in which she and her work existed renders apparent that Dehn could not always overcome the racial and cultural barriers of being a white woman in a field dominated by Black artists; her lack of endorsement may have made invisible the work she actually accomplished. This meant not being fully able to get support on various projects, or synergy in some collaborations.[14] The lack of cooperation from some dancers existed, in part, from a history of appropriation and exploitation common in associations between Black artists and white impresarios. Though Dehn herself did not appear to benefit financially from her articles, films, or productions with the dancers, often in relationships of this kind, Black artists were not credited or fairly compensated for their portion of work. This history, and "sensitivity to the fact that as a political group blacks had limited power to appropriate or export any culture, even their own,"[15] may have tainted Dehn's relationships with her dancers. Her manuscripts are dotted with both references to the struggles of her work and her unwavering persistence.

By her own admission, Mura Dehn was not obsessed with the details of grammar; in fact, she described herself as "analphabet"; she loved to philosophize, but was not overly concerned with minutiae.[16] While she chose words eloquently, honestly and with much color, she often missed the fine points of mechanics such as exact spelling or citations and was always a bit self-conscious about her writing. Deciphering her barely legible handwriting and the implied meaning in her verse was extremely difficult as she did not always conform to traditional and linear modes of scholarship and at times her logic was difficult to follow. Determining dates was often done by deduction, for while she was prolific, she was not systematic, and her scrapbooks are filled with magazine and newspaper articles with both the serial titles and dates removed. Stella Snead described her as "loving chaos,"[17] a point alluded to in most of the interviews I conducted. Dehn's range of languages was also a complication: most likely Yiddish-influenced Russian was her first language, German second and French third, and the vast amount of her written material is in English. Handwritten journals and letters would often begin in one language and drift into another, making translation arduous. What was decipherable was put into the order below.

Chapter 1, "Jazz Dance: The Soul Feeling of the Body," *briefly* covers the basics of jazz dance and offers an operational framing in relation to this project; Chapter 2, "The Realization of Maria Mura Tsiperovitsch," assembles the pieces of Dehn's early life in Europe through her own words, programs, newspaper articles and letters to and from her first husband; and Chapter 3, "The Dance Hall, the Dance

Stage and the Academy," depicts the dance scene in New York City and her early choreography. Chapter 4, "Swingsters, Masters and Champions," highlights the most accomplished dancers of the Savoy Ballroom that she presented and filmed; Chapter 5, "Jazz Profound," describes her work as an ethnographer/anthropologist, her travels to where she felt the roots of jazz began and her fourteen-year partnership with class act dance legend James Berry. Her epic film series, *The Spirit Moves,* and the artists involved are covered in Chapter 6, "*The Spirit Moves*: A Life's Mission," and Chapter 7, "*Rag to Rock*," is necessarily split into two sections, the first about the program she developed and its cast, the second detailing their historic tour to Africa in 1969. The post-tour Traditional Jazz Dance Company, the ensemble which danced a panorama of jazz from ragtime to rock 'n' roll with her in New York, Chicago, Mexico, Washington, DC and Africa, is covered in Chapter 8, "The Traditional Dance Company, 1969–74," and Chapter 9, "Rhythm: A Driving Force," focuses on the film festivals where she presented and her final venture into poetry. Chapter 10, "Lessons from the Academy," is a denouement. Trying to present her legacy and the contributions of the artists is a considerable task. The message in a recent Eiko performance—that this is only a sliver of time, an understanding for this moment—provided courage and freedom from craving the absolute.[18] Limitations of space and time largely determined the scope of this offering, but there is so much more to be discovered.

This monograph is actually about Dehn, jazz/social dance, and the Black dancers whose bodies stored cognizance and performed philosophies, conveying sociopolitical histories. Dancers are often second-tiered, or worse, anonymously referred to as the "company." Yet it is their effort and sweat that yield the composition, each work rides on the backs (and feet) of the muse who inspires and assists in every creation. "What African Americans long for is acknowledgment of and respect for, the Black roots of swing dance—in word and in deed," wrote esteemed dance scholar Brenda Dixon Gottschild, "Ownership and entitlement are crucial issues when the stakes in economic profit and artistic recognition are so high."[19] Tap legend Jason Samuel Smith insisted in a lecture in 2023, that Americans are not given full credit for the innovations and creativity they have produced and continue to produce, in which the entire world participates.[20] This work strives to give Mura Dehn *and* the amazing, innovative dancers she worked with that recognition.

1

Jazz Dance

The Soul Feeling of the Body

> *The influence the Negro has exercised on the art of dancing in America is absolute. Throughout the ages the influence of the dance upon music has also been absolute.*
>
> James Weldon Johnson[1]

Mura Dehn first encountered jazz in Russia as a young girl and was drawn to its rhythms; she developed her tastes in Paris, then in New York found all she was yearning for in what she referred to as the "Golden" era of jazz. At that time, from the 1920s to the 1940s, music and dance were inseparable, innovation reigned, and the individual's instinctive response made every dance a new experience. The dance evolved organically at the turn of the twentieth century alongside the music. Today "jazz" has been used to describe the social dances done to jazz music or swing music, much of the dance in musical comedy and theater, and a contemporary concert form encompassing a seemingly infinite variety of steps, attitudes, motivations, and sound accompaniment. The 2014 compilation *Jazz Dance: A History of Its Roots and Branches*[2] found the dance still demoted to a backseat in the high/low art dichotomy, the definition varied according to personal beliefs, and concluded "jazz dance has multiple meanings and styles of expression." This book defers to Dehn's theories which describe jazz as having both African American and European American influences, drawing its kinetic urgency from vernacular dance and current trends, and is driven by a complexity of embodied rhythms, individuality, and improvisation. This description is a recipe with multiple "ingredients," the term borrowed from jazz dancer, and music critic Roger Dodge, who asserts that "the ingredients in an art form are what create the form's significance."[3] The ingredients of jazz dance include the above, plus its roots, the myriad cultural contributions, and the ethos of American society in the twentieth century. Dodge also recognized the importance of improvisation:

> [In] improvisation, in the folk medium, there is vitality, a liveliness and exciting spontaneity which is never present in a set work of art. When warmed up to improvising an artist can do things impossible to recreate even if adequately notated and offered anew for interpretation. It is these very things which give jazz vitality.[4]

Pre-jazz included marching bands in the streets and dance bands in the town squares of New Orleans; often musicians played in both, varying instruments as necessary. At the turn of the twentieth century, New Orleans was a thriving seaport in the shape of a large crescent, which catered to travelers from all over the world. Different languages made conversation and theater obstruse activities, but they could listen to music, and *dance*. There existed a party atmosphere unparalleled by any other city in the United States, an atmosphere that generated much work for musicians—one of the few occupations open to African Americans at the time. The influences on the sound drew from Creole blues, Sousa marches, Joplin rags, music of Mexican brass bands, work songs, church songs, Spanish and French music of the Gulf of Mexico, and indigenous American and African American rhythms.[5] The numerous taverns and dance halls of the cosmopolitan city were filled with Black musicians who played in parade bands, and also accompanied European dances such as the mazurka, schottische, and quadrille. To satisfy the demands of dancers, they combined music from many sources and created new, commanding rhythmic material. Leonard Feather inferred that "Jazz is not Negro, it is segregated Negro," as enslaved Africans were not free to perpetuate their own cultures, and hence merged with those with whom they had contact.[6] Ragtime developed first, and like the earliest jazz reflected the practices of both European Americans (instrumentation, chord progressions, melodic line) and African Americans (improvisations, syncopation, rough timbres, repetition, polyrhythms and call and response), and to a lesser extent, the many other cultures inhabiting the Crescent City.

Jazz was folk music cultivated by the people making it, where they were playing it. It gradually spread and developed by travel and entertainment on Mississippi riverboats at the turn of the century, by the flood of jazz men to Chicago when Storyville, New Orleans closed down in 1918,[7] and by the 1921 boll weevil scourge in the South, when hundreds of thousands of white and Black Americans moved north. The unique conditions that had to exist could not have happened anywhere but in New Orleans,[8] though Duke Ellington made the case that jazz happened once African American rhythms of the South merged with the horns from New Orleans and the strings of the East Coast, via Chicago, in New York; then, and not until then, Ellington felt, was the music jazz.[9]

From the First World War through Prohibition bands were essentially providers of entertainment in cafés and night clubs. During this time collective improvisation by musicians treated ragtime, blues, spirituals, marches, and popular tunes in new and exciting ways, which was widely appealing to young audiences and social dancers.[10] Dodge thought that even up until the mid-1940s most jazz musicians were employed for the purpose of supplying music for dancing.[11] Musicians played, dancers moved, and the music and dance reflected, nurtured, and inspired each other as if the musicians were "reading the dancers' hips," wrote Lorraine Kriegel.[12] Lawrence Lucie, a musician at the Savoy Ballroom, said: "I think jazz music is spiritual and when we'd play, the dancers got a spiritual feeling, and their motion affected the musicians, and made them play better."[13] The constant need for fresh material led to stretching, salvaging, blending, and revising assortments and approaches.[14] In turn, the development of the new sounds motivated the dancers to experiment and modify the movement. Jazz music reached Broadway in 1921, where *Shuffle Along* introduced the new star Josephine Baker, and the Charleston by James P. Johnson was first heard in the all-Black musical *Runnin' Wild* in 1923.[15] When the Savoy Ballroom opened its doors in 1926, New York City was riveted by jazz dance and music. There, as Dehn would later recognize, the music and dance provided Black Americans an avenue into a euphoric state that eluded oppression.

The Essence of Cool

Scholars have identified sensibilities of Black music. Olly Wilson believes there is "a tendency to approach singing or the playing of any instrument in a percussive manner," the performer stressing accents and tension with individual quality rather than fulfilling the written instructions.[16] Dixon Gottschild attests that jazz has the aesthetic of the cool, it is hot, energetic, vital, and at the same time calm and appearing effortless, which Thomas DeFrantz believes is "experienced as pleasurable by actors and witnesses alike." Gottschild also points to principles of jazz which include valuing the individual among the group, improvisation being expected and the body allowed free rein to create, and it is integral to incorporate physical body motion into the music making process. Rhythm and complex counter-rhythms are valued more than the centrality of melody, and isolations and polyrhythms are exhibited in movement. At a recent colloquium in Philadelphia, Gottschild said that African American aesthetics have been "invisibilized," and insisted this information is essential to understanding the culture of the United States.[17] Through jazz these African/African American aesthetics were learnt and changed America's dancing disposition. Mura Dehn witnessed this change and wrote:

> The importance of Jazz lies in the fact that white people absorbed this black contribution as the main element of their own dancing. It marks a new development in the history of Western dance: for the first time in many centuries, it has brought a new approach to rhythm and most important—a new conception of the body.[18]

Wilson wrote: "Although historically American social and political forces have worked to denigrate and exclude African American cultural patterns from the broader society, these attempts have always failed, and cultural interaction more than cultural isolation has characterized the American experience." He went on to explain:

> The colonial practice of allowing Black musicians to perform Euro-American dance and military music, ultimately resulted in reshaping the Euro-American qualities of the music to African American norms. This process of cultural transformation became the salient characteristic of this tradition. The musical forms most often associated with this tradition were pre-existing Euro-American forms, but the significant features of their presentation are Afro-American.[19]

Dehn and the Black artists she worked with were interested in the dancer's ability to get the beat physically. This embodiment of rhythm—when the pulse transcends the cognitive and becomes kinesthetic—was the underlying tenet. Dehn believed jazz dance to be rhythm in motion. Rhythm was the impetus to move; the steps and vocabulary were secondary. "It is essential, therefore, for the jazz master to feel the emotion conveyed by jazz, its rhythms, its spiritual and other connotations," wrote Dehn, "Rhythm produces great excitement which has the effect of making the artist appear 'possessed.'"[20] Beguiled by and completely embodying the beat and sounds was the imperative that defined the form for Dehn. She hints at the depth to which the rhythm has to be ingested, saying, "The movement is just a result, a visible manifestation which takes approximately the same shape each time in execution, once the best solution for a rhythmic pattern is found."[21] Dancer Pepsi Bethel told her: "You don't dismiss music; you listen to it until you feel the erudition."[22] To Dehn the dancer was the physical embodiment of the music manifested in multiple articulations of the torso and extremities. Polyrhythms of African music are analogous to polycentrism of the body, what Gottschild described as a "democracy of body parts"; with multiple centers and use of isolations, each part was liberated to move independently, while the European torso was generally long, monocentered, and erect, retaining its verticality at most times.[23] Dehn wrote and spoke about the use of the torso, describing her partner, Alfred Leagins: "He danced triumphantly erect, always ready, in case the English King should visit The Track" (the nickname of the Savoy Ballroom dance floor). His posture was "perfect,"[24] then he would bound into the air, or sloop, slide, and bend halfway to the floor, exhibiting both European and African corporal attitudes. Gottschild explains in the same books[25] that the aesthetic, political, social, and religious preferences of the first Africans and Europeans in the United States were a study of contrasts that were melded through jazz and swing.

Culture as Context

That dance is the art of the body whose forms and functions are largely culturally determined is primarily responsible for the distinctions between jazz, ballet, modern dance, and other folk forms. Ballet was first a social dance developed in the courts of Europe in the latter part of the sixteenth century and was tied to the aesthetic of those involved in its origination. Those aesthetic values were revealed through the themes and customs enacted on stage, the bodies who performed the dance, the kinds of flora and fauna which appeared regularly, and the associated costuming and music accompaniment.[26] While modern dance and jazz are both phenomena of the twentieth century, modern dance was initially created in the United States and Europe by a group of artists predominantly with European ancestry. Although the work of scholars such as Dixon Gottschild and Susan Spalding[27] helped to illuminate the contributions and accomplishments of African Europeans and African Americans to many European dance forms, ballet and modern dance historically had been heavily weighted with aesthetics that developed from Eurocentric ideals of beauty, taste, and the sacredness of art.

Merleau-Ponty's organization of the body had both felt, internal, subjective aspects and those that were observed, external, or objective. Though all dancers feel their bodies, Dehn's Golden age of jazz/swing emphasized the subjective, aural relationship with movement, while ballet and modern dance the objective or visual.[28] Ballet and modern dance of the early twentieth century employed systems of teaching deliberately designed to exhibit particular, codified, shapes and moves. Themes were expressed through a specified, often recognizable vocabulary, created for display, intended to create the visceral impression through an elicited *visual* impression. Though there is always an interplay between the subjective and the objective bodies, the ideas of display and vocabulary, in contrast to a spontaneous, internal reaction to rhythm and sound, were central to the early distinction between ballet, modern, and jazz dance. Ballet's codified vocabulary was shaped by the choreographer and fulfilled by the dancer to communicate an idea. A trademark of Modern dance has always been in the openness of its position, with the choreographer free to invent the vocabulary needed to fulfill the sentiment of the dance. Here too, however, while the dance could be rhythmic and motivated from an internal orientation, a central ideology existed in the invention, retention, then display of movement material.

According to Dehn, jazz dance emerged from an *aural* locale and stressed the experience of the dancer or the felt, subjective encountering as privileged over visual or objective aspects. Jazz dance, according to Dehn, placed its greatest emphasis on the response of the human figure to solve a rhythmic puzzle; the steps and vocabulary emerged as an answer to that puzzle. The dance and the music were more than partners, they were different modalities for the same inspiration, she wrote: "[Jazz dancers] dance as much for the ear as for the eye."[29] The movement begins as a subjective response, and is dominated, determined, and driven by a rhythmic imperative. The movement is then perpetuated and sustained by improvisation and a flair toward individuality, characteristics that African Americans brought to the form, distinguished from the corps of ballerinas who strove to execute body lines and designs, or the modern dancer's emulation of the choreographer's ideal. These distinctions among ballet, modern, and jazz dance were clearly more discernible in the early part of the century than the latter. By the 1950s and 1960s the impact the forms had on each other began to escalate, and post-modern, contemporary ballet and jazz dancers both blended and opened aesthetic boundaries.

Jazz absorbed characteristics representative of many cultures: the contributions of the Africanist body attitudes—the embrace of improvisation, individuality, and rhythmic propensity—blended with European dance and music forms. The combination produced a uniquely American art. "If we're talking about American dance," Melanie George told the *Observer*, "jazz is our most indigenous postcolonial form. Jazz could only have happened in the United

States. . . . And it forms the foundation of what we know not only about social dancing in our country but also theatrical dancing.[30]

A Living and Contemporary Folk Dance

Benny Goodman said that "[jazz] is one of our most original contributions to twentieth-century culture and the 'real folk music' of our country."[31] The music stemmed from a specific social environment in which a group of people developed highly distinct cultural traits. The development was African-based yet adapted to a particular situation. It is intriguing to compare other folk dance forms which originated from diasporic African and European fusions, such as the samba and tango, with jazz dance. All three share a legacy of colonialization and slaveocracy, but in different environments they developed their own unique sounds and dances. Within all of these forms, however, is not only "the will to persevere, but also a spiritual yearning emboldened by struggles."[32] Spirituality, explains Michael Ventura, emanates from the metaphysical content in African-based art forms.[33] Jazz allowed the dancing body to simultaneously harbor both the sacred and the popular/folk/secular.

Due to its relationship with folk, popular, social, and commercial dance, and its influence of African Americans, historically the original jazz dance was a low priority for research. Jazz dance made appearances on the concert stage during Dehn's time, but most often its associations placed it at the nether end of a high/low art dichotomy. The source material was found in dance halls, night clubs, and on the streets; and, until the late twentieth century, popular art and folk art were considered apart from and below the art of European theatrical dance and visual art forms. The education of popular and folk artists was not considered formalized and was therefore substandard, the forms themselves undeserving of conventional study. "The demeaning and narrow viewpoints towards African Americans that were indisputably present in the early part of the 20th century were aligned with the Eurocentric bias present in educational institutions,"[34] which held the art form at bay from scholarly investigations.

Mura Dehn resided outside of mainstream academia and differed significantly; she thought social and vernacular dance forms could be revelatory, transformative, a measure of society, and emblematic of the culture in which they exist.[35] Folk art history and art artifacts further the ideological foundations of a society as art is a history of how humanity feels and dance the embodiment of history. Working in the Black cultural milieu of New York City and sensing a call of importance larger than her own performing career, Dehn dedicated her life to the documentation of what she called a "living, contemporary folk dance."[36] Her literary, dance, and film works reveal jazz dance as a creative pathway for African Americans that both gave shape to philosophies and provided a vehicle for expressing them. Contextualization is key; when an object is examined in relation to the environment in which it exists, the rationale that separates high and folk arts is exposed as an elitist misunderstanding. Benny Goodman stated that jazz had been ignored or looked down upon with condescension by those who were unwilling to accept all of the contemporary art forms on an aesthetic level.[37] Dehn thought jazz was America's first folk dance and a vehicle for expression, resistance, transformation, and bliss, the same as any other high art, and deserving of study and recognition.

The Spirit of Swing

Through her study of African American culture, Dehn came to be moved by a spirit she recognized in the liberating energy of rhythm. In this text "rhythm" refers to the patterns produced by the alternation of stress, duration or pitch; the presence or lack of expression; the distribution and accents of sounds; and regularity and differentiation of breath, of pulse, or of tides, as the patterns in nature or the course of events.[38] Swing, an important characteristic of jazz, has several connotations. It can refer to an era in jazz history, an element of rhythm, or a manner of playing music or dancing. The Swing Era (mid 1920s–mid-1940s) refers to the years during which popular music took on a steady, danceable beat, driving a generation to dance to the music of big band sound.[39] Some are happy to use the terms interchangeably, citing swing as jazz and jazz as swing,[40] but swing as a style is characteristic of the jazz represented by bands such as Fletcher Henderson's, Duke Ellington's and Harry James', to name only a few, and the dancing done to that style of music.[41] As a rhythmic concept, swing has an abundance of syncopated rhythms and swung eighth-note patterns. Though difficult to notate, according to Gridley, the patterns seem to fall somewhere "between a tied eighth-note figure and a sequence of eighth notes having identical durations."[42] The desired choice of duration on each note depends on the band, the musician, and style of the arrangement. While no one has succeeded in wholly defining swing, Stanley Dance said, for most people "It is an exhilarating rhythmic feeling around a fundamental pulse that suggests but does not actually realize—a quickening of tempo . . . in essence swing bears a close relationship to physical movement," especially to dancing.[43]

If music or dance is said to have swing, it has an undeniable rhythmic pull. The manner in which it is performed has a "specific type of accentuation and inflection" and "forward-propelling directionality with which the notes (or steps) linked swing together.[44] The Lindy hop was a perfect example of music and dance as equivalents. Gottschild relates that the embodiment of sound had also been evident in cakewalk and in the Charleston, but the big band sound of the era was brought to life by the motion of the Lindy. She wrote:

> The Lindy was an innovative means of making dance the visual equivalent of this music. . . . the Lindy (and the other swing-era dance form, rhythm tap dancing) uses arranged structures and improvisation as equal partners. . . . Lindy is music in motion, brought to life by the big band sound of the era. The "swing" in the Lindy had a lot to do with the dancers utilizing their bodies like finely tuned instruments, adding counterpoint and sophisticated rhythmic variations to their movement phrases, allowing the spectator to see swing as well as hear it.[45]

Gottschild then calls on us to correct the historical record on swing culture and give respect and credit by knowing where the "swing" in swing comes from, namely from the aesthetics of the African Americans living and creating it in the ballrooms of Harlem. The main vehicle for swing music, the big bands found in large dance halls and hotels, attracted millions of dancers nationwide. With the growth of big bands came an increase in the use of written arrangements; although improvisation still existed, musicians had to learn to read and write jazz music to have enough material on hand for a large repertory. Dehn and others professed that it was during this time that dancers and musicians shared the most exciting and lucrative partnership: driving each other to continuously invent rhythmic creations suitable for dancing.

The Partnership Was Absolute

To Dehn, jazz dancers were also musicians:

> He does not think in patterns of shapes, he thinks in patterns of rhythm. . . . It is hard to say whether it is the musicians or the dancers that bring about the change in the dance desire. A jazz band playing without dancers for a long time is apt to lose its rhythmic dynamics. . . . I profoundly believe that the jazz musician needs the dancer as much as the dancer needs the musician. When these two are together jazz is in its best and greatest form.[46]

Dehn's friend and occasional collaborator Marshall Stearns was founder and director of the Institute of Jazz Studies. He believed that great musicians inspired great dancers, and likewise dancers inspired musicians: "Indeed one of the reasons for the development of great big-band jazz at the Savoy [Ballroom in Harlem] was the presence of great dancers." He quoted Lester "Prez" Young of the Count Basie band as saying: "The rhythm of the dancers comes back to you when you are playing"; the partnership of the music and dance was absolute.[47] Dehn believed the music and dance were inseparable: "[The dancer] must also understand its relation to jazz music," wrote Dehn, "Both dancers and musicians receive their primary impetus from rhythm.[48] In an article she wrote for the *Jazz Record* in 1947 she states that an audience which does not want to dance to true jazz has somehow lost its vital and organic connection with that music.[49] Lorraine Kriegel thought that in indefinable, usually nonverbal ways, dancers guided early musicians toward the discovery of swing.[50] Dizzy Gillespie's memoir *To Be or Not . . . to Bop* claims that "jazz music was invented for people to dance to! So, when you play jazz and people don't feel like dancing or moving the feet, you're getting away from the idea of the music."[51] He espoused a reciprocal relationship, advising never to lose that feeling of somebody wanting to dance, believing it to be one characteristic of the music. "You wanna dance when you listen to our music because it transmits the feeling of rhythm."[52] Duke Ellington expressed similar thoughts, saying: "The reason Chick Webb had such control, such command of his audiences at the Savoy Ballroom, was because he was always in communication with the dancers and felt it the way they did."[53]

From the turn of the century through the late 1940s jazz dance and music were inextricably linked by a common name, common heritage and common characteristics. They have developed independently since then, but retain important, intrinsic, similar ingredients, ingredients which set them apart from other music and dance forms. Jazz must also be approached emotionally or spiritually as a subjective, felt experience and a sonority of phrasing which mirrors the individuality of the performer:

> And a ballroom dancer from Harlem in the 30's sums up the meaning of jazz: jazz is the soul feeling of the body, it comes without a thought. . . . It comes from you, yourself. It comes from a surrounding, a feeling from the environment that you are in, and through that environment you do not pick anything in particular, but from it you naturally find your own movements, because you are inspired, because you never know what the movements are going to be until it happens.[54]

The "soul feeling" of the body suggests a subjective relationship to the movement, a relationship that Dehn felt was initiated and motivated by an organic response to the rhythms as they exist at that time. Gottschild wrote in 2003:

> For African American performers, soul is the nitty-gritty personification of the energy and force that it takes to be black and survive. Rhythm, and the many textures and meanings implied in the concept (percussive drive, pulse, breath, and heartbeat, for example), plays a pivotal role in generating and disseminating soul power. Soul is about going in deep, gettin' down: Soul is the digger. Soul leads to spirit by means of those characteristics that are fundamental to the Africanist aesthetic: radical juxtaposition of unanticipated elements; call and response; polyphony and syncopation; ephebic energy; and the balance between hot and cool, dubbed 'the aesthetic of the cool.'[55]

By the Second World War, however, the connection between jazz music and jazz dance began to shift. Dehn lamented: "In the 40's just when this galloping festivity is at its zenith—the War stops it cold. It takes the ablest dancers. The dance hall is orphaned without its leaders."[56] The war not only drafted dancers, band players, and leaders, but also forced such an economic shift that many big dance bands could not afford to travel and tour. In addition, a crippling 20 percent "entertainment tax" on businesses with dancefloors sharply curtailed dance as a popular form of recreation.[57] Most dance halls covered up their floors with tables and chairs, and bands were reduced to a fraction of the size. A different attitude emerged within dance and music.

In 1945–6 music began to assert itself, and smaller combos played jazz with superb improvisation but with rhythms that were increasingly complex and diverse. Dehn felt that the bebop musicians were ahead of the dancers in their search for new forms. In diverging from the old jazz formula of a steady, danceable beat, the musicians no longer looked to the dancers for inspiration and tempi. In what she termed a "furious assault of saxophone virtuosity the musician seemed to disregard" the dancer.[58] The Lindy, done so eloquently and joyously, gave way to the more disjointed and apathetic quality of bebop. Dehn described the dance as hesitating, yet tantalizing, with a preoccupation to break up the beat. She felt the position of the body to be nonchalant and deliberately negligent, though still reacting to the contemporary ethos.[59] With bebop, jazz began to be more than just functional music for dancing; it became concert music as well. Unlike European music, it still had rhythm at its core rather than melody or harmony; unlike African music, this jazz was to listen to rather than dance to. The listener's job of creation was to "join into the musician's trance."[60] Even as swing styles continued, after Benny Goodman played Carnegie Hall in 1938 some jazz began to progress toward art-music. Feather marks the shift a decade or so later, believing that during the inaugural half-century jazz was restricted to the role of utilitarianism, and not until the early 1950s did jazz reach the concert hall.[61] By 1960 it was no longer looked upon as merely dance music, but as an art form in and of itself.[62] Notably, it was at this point that in-depth inquiry into jazz music began to emerge, though, except for a few writers like Dehn, investigations into jazz dance lagged far behind.

Mainstream social dance experienced a ten-year lull in comparison to the activity of the previous decades, though cabaret parties, rent parties, and block parties were frequent dance events in the African American community.[63] By the time European Americans had rediscovered dance in the late 1950s, they were lured by the driving, yet less complicated sounds of rock 'n' roll. Whatever relationship jazz music had with social dance was dismantled. The swing dance revival that began in the early 1980s and exists worldwide today revitalized the dance/music partnership, and many dancers craving the original connections have brought the forms back together. However, it is as common to find "jazz" dancers and choreographers using many varieties of music for accompaniment as it is for them to use jazz music, with the most contemporary sounds being the most common. Jazz music is no longer only a form with an incomparable beat designed to dance to, and jazz dance is a hybrid of the original vernacular phenomenon, no longer only a response to jazz/swing music.

Codification and Hybrids

By the late 1940s influences affecting jazz dance included the theater, modern dance, ballet, ballroom and tap, and many forms of dance not indigenous to the United States, such as Latin dances and those of India. Jazz hybrids developed with formalized classes; the teachers' objectives were to train dancers, and improvisation took a back seat to imitation. African American dance characteristics such as individuality began to wane, while new emphasis was placed on technical achievements, and improvisation gave way to structured classes. Since jazz was the predominant dance form used in the theater, landing a job on Broadway or in films often meant developing a "jazzy" prowess, and from New York to Chicago to Los Angeles students flocked to jazz dance classes for training. These classes were developed by teachers who injected some of the objective aspects of ballet and modern dance, along with other elements, into the jazz dance form. The resultant hybrids retained a connection to rhythm but were generally concerned with an external viewing of the movement. Moving from the motivation of the rhythm, individuality, and improvisation, aspects which some, such as Dodge and Dehn, felt were important became secondary considerations. Dodge lamented:

> while Lindy Hoppers stood on the sidelines, a new breed of dancer, fortified with ballet and modern dance training, took over show business and danced to some form of jazz music. . . . The new dance has none of the style, refined or not, of the [Negro] dance. With its few movements derived from jazz it became a choreographer's idea of what dancers with ballet and modern training should do to jazz.[64]

Due to the efforts of magnetic teachers such as Jack Cole, Luigi and Gus Giordano, as well as those of Matt Mattox, Alvin Ailey, and Katherine Dunham, many different techniques of jazz, modeled after the teaching styles of their inventors and codified into recognizable vocabulary, became extremely popular. Though Ailey and Dunham felt reluctant to limit their art as jazz dance, both developed codified systems of dance which included variable proportions of jazz, modern dance, ballet, and traditional dances of Africa. This codification, a first step in the objectification of a dance form, is very much a European propensity—similar to the documentation found in academia, abetting the previous argument for the lack of jazz dance research. Until it became codifiable, research was at best problematic. Hybrid forms of jazz dance developed, still drawing from social and vernacular material, continuing to be shaped and influenced by Black music, social dance, and artists, but largely commercialized and marketed by the whites, with objective aspects of the dance often overshadowing the subjective. Literally thousands of studios—with tens of thousands of dancers worldwide—offered descendant, hybrid approaches. Authentic/vernacular/swing jazz dance, however, with the compulsory ingredients, has crept back into fashion in the last two decades, and is seen in the worldwide swing dance revival, increasingly on the concert stage, and in academic research.

Jazz Tap Dancing

The jazz Dehn fell in love with had a historical legacy dating back to minstrelsy. She did not believe tap to be of the masses, so not a folk form, and did not combine tap and jazz in her discussions, though tap dancers often performed with her company. Dehn sought information from the originators themselves; over the course of forty years she interviewed many dozens of dancers and recorded their narratives. Tap dance legend Baby Laurence had this to say when asked about its origins:

> The metal plates in tap shoes came from King Rastus Brown. It was made by blacksmiths who used to make horseshoes. These were small metal discs. Tap dancing is now very much advanced in comparison with old times. I would rather work with patterns or situations of rhythm that I am used to, then to put taps to other modes of rhythm, because I like to experiment with sound—pure unadulterated sound. That is what I always have been involved with. I dance primary for the ear. . . . My style is mostly oral—it is humorous sometimes. Tap dancing is percussion—it's like drums. I was influenced by Art Tatum and Charlie Parker merely because they were articulate rhythm masters—so flawless. Tap dancing is definitely percussion. In fact, in the old days of Charlie Parker and Dizzy Gillespie—I used to carry my dancing shoes in the trumpet case and take it out on the stage—like any other musician.[65]

When she asked whether it was an inherent (negro) form of dance, or was it appropriated from the white dancers, he replied:

> It's a combination. Because the "Jazz tap dancing" started in this country. You can always say in reference to African heritage we had the rhythm. But the movements and the actual execution is involved, it is a mesh of Irish step dancing, English interpretation, Scotch, European clog dancing because the negro people that started to get a feeling for this type of dancing got it from watching the people on the plantation when they had parties. They watch them and mimic them—the same as Jazz started. They brought rhythm that made it jazz. They mimicked the sound of tap and what they heard them do—and from that extended into a thing that became Negroid.[66]

Multitudes of jazz dancers filled the dance halls, while a comparatively smaller number of tap dancers were on the side or in the backrooms competing, inventing, and sharing, and often on stages with bands in theaters—different forms, but aligned through the attachment to jazz music and Afro and Euro affinities, mimicking, blending, and originating new sounds. Dehn believed the Black, social, folk dance she witnessed became jazz, blues, bebop, rock 'n' roll, then break dancing. Her entrance into the forms was always through her lived experience, the artists, the folks, folklore, the churches, and the embodiment of social comment and rhythm. The latter she first found as a young girl in Odessa.

2

The Realization of Maria Mura Tsiperovitsch

There was a tremendous desire to step out of harmony, to step into some kind of a freedom.[1]

Art as Direction for Living: Dalcroze, DelSarte, and Commedia Dell'arte

Mura Dehn wrote constantly and kept even scraps of paper with notes on them, yet mysteriously her collection at the New York Public Library (NYPL) does not hold a diary, passport, or birth certificate. Dehn's life history is created here through her work as expressed in her concerts, presentations, papers, manuscript, articles, poetry, and films. This sketch is drawn from the clues and fragments found in her archives at the NYPL, supplemented by letters from her first husband's collection at the Smithsonian Institution's Archives of American Art, and conversations with those who knew her. Her evolution was due to creative avant-garde schools in Odessa, training in the arts in Vienna, and living and performing in bohemian Paris, though it continued through the very end of her life in New York.

Maria Mura Tsiperovitsch was born on October 7, 1902 in Kherson, then a part of the Russian Empire, now a part of Ukraine.[2] Odessa was the fourth-largest city in the empire at the time, with a third of its total Jewish inhabitants working mostly as artisans and middlemen in its neighborhoods and suburbs. It was a free port (exempt from taxes) with many cafés, teahouses, and restaurants that attracted wealthy foreign businessmen. The multilingual/multiethnic population of Odessa was made up of Russians, Germans, Italians, Greeks, Poles, Turks, and French. There the cafés were centers of Jewish life, culture, and intellectual creativity. Yiddish Theater flourished during this time, nurtured by the freedoms of modern, creative café-spaces.[3] Dehn's friends recalled she had a great family life and adored her father, brother, and mother.[4] Her mother, named Fanny and nicknamed Chaprik, insisted on creative education, so free schools of dance and theater were chosen, like those adhering to the imaginative aspirations of François Delsarte. Mura's first dancing lessons were at the Odessa Dalcroze Institute, and her theatrical training was in commedia Dell'arte with Professor Niklashevsky. The schools strove to develop creative and intellectual freedom, control, and balance through music, dancing, and theatre, but entailed philosophies that were larger than dance alone. All three methods espoused theories that could be applied as directions for living.[5]

François Delsarte (1811–1871) was unsatisfied with the subjective and posed style of acting taught at the Paris Conservatory, so began a study of how humans actually moved. In everyday places such as churches, parks, cafés, and even disaster scenes, he examined movement dynamics, voice, and breath, and their roles as purveyors of human expression. He developed a "Science of Applied Aesthetics" which was also the method used to establish the first acting school in America; this led to an approach called "aesthetic calisthenics," which was somewhere between gymnastics and creative dance.[6] Lauded by scientists, religious scholars, musicians, artists, and yogis, the Delsarte method seemed like "a window into the deeper mysteries of art."[7] At the end of the nineteenth century Delsarte's teachings were very much in vogue, and his understanding of the relationship between inner experience and physical manifestation could guide one in developing body awareness for any aesthetic practice, general health, or education in a broad sense, such as decorating your home. Delsarte, Dehn said, taught her the laws of expressive gesture. The Delsartian method helped one to develop freedom and relaxation of every part of the body, an aspect of jazz dance that Dehn talked about frequently.

Dehn also felt that the Dalcroze rhythmic gymnastics she studied at the gymnasium in Odessa from 1914 to 1916 directly influenced her fascination with jazz dance. Émile Jacques-Dalcroze was considered a major influence on many musicians and dancers at the turn of the century. As a music composition teacher in Vienna, he was dissatisfied with his inability to guide his students toward internalizing rhythm and musical movement. He developed an education system designed to foster relationships between rhythm and human motion, creating bodily exercises to accentuate rhythmic awareness and musical creativity.[8] His system, most often referred to as Eurhythmics, influenced musicians, composers, and dancers in the late nineteenth and early twentieth centuries as the proponents of his system spread its teachings throughout Europe, Russia, and the United States.

Maria Kandilakis interviewed Dehn in 1973 and asked her about the kind of training she had had that would give her such perception or feeling for the Black folk artist. She replied: "Well, I came from Russia . . . [and studied] Dalcroze which is interested in rhythm mostly in improvisational movement. Dalcroze was very important at that time, his style was the rhythmic gymnastics and it permeated all the schools.[9] In the same interview Dehn explains that jazz was popular in Europe before the First World War and that she became aware of it at age twelve through the dancing of Irene and Vernon Castle, who toured Russia, and her mother, who had taught her a cakewalk. Dehn claimed to know all of the dances which came from the Americas (North and South) which were Black-influenced or Black re-creations of white forms, and the moment the Blacks started to create social dances out of European dances, it became contagious:

> Jazz influence was felt in Europe . . . I mean a whole new rhythm spread in Europe . . . apparently there was a desire for a more pronounced (rhythm) with dance of a different quality than the European dances. Polka has rhythm, and Mazurka has rhythm, and Waltz is with them, but somehow it was enchanting to the Europeans to be under the spell of that new music.[10]

Dehn was also schooled in commedia Dell'arte, a theatrical form characterized by improvised dialogue and a cast of colorful stock characters that emerged in northern Italy in the fifteenth century and rapidly gained popularity throughout Europe. At its pinnacle, plays of the commedia Dell'arte (literally, "comedy of artists") were performed in the open air by itinerant troupes of players. Commedia Dell'arte was often a familiar plot or story with which the actors improvised and developed dialogue. Performances were personalized to particular audiences—commenting on contemporary politics that would otherwise be censored—with satire and humor, and stock characters each had distinct sets of attributes that became their trademarks. Dehn studied commedia Dell'arte from 1918 to 1919 with Professor Niklashevsky. She felt that this theater form was reincarnated in the theatrical tradition of African Americans. She drew links between the theater of antiquity and jazz dance by noting the similarities between the African American players and the jesters of years past, most notably in their use of improvisation and satire:

> I entered the theatre and dance era in Europe, which rediscovered rhythm, natural movement in proposition, and folk humor. It was researched in the museums, in books in order to connect it with the new theater . . . how much more simpler and natural it was in the dances of the American [blacks]. . . .

> In the Savoy ballroom rhythm and freedom of movement, improvisation and humor were alive like in the times of the Dionysian festival and Italian comedy, satyrs and harlequins.[11]

A childhood filled with education and encounters in rhythm, expression, movement improvisation, satire, and wit, it was multiethnic, multilingual, creative, and was experienced in cafés, schools, and theaters. These influences—the rhythmic sensibilities of Dalcroze, and the creative freedom they and Delsarte espoused, together with study in a historical "theater of the people" which dealt with improvisation and social commentary—prepared Dehn for the life's mission she was to discover in the United States. Expressive movement, juxtaposition, individuality, humor, improvisation, all in rhythm, are ingredients of the Lindy and swing/jazz dance.

At the turn of the nineteenth century Odessa also had upsurges of anti-Jewish violence following the assassination of Tsar Alexander II. Anti-Semitism and political tension increased, and during one pogrom at least 400 Jews were killed. Jewish schools, synagogues, and other religious groups, including nearly all non-Bolshevik cultural institutions, were closed. The political state forced the Tsiperovitsch family to flee on an English ship in 1920; the family escaped via Constantinople, Sofia, and Budapest to Vienna.[12] David Tsiperovitsch, Mura Dehn's father, had completed his studies in engineering at the Institute of Technology in Kharkov, and worked for British Shipping company in Odessa before the revolution that perhaps enabled the family passage.[13] His visa to London and a note from the British consulate imply that the family was safely out of Russia (which must have occurred in haste as they even forgot their passports). Letters written ahead of their departure from Russia indicate that Tsiperovitsch was looking for and found work in London.[14]

Ellen Tels, the Duncan of Moscow

While David and brother Boris went on to London, mother and daughter stayed in Vienna, and Mura was advised by a mentor named Novikoff to study at the Academy of Arts with director Ellen Tels (Elena Rabeneck). Tels had previously been associated with Stanislavski at the Moscow Art Theatre, where she was dance director.[15] Tels' *dance plastique* absorbed the intricacy of ballet and was inspired by Isadora Duncan. Dehns tenure at the academy lasted four years, during which time she performed dances to classical music which could be described as Duncan-esque in style. Dehn wrote that Tels was the Isadora Duncan of Moscow, but being Russian, never completely dismissed ballet, so convinced Dehn to take classes with Léonide Massine in London, Lyubov Yegorova in Paris, and later with Pierre Vladimiroff in New York.[16] Numerous concert programs in Dehn's Collection reveal she danced in a dozen concerts with Tels in 1922 and 1923 using various spellings of her name. April 20 and 22 were at the Grosser Konzerthaus-Saal, her name listed among the other dancers as Maria Ziperowitz. April 28 and 29 were at the Tanz Abend, where her last name read Ziperowitsch, June 10 at the Buggarten in Moscow, again under Ziperowitz, and as Premiere Danseuse at the Volks Opera in Vienna. On October 27 and 28 she was back at the Grosser Konzerthaus-Saal as Mura Ziperowitsch.[17]

Isadora Duncan had stunned the world with her natural, rhythmic interpretations of music, and her audiences experienced movement on a new level. She was inspired by nature, classical music, and sculpture, but in a revolt against the rigid rules of ballet and Victorian society, took off her shoes and corsets, expressing women's freedom and individuality. It is important to note that Duncan scorned what she called the "sensual convulsions of the [Negro]" and danced with the erect, long torso thought beautiful by Eurocentric standards; energy that lived in the hips and spine would proceed through "proper" channels—channels that were well defined outside of the dance and the body.[18] Duncan, however, also felt that as long as people danced in rhythm, the form and design did not matter, but one must perfectly correspond to the other. Her conception of rhythm included variety, stillness, and movement, and dynamic shadings. Mura was trained in this style, dancing mostly to European classical music in Tels' ensembles, and finding yet another way to experience rhythm. After one of the concerts in the winter of 1922 at the Opera in Vienna,[19] while attending a gala given for the artists, Mura met Adolf Dehn, who was to become her first husband, later known as one of America's noted lithographers.

Adolf Dehn

Born in 1895 in Waterville, Minnesota, Adolf Dehn began creating artwork at the age of six. He was eventually known for both "his technical skills and his high-spirited, droll depictions of human foibles," and worked in the American art movements such as regionalism, social realism, and caricature.[20] Dehn's drawings, lithographs, and watercolors satirically chronicled the social and political milieu of first Germany, then Paris, then America, as well as poetic landscapes, many of which depicted the rolling hills and farmlands of his native Midwest.[21] His life work is well represented in his collection at the Smithsonian Institution, which houses his extensive collection of correspondence, exhibition announcements, scrapbooks, artwork, photographs, and legal documents. The latter contain an affidavit signed by Dehn in connection with his 1926 marriage to Mura Dehn (neé Tsiperovitch).[22]

Adolf's mother was a pacifist, socialist, and feminist, while his father, not wanting to depend on anyone, was a free-thinker who made a living as a hunter and trapper. Adolf was exposed to a wide range of radical thinking while growing up, his parents instilled in him a suspicion of conventional forms of authority, and his artistic prowess was encouraged.[23] Given this background, it is not surprising that Dehn became known for his political consciousness and independent-mindedness as an artist, though his left leanings never hardened into stiff ideology and he remained a cautious radical, with art meaning more to him than politics.[24] After graduating as valedictorian from Waterville High School, Dehn attended the Minneapolis School of Art from 1914 to 1917, whose character strongly reflected that of its director, "Munich-trained Robert Kohler, an artistic conservative but a social radical.[25] When drafted in 1918, Dehn stated that he was a conscientious objector, a claim that landed him in the army guardhouse for five months, though his congenial nature saved him from the harassment suffered by other conscientious objectors.[26]

Dehn left for Europe after he was released from the army in 1921. He spoke fluent German, the language of his parents, so he gravitated first to Vienna, then Berlin, and eventually to Paris. In Vienna, he said: "There I learned about living. It was a time, of course, when living in Vienna was fabulously cheap, very cheap and I could live well."[27] Most of Europe after the First World War had been overwhelmed by inflation, poverty, and financial collapse, which brought destitution to the middle and working classes. Dividends and wages had depreciated and unemployment was rampant, so prices were low and people lived on very little. He enjoyed the bohemian lifestyle as an artist and rambled with friends throughout the cities and mountain areas of Europe, becoming part of a group of expatriate intellectuals and artists, including Andrée Ruellan, Gertrude Stein, and e.e. cummings.[28] They and other cosmopolitan artists, such as Jules Pascin, Guy Pène du Bois, and the Dada painter George Grosz would become his compatriots who poked fun at the international bourgeoisie, and established a "distinctive culture in which new modes of artistic expression were tied to a deep-rooted skepticism about traditional Victorian values."[29] Dehn got by selling his drawings and lithographs that satirized the high society and decadence of the 1920s. He also became friends with Scofield Thayer, editor of *The Dial*, and took a job as his magazine illustrator. Thayer, who was in analysis under Sigmund Freud at the time, also involved Dehn in several publication schemes that helped to modestly support the artist for several years. Thayer also introduced Dehn to many artists, including e.e. cummings.[30] Adolf developed into an expressionist printmaker with passions for nature and satire.[31]

There are folders of mostly undated letters in Adolf's collection written in German/English from the "beautiful, exotic, artistic" nineteen-year-old Mura Tsiperovitsch, whom Dehn met at a ball following one of her performances with Tels.[32] He immediately fell head over heels for her, and though seven years younger, she quickly became his constant companion and lover.[33] "A truly exotic creature," with Russian origins and dramatic and dancing talents, men raved about her sensational beauty, which produced an almost "universally stunning effect upon males."[34] In February of 1922 Adolf wrote in a letter to his former girlfriend Wanda Gag that he was "madly in love" with Ziperovitch. "I guessed her age at 23 but she is only 19. She has an all-around knowledge that perhaps is more theoretical and intuitive than from experience. Along with her wisdom she is deliciously naïve." Adams notes that when reading the letters, "it's hard to distill any coherent narrative, though the flow of words traces a sort of seesaw pattern of flirting and breaking up."[35] Mura and Adolf courted for four years, traveling often between London, Paris, and Vienna.

Mura finished the Academy of Arts in Vienna in 1923 and became a teaching assistant for Tels. In January of that year she graced the cover of the illustrated monthly *Kunst and Lëben* magazine, and danced with Tels in concert at the Grosser Konzerthaus-Saal as Mura Ziperowitsch. In June Mura Zipero*vitsch* shared a program (still all classical music) with Maru Kossjera at the Vindobona in Germany. Her name on the program was larger and placed higher when she headlined a concert in 1924 at Saal der Session, where she again used the name Mura Ziperowitsch, and later that year began a solo concert dance tour to Paris, Nice, Cannes, Juar-les-Pins, Alz-les-Bains, and Brides-les-Bains.[36]

Bohemian Paris

During the first years in Vienna and Berlin, Adolf had plenty of work to enable him to travel around Europe, attending the opera and hiking in the Austrian Alps with Mura and friends.[37] Berlin had become an ultra-modern metropolis, a melting pot of Eastern Europe for the thousands fleeing Russia, with a rambunctious and seamy nightlife. Mura recalled: "there were few appetites that could not be satisfied in Berlin." Adolf, even when Mura was not there, partook in the life and found subjects to sketch in the "lesbians, the society parties, and the dissolute club patrons."[38] The operas also provided fodder for Dehn's drawings, and the singers, dancers, and Mura were often his inspirations. Throughout this time in Europe, Adolf Dehn was in contact with many other notable intellectuals, performers, and illustrators of the time, including Josephine Baker, Kurt Weill, and Leo Stein.[39] When in Paris, Mura and Adolf spent time with the many avant-garde, socialist, progressive artists who gathered at cafés near Montparnasse to critique Western culture.[40] Cafe Rotunda was always full of Americans, Hungarians, Russians, Swedes, and Germans, and many celebrities such as Rockwell Kent, Max Eastman, and Isadora Duncan. Painters, photographers, and writers assembled at Le Select, Café du Dôme (their main stomping ground),[41] Café La Cupole, and basement cabarets and dance halls in the Latin Quarter where jazz reigned.[42] During this time Guy Pène du Bois drew a portrait of Mura which is now in the National Gallery of Art in Washington, DC, and Adolf and Mura frequented the underground jazz cabarets. Adolf wrote in a letter to his sister, "Life in Paris is simply glorious,"[43.] while he supported himself by providing light-hearted cartoons and scenic European landscapes to editors back in the United States, a number of which appeared in *Vanity Fair*.

Paris in the 1920s was seen as a magnet for American artists seeking freedom, diversion, beauty, adventure, and intelligence, and at the time was the world capital of photography.[44] The Bauhaus and Dada movements in art were reforming artistic principles, and a community of artists working together aiming to bring art back into contact with everyday life was a trendy idea. The shift from Victorian values to a modernist concept of the unglamorous and functionality was evident throughout Europe, especially in class-conscious Paris. Jazz fit in perfectly, as its popular and social roots reflected an art/folk connection. Mura felt that "jazz happened because of a new, global awareness of rhythm at the turn of the century," an awareness which was ready for the seductiveness of jazz. Dalcroze had spread his Eurhythmics to movement and dance educators throughout the United States and Europe; and with her natural approach to movement, Duncan "gave dance back to the layman."[45] In addition, through minstrelsy audiences on both continents were hearing much more complicated dance and music rhythms than were common in European forms; the minstrel show had served as a training and development ground for some early-jazz music.[46]

Minstrelsy is very controversial. It started out as a humorous dance, music, variety show, in between other kinds of more formal theatrical acts, but was explicatory of the racial derision that affected all of American society of the 1830s and 1940s. Because many of the audience didn't know African Americans, and there were many places where there were very few, people assumed that the characterizations, depictions, and foolish characters on stage were the real thing. But at the same time, there was an embrace of what was happening on the stage; people were having great fun, being entertained. They were embracing a culture that they were deriding at precisely the same time. It is also important to note that within the context of the period, minstrelsy represented a popular source of entertainment for both races; an interplay and intermix of Black and white culture that so defines American music but defies imagination to this day.[47] White audiences witnessed continuous innovations in popular music and dance, Black entertainers somehow persevered through racial atrocities with vitality and resilience.

By the time the sounds and movement of early jazz infiltrated Europe and mainstream America, the world had been prepared for its rhythmic originalities and nothing could prevent this particular contagious approach of movement to music from spreading worldwide as jazz music swept dancers into a pulsing frenzy. Young, bohemian Parisians were seeking new ways to define themselves and demanded a driving beat designed for their moving bodies; the European dance ethos had been primed for their rhythmic desires. In a 1978 interview, Mura told Karen Wickre:

> So, when Charleston came, we were all prepared for it. It was our dance and we jumped into it with absolute, what shall I say, torture because it was difficult for the Parisians to do Charleston. But there was a tremendous desire to step out of harmony, to step out into some kind of a freedom, which was also a freedom of sex, and it maybe seemed decadent because in these little cafes with the cavernous lights, and green lights and peoples' hinies stuck out and cheek-to-cheek and jerking with terror in their face. Yet, I remember there was an expression that was translated like: "Rhythm is a bitter pill, but we will swallow it." So that was jazz and I was part of it and I right away made concerts in jazz form in 1926 in Vienna.[48]

Dancers' demand for jazz brought many African American musicians to Europe, where despite economic limitations and biases they could actually make a decent living. Paris at that time understood racism but did not have the overtly segregated, stratified society of the United States. Many considered the distinctive music exotic, much like the art that captivated France when Picasso and compatriots began using African sculptural images in their paintings *circa* 1906. African art was desirable for its originality and remained part of the surrealists' consideration. Jazz had a totally new vibe, and like African Art, represented a critique of both traditional values and Western mores. Yet, the "noble savage" fabrication viewed African culture as natural, innocent, and uncorrupted:

> The French saw all blacks as primitive and exotic; it was unimportant to them that Black people came from many parts of Africa and the New World. The result of this ignorance and stereotyping was that jazz music became the music of the "noble savage" and fit into the vogue for Blacks and Black arts as symbols of an uncorrupted past in the history of the human race. In fact, the Parisian demand for Black jazz musicians was so intense during the 1920s that white jazz musicians had trouble competing for jobs.[49]

"Primitive" and "savage" were boorish terms that perpetuated the narrative of Black artists as being inferior and their endeavors separate from Europeanist art. Still, at the time, the terms were not always deliberatively negative but also represented the longing of bohemian Paris for a pre-technological, pre-urban, primal, more essential life. Black music had the "pulse of some quintessentially human impulses that over-civilized people had forgotten. . . . titillating, dangerous and sensual.[50]

Black dance and music were simultaneously antediluvian and modern. Jazz even affected fashion, evident in the hair styles, jewelry, and fringed dresses of the "flapper" that symbolized the changing roles of women who were going to college, making a living, and had the right to vote. "The flapper was a young, adventurous woman who experimented with her new-found freedoms and lifestyle, and of course, swayed to the music."[51] The unfortunate terminology relegated the African to "other," and at the same time the words symbolized newly found freedoms and lifestyles. The Bohemians also thought self-discovery and personal expression carried into frolicking and sexual liberation. Adolf's love letters to Mura and other women were "filled with unabashed actual or imagined sexual descriptions of what indulgences he thought necessary for authenticity" of his voluptuous satirical renderings. He wrote: "My attitude to life is rather sensuous—and sensual too—and only after I have filled myself with sensuous experiences can I go about working. I am crazy about life and want to have as much out of it as I can. . . . The work comes after my living life, or rather out of it."[52]

On one of their trips to Paris in 1924 Adolf took Mura to see Josephine Baker, and she was immediately enraptured. "I was captivated by Josephine Baker, hence captivated by jazz. In it I found the very thing Dalcroze and Duncan were seeking—creative freedom through rhythm, along with a magnificent sense of humor—controlled and timed theatrical traditions."[53] Josephine Baker became one of Dehn's inspirations, and one she would refer to often. Forty-five years later, in 1966, she would write: "I have never seen a jazz dancer who could compare to Josephine Baker. The extraordinary beauty of her body, the unpredictable humor of her limbs, the savage playfulness of her spirit. . . . When the Charleston hit her she would fly in all directions at once."[54] She wrote: "Before, European couple dancing was very formal—too pleasing and too relaxed. But life was not like that. We needed something to energize us, to give us abandon. The Charleston gave us the spice of rhythm and syncopation." Eurocentric cultures privileged the mind over the body, and jazz disrupted that value system with a license for joy, sex, and expressing all of those things Victorian society was trying to repress:

> Pulled up very high, all in profile, all nude, a little banana skirt, quick bouncy steps, her fanny fluttering behind her like the wings of a hummingbird. Just a brief moment—but the picture remains for a lifetime. Untamed, careless, expert, she brought the antics of irrepressible gaiety and seduction. Josephine and Charleston invaded Paris like a drug.[55]

Josephine Baker was quite successful in aligning her onstage personification with Parisian images of the primitive and exotic, hence creating her own narrative. "She used her scanty costumes, make-up, and jungle-stage settings, as well as conventions of burlesque to create a danse savage that played with the paradigm of the black exotic in the context of white colonialism."[56] Despite language associating her with the jungle and childlike qualities, Baker "allowed her audiences to feel superior and in control while at the same time providing a vicarious sexual experience forbidden in everyday life.[57] Baker embodied the avant-garde, the rhythm, the vitality, the humor, and the satire of the jazz temperament, which both Dehns embraced into their own artistic practices, first in Paris and later as they skipped back and forth across the pond.

In 1925 Adolf was in New York and his illustrations appeared in many leftist publications such as *The Liberator*, *The New Masses*, and *The Dial*, noted his hometown paper *The Minneapolis Journal*.[58] That year Mura Dehn, according to her Biographical Materials, performed in Frankfurt, Dinant, and Belgium. The next year in April she was back in Vienna as Mura Ziperovicz in a *solo* concert. The second half of the program included a Charleston with a jazz band on stage, a piece entitled *Pierrot in Blues*, and a foxtrot. On April 17 she was back at the Grosser Grosser Konzerthaus-Saal with Tels but was increasingly incorporating jazz into her solo work. She was the "première danseuse" in the first performance of Stravinsky's *L'Histoire du Soldat* at the Volksoper in Vienna, about which she said: "the tango and ragtime danced by the princess created a great scandal and assured my success."[59] Later that year, in a conference dubbed *Dance Through the Ages* directed by Mr. José Germain, Ms. Mura Ziperowitsch was billed as the premiere great dancer of the Grand Opera of Vienna accompanied by Mr. Henri Delvaux, pianist, a winner of the first prize of the Royal Conservatories of Brussels and Liège. The conference was organized to benefit the "Christmas and New Years' poor children" and produced by the Federation of Veterans, the Federation of War Invalids, and the St. Nicholas Committee of Orphans and Needy.[60]

Marriage Apart

Some time in 1926, after four years of courtship, Mura married Adolf when she was twenty-four and he thirty-one. Their relationship continued to be ruptured by his trips to New York and her dance career, and often they lived apart.[61] Chaprik, to whom she was very close, was always in tow, whether in Paris or when they traveled about Europe. Mura was in Coburg when Adolf was in France, or she in France while he was in in New York, and all of them at one time, including Chaprik and Boris, were in Adolf's apartment in Paris. Some, including one of Adolf's sisters and one of Mura's lifelong friends, Lyena Dodge, wondered if the marriage was ever consummated, as she related that when they lived together Mura often stayed in the same bedroom as her mother. The former, his sister Emilie, wrote to Adolf's mother:

> All I know is that they are very, very good friends and get along well. They have a deep fondness for each other. Whether or not they sleep together? I don't know—one doesn't ask I daresay—if they don't—they are still better friends and have a deeper fondness for each other than 9/10ths of married people.[62]

An article in an English-language Parisian newspaper *circa* 1927 in Mura's clippings folder reads: "the American art colony at the Left Bank has lately received a welcome addition in the person of the well-known caricaturist Adolf Dehn who is taking a studio at 15 rue Bardinet. He plans to remain in Paris indefinitely." Adolf was becoming important in the art world, and the American Federation of Graphic Arts chose one of his etchings, a landscape, to be included in its collection of the fifty best prints of the year, which "will be exhibited in all of the principal cities of the United States."[63] By this time his works appeared in one man shows in both Vienna and in Berlin, where the critics were liberal with praises. Many were of his wife, "[Maura Ziperovitcsh] the well-known dancer, [who] is one of his favorite subjects."[64] Another clipping titled "In The Quarter" (again the Left Bank) concerns a concert at the Théâtre de la Madeleine. The writer had watched a rehearsal for "Futurist pantomimes" and declared: "Among the performers were a number of dancers who live on the Left Bank. Mura [sic] Zepurevich is certainly worthy of mention. She appeared in three pantomimes and in each one did a notable bit of dancing which brought the applause of the house."

Much of 1927 and parts of 1928 were spent in Paris, where Mura came into contact with many photographers. The Hungarian Ergy Landau worked in Vienna then Berlin, emigrated to Paris in 1922, and was known as the portrait photographer who brought the first Rolleiflex camera to France.[65] Landau's pictures of Mura were often on the covers of Parisian magazines. A Landau portrait, multiple other pictures—such as Mura modeling a can-can costume—and multiple magazine covers are in her New York Public Library collection and most likely come from this period. The quality and number of photographs in her collection suggest she was also modeling at this time, perhaps for photography students, but also for professionals such as Landau and Wilhelm "Willy" Maywald; several other photos are from the Willinger studio in Berlin.[66] Mademoiselle Mura had attracted some fame and was described in Paris newspapers at this time with very favorable adjectives such as: "première danseuse" when she performed at the Madeleine (where she was also listed as choreographer), as a "famous Russian dancer," and "a grand artiste both here in France and other countries on the continent of Europe."[67] In December of 1927, using the name "Maria Mura," she headlined a performance at Salon D'automne that included a Charleston and a foxtrot. An unknown newspaper review in her clippings read:

> The art of Terpsichore will be accorded due recognition at the Salon d'Automne (Grand Palais), on Saturday, when Maria Mura, famous Russian dancer, and wife of Adolf Dehn, noted American artist, will appear in a classical and modern dance recital. Mrs. Dehn's art has found considerable public approval throughout the Continent. The first two numbers of Maria Mura's program—Beethoven's *Sonata Pathétique* and Chopin's *Marche Funèbre*—are dances whose masterly interpretation by the great American dancer brought her world fame.[68]

The *Evening Paper of Paris* reported:

> Mura Ziperovitch, the Russian dancer who distinguished herself in the Futurist Pantomime performances at the Théâtre de la Madeleine, has left for Lisbon, where she will stay 2 months, appearing in some jazz caricatures and classic dances—if the combination be possible. But very little seems impossible to this young woman whose talents are so readily appreciated in The Quarter. Upon her return she will fill an engagement at one of the leading theatres of Paris as premiere danseuse.[69]

Mademoiselle Mura's artfully exposed full figure graced the cover of several magazines between 1928 and 1933. "Notre Miroir de Beauté" (our mirror of beauty) were the words printed above one of two covers of *Paris Plaisirs*, which focused on the music halls of the Art Deco era, and later she adorned *Paris Music Hall* and *Voilà*. Notably she was called "the Shapeliest Woman in all of France" in 1928 by *New York American Weekly*, published in Great Britain, at a time when the pencil-thin flapper body of the 1920s was going out of fashion in Europe. The article states that "Mlle. Mura appeared in costumes that displayed to the best advantage the beautiful curves of her figure." She danced solo concerts in Lisbon and Portugal and was a resident Maîtresse du Ballet and choreographer at the Coburg Opera over two years. In May of 1928 she performed in a Gustave Rives Challenge fencing exhibition in Paris with Professor Albert Lacaze. A newspaper review read: "This time, Professor Lacaze had as his opponent Ms. Maria Mura, an extraordinary Russian fencer, who displayed in these attacks, which are dangerous since they were executed without a mask, a diabolical combativeness and virtuosity, at the same time as an aesthetic sense."[70] Another review observed: "Maria Mura deploys in these battles a suppleness, a fantastic, dazzling brilliance. She rushes, leaps, attacks, or evades with prodigious and charming ease" (translated from French).[71] A performance such as this would only be possible due to her dancing prowess, as she had no former training in the fencing arts.

Adolf sailed to New York in 1929 for a show at the Weyhe Gallery, and (as in Paris) he kept company with art luminaries, and his haunts were jazz clubs in Harlem. During this time they wrote many love letters to each other. Mura was still under contract at the Coburg Opera company and promised to meet him later. Her vita lists a performance, arranged by the young theatrical agent Rudolph Bing,[72] at the Coburg Sachsen-Gotha Opera House, where she presented a program of concert jazz to an audience that included the former King of Bulgaria (Ferdinand), King Cyril of exiled Russians, Prince Von Hohenlohe, and the Herzog of Coburg Sachsen-Gotha. Music on the program was by Duke Ellington and Louis Armstrong;[73] at the final curtain call, after a minute of silence there was thunderous applause. (An interesting aside here is that Mura knew Bing from Vienna; he married one of her close friends who was also a dancer. The three remained close, and when Bing became general manager of the Metropolitan Opera in New York City decades later, she often was invited to his box seats.) At the end of the 1920s Mura was steeped in the creative expressive arts and improvisation, bolstered by an exciting performing career, enmeshed in the socialist avant-garde art scene in Paris and enamored with jazz.

Family

Boris joined Chaprik, Mura, and Adolf in Paris when they moved there from Vienna *circa* 1926. A handwritten, diary-type note in a spiral journal in her papers reads:

> The greatest influence in my life was Boris' illness. I felt it first in 1923 when he came to visit us from London and cried long and bitter at his change—and then in 1925 while a bride to Adolf which was also a sad time. . . . I stayed at home one night when they went to a dance—and all at once understood the tragedy that swallowed Boris and cried loud . . . for a long time—he had his crisis in 1928.[74]

According to letters, when Mura was in Coburg with her mother, Adolf often visited with Boris in Paris, though it is unclear whether her brother was able to live alone, as he seems to have struggled with schizophrenia-like symptoms most of his adult life. In letters, Adolf wrote to her in sumptuous verse such as "I am amazed that you exist. I look at the bed where you took me so close and I will be there alone, Dear Lover I shall try not to cry . . . happy you are starting your work, you will be great and grand."[75] He went on to describe taking Boris boating or buying him a new suit and caring for him financially and emotionally. When Adolf was in New York Mura wrote passionate letters from Paris, and many included news about Boris' erratic temperament. He responded, "you are a great curiosity a myth almost to those who have not seen you," begging her to come to New York: "Tell me what you need so you can be terribly chic. I see your legs which I want to kneel before."[76]

Mura and Chaprik visited Adolf in New York in late 1930. Chaprik returned to Paris after six months, and some time in 1932 Adolf and Mura divorced and she also returned to Paris. In sometimes desperate letters on Café du Dôme letterhead, Mura wrote that Boris' condition was worsening, she was unable to leave her mother with him alone, her dancing jobs were inconsistent, and she pleaded for Adolf, whose career was taking off in New York, to send the family money.[77] In conversation with Mura's friend Lyena Dodge, and in Mura's materials and letters there were several references to Boris' illness and trying to find for him an appropriate living situation.[78] A clipping from an unknown serial in Geneva *circa* 1951 reads: "Mura Dehn. It's likely you have never heard her name. But it's likely too, that her name will go down in jazz history under the heading 'Jazz Dance.' Miss Dehn arrived in Geneva this week to stay with her brother."[79] Most likely Boris was hospitalized from the early 1930s through the rest of his life.

Lillian Morrison and Eiko told me Mura was extremely close to and fond of her mother, and they were inseparable.[80] When Chaprik traveled to New York with Mura, they even went on to Waterville, Minnesota to meet Adolf's parents. There Mura charmed all of the Dehn family, though she shocked "local residents by hitchhiking alone from Duluth to Waterville and by swimming nude in German Lake adjacent to the town."[81] Repeatedly friends referred to a type of confidence Mura emitted, a determination and strength which they felt was a result of the positive and nurturing relationship with her mother. A verse of a poem in *Lion Tamer*, a book of Dehn's poetry published posthumously, reads:

To Mother
Each of my days stand up for you
You are a lamplight
in the evening,
by day,
a festival.[82]

There is no clue as to when the poem was composed, though Fanny "Chaprik" Tsiperovitsch died when Mura was in her mid- to late thirties.[83]

Dehn's Collection contains many Russian documents such as diplomas, certificates, and working papers, but there is little mention of her father during his decade in London. He moved to Paris by 1929, as a registration document from that May attests. In her materials are *certificats d'identités* for both her mother (1932) and father (1936) that show them living in Paris at different addresses, and his work visa from Constantinople. A letter states that he taught at technology schools in France from 1938 to 1943 until forced to stop under German persecution during the Second World War,[84] and on the back of a photo of David with Boris is written "There you have another photo taken 12-7-47. With love and kisses to you, Father and Boris. How do you find Boris with a beard? He is very proud of it!"[85] A good guess would have David riding out the war from 1943 to 1947 with Boris in Switzerland, which had escaped a Nazi invasion, before emigrating to the United States. The collection also contains an application for a faculty position at Bryn Mawr College in Philadelphia, which indicates that he was attempting to find work as a teacher of Russian studies there in 1949. He lived with Mura at 308 West 15th Street in New York for the rest of his life; the latest pictures of him appear to be from the mid-1950's, and a receipt for his tombstone reads "David, Son of Joseph Tsiperovitch 1869–1960."[86]

Adolf wrote hundreds of letters from the 1920s through mid-1930s to his sisters, mother, Mura, Chaprik, and others, including Willis Bock and Eileen Hall Lake, which revealed both an irrepressible romantic, and one who remained a loyal and dependable family man—even throughout his wild bohemian days. When Adolf was in New York, and still married to Mura who was in Paris, Bock wrote him impassioned love letters from Berlin throughout the 1930s. Some included nude photos of herself and were signed "Your little wife"; whether or not Mura knew about the liaison or whether it influenced the Dehns' divorce is unknown. Adolf also had a romantic relationship with Lake, an artist and poet he had met in Paris in 1930. He spent three summers with her on Martha's Vineyard from 1933 to 1935, which Mura knew about. The Dehns were divorced by then, and in letters addressed to Adolf at Lake's Martha's Vineyard address, Mura asks him to send Eileen her warm wishes.[87] So many factors could have contributed to their break-up: his liaisons with other women, her "almost stunning effect on men,"[88] financial struggles, or that Chaprik and Mura were inseparable and lived with them most of the time they were married. "It was my greatest pleasure to be the daily companion to my mother—that is the Russian way of family," she recalled. "Men, including Adolf, had to come second."[89] They remained close friends after their divorce, but their separation left an emptiness that "only his second wife, Virginia Engleman, would fill fifteen years later."[90] Adolf kept Maria Tsiperovitsch's letters; she kept the professional name of Mura Dehn until the time of her death.

Foreshadowing her life's work in folk arts, one of the first mentions of Mura in New York, in The Afro-American, Baltimore,[91] has her at the Tharpes-Roberts Affair. One of those unofficial interracial confabs at Agnes' (Tharpe) Palace of Hades on West 10th Street. Apparently she and several dozen attendees enjoyed entertainment including impersonator Mademoiselle Cullen, Mexican violinist Señor Gabriello, and African American songwriters and musicians Maceo Pinkard and Nappy Napoleon. In the same year Adolf and 100 other artists signed a petition for the press to awaken the public about "Red baiting" and imprisoning men and women for their political opinions,[92] and his lithographs were in several exhibitions. An April 13 review states: "He ridicules everything he sees. But he does so with a human sympathy that lifts his lithographs out of the realm of burlesque,"[93] and the next year Dehn's "Splendid Drawings" at the Weyhe Gallery were greeted with, "Light is Mr. Dehn's province; light and the marvelous nuances in shadow . . . he can achieve prodigious depth in a landscape unblinded by beauty he proceeds with sensuous cunning towards his goal."[94] Having spent over a decade in Paris with numerous artists, creating and performing and crossing the Atlantic many times, Adolf and Mura both moved to New York. Friends remembered them in similar ways, as being open, effusive, and zestful, with the "mainsprings of [their arts] being the experience of living."[95]

3

The Dance Hall, the Dance Stage, and the Academy

No step is an end in itself. Every vibration is a potential of new formation. The exchange of innovations among dancers is constant. In the dance hall the poetry and wit of jazz comes out with a natural grace.[1]

Mura and Adolf ventured to New York with a perspective that Sally Sommer coined perfectly: "African American jazz was received as a new modern art with curative and liberating powers that ruptured the old lifeway tempos, breached racialized barriers, and reformulated ideologies about grace and propriety."[2] Like Paris, Harlem was considered a place to hear and dance to jazz music, get into the swing, and throw off the constraints of turn-of-the-century sexual repression. Jazz was seen by some as a symptom of degeneration, but the interest in its rhythms, modernity, and sensuousness drove thousands to its dance halls every night.[3] Transcontinental popularity at home and abroad should have secured its place as a significant art form worthy of study, but its association with the milieus where jazz was performed had quite the opposite effect in the United States. In the 1920s many people knew nothing about jazz as music, but had the firm opinion that the "men and women of jazz were degenerate and unwholesome," dance halls and honky-tonks were considered to be houses of sin and corruption, and jazz dance was distasteful to some teachers and scholars.[4] In addition to being looked down upon as unsophisticated and "primitive," early jazz was also perceived by some as a cultural remnant of American slavery, a time and circumstance which many people preferred to forget.[5] Regardless, Mura began to frequent the Savoy Ballroom and to study with its lead dancers and teachers.

Stepping into Another World

Located at 596 Lenox Avenue between 140th and 141st Streets, the Savoy was built for African Americans in Harlem yet was completely integrated, and neither seating nor entrances were separated by skin color. Billed as "the World's Finest Ballroom," it operated from March 12, 1926 to July 10, 1958, and rivaled any downtown nightclub in class, dancing, and music. It was "a building, a geographic place, a ballroom, and the 'soul' of a neighborhood,"[6] it was also a place where Black bodies became sites of resistance, performing a new narrative of inventiveness and autonomy. Opened and owned by white entrepreneur Jay Faggen and Jewish businessman Moe Gale, it was managed by African American real estate man Charles Buchanan. Buchanan sought to run a "luxury ballroom to accommodate the many thousands who wished to dance in an atmosphere of tasteful refinement, rather than in the small, stuffy halls and the foul smelling, smoke laden cellar nightclubs."[7] The Savoy survived the Great Depression, the First World War, and racial riots. It was as popular as Radio City Music Hall and the Empire State Building as a tourist attraction where the best dancers and musicians congregated to celebrate, perfect, and disseminate the latest in jazz culture for over three decades.[8]

While many white tourists thought of Harlem as a tantalizing ghetto and an escape from their conventional routine, the Savoy articulated the cultural aspirations of the local Black and surrounding communities. Through word of mouth and Black-owned newspapers it became an entertainment destination for Brooklyn, New Jersey, the Bronx, and Connecticut.[9] Advertising emphasized that it would offer Black patrons entertainment comparable to that in elite segregated venues: "Thousands have found enjoyment at the Savoy . . . the management have always tried to please and hold their large patronage by offering things not to be found at any other place of its kind in the city catering to Negroes."[10] Buchanan insisted on "a dignified atmosphere and at first encouraged bouncers to break up any couples dancing the Charleston or other exuberant, up-tempo popular dances."[11] "The bouncers, some who had previous jobs such as boxers or basketball players, wore tuxedos and made $100/night. . . . [N]o man was allowed in who wasn't dressed in a jacket with a tie." Buchanan eventually embraced social dancing and understood its currency, and the ballroom became an important space for the development of the most popular dances of the day.[12] The Savoy hostesses would teach patrons who purchased a 25-cent ticket. On a panel discussing the Savoy, "To be hired," former hostess Helen Clarke told Robert

Crease, "Mr. Buchanan would check your background, schooling, everything." He would "keep an eye on you because he knew if one or two girls created scandal," the place would be shuttered. "We had rules and regulations." When Crease asked, she replied they wore "beautiful evening clothes. We were making money, so we could buy anything."[13] Professionalism, dignity, and frequently updated luxurious decor distinguished it from whites-only venues such as the Cotton Club, which objectified and commoditized the Black performer.[14]

Twenty million customers danced to over 300 bands for thirty-two years.[15] Colored lights shone on the hardwood dance floor, made of many layers of mahogany and maple, that was replaced every three years due to its constant use.[16] It was cleaned and polished every night. The 10,000-square-foot ballroom was on the second floor and a full city block long. It could hold up to 5,000 people. It provided a space for Harlemites to gather, hosted charity balls, had its own basketball team, and its status as a prominent tourist landmark made it a place to host celebrities and visiting dignitaries, which also affected the financial growth of Harlem.[17] The lobby, a large open space with a marble staircase and cut-glass chandelier, led Leon James, one of the master dancers of the Savoy, to tell Marshall Stearns: "My first impression was that I had stepped into another world. I had been to other ballrooms, but this was different—much bigger, more glamour, real class."[18]

Dr. Jazz Cures All Ills

Karen Hubbard wrote that the Savoy provided "a more dignified environment for social dancing than the usual jook joints, nightclubs, and dance halls open to black Americans," enabling a portrayal of Black culture unmarred by white dominance. The quality of the decor and "insistence on polite and considerate etiquette, along with the best music of the day, enabled many others to see such dancing in a new light."[19] For the Black locals who regularly visited, the ballroom was not only a temporary escape from work but also from the restrictions of explicit and inexplicit racist policies.[20] It changed Black American identity and culture in Harlem by providing an environment free of racial exoticism, jungle motifs, and Black caricatures, and disrupting demeaning stereotypes.[21] The dancing "became a potent tool to reproduce, reshape, and resist the structures of identity that produced the politics of difference."[22] Dance there was an agent to convey attitudes about social life and reconstructed images of a reality they could operate in. Dehn wrote: "Music is their only discipline, but outside of this condition they are totally free. They seem to dance themselves out of any society rules."[23]

The lack of segregation was a radical idea not shared by the many other clubs in Harlem. It was important to morale because it was a symbol of hope for the desegregation of America during a time of severe racial tension.[24] The Harlem Renaissance had produced incredible literature works by Black Americans, such as W.E.B. Du Bois, Langston Hughes, and Alain Locke, yet some intelligentsia thought that popular dance was not serious art, and the dancing body was still connected to minstrelsy, sexuality, and reinforcement of Black people as primitive.[25] That Renaissance may have failed to remedy the racial and economic strife and may even have contributed to the "New Negro" as still subordinate to the dominant white culture.[26] At the Savoy, however, whites and Blacks could enjoy each other's company and dance to a common beat. Lindy Hopper Norma Miller wrote: "For the first time in history, the status quo in America was challenged. At last, there was a beautiful ballroom with no segregation. Black people and white people danced on the same dance floor; they sat and ate across from one another in the booths; everyone's money was the same at the Savoy."[27]

Mura felt the energy, and related a similar vibe, telling Wickre:

> If you were dead tired, if you were old, if you don't want anything, you go to the Savoy and you become renewed. And working people were dancing there mostly, and they called it "Dr. Jazz, which cures all ills." And it did. And it was a wonderful interchange of whites and blacks—there was an admiration. And the Blacks were open and very giving, very giving. . . . And so it was a good time of friendship.[28]

Conrad Gale, nephew of owner Moe Gale, on the same panel as Clarke, told Crease: "the thing that impressed me most was how the regulars at the Savoy felt about themselves. The [colored] people who went there, I believe, got the first feeling of themselves as free and accepted . . . and the Lindy Hop was an expression of the liberation of the Black soul." Dancer Frankie Manning added: "Going into the Savoy was a medicine. If I was feeling low, as soon as I'd walk in and see that floor bouncing and the people dancing and the musicians on stage playing, I'd begin to feel great!"[29]

From the outset, the Savoy played a significant role in Harlem's community life as a venue for society gatherings and events. Churches, community centers, and civic unions used the grand ballroom for charity balls and other major functions.[30] It seems like everyone had a place: housewives could get a discount on Mondays, and Thursdays were especially reserved for "Kitchen Mechanics." Activists such as Buchanan and Adam Clayton Powell ran clubs and political groups on Wednesdays and Fridays, which provided a safe environment where whites and African Americans could discuss current political issues. "Squares Nights" (Saturdays) were so packed that there wasn't room for much dancing, but Tuesday night was reserved for the elite dancers of the 400 Club, who wowed the crowds.[31] John Martin wrote for the *New York Times*:

> [The 400 Club] movements are never so exaggerated that they lack control, and there is an unmistakable dignity about his most violent figures. . . . [A] remarkable amount of improvisation and personal specialty mixed in with the Suzy-Q and familiar Lindy-Hop figures; some of it is acrobatic and strenuous, some of it is superficially erotic, and all of it full of temperament and quality. Of all the ballroom dancing these prying eyes have seen, this is unquestionably the finest.[32]

Harlem became the largest African American community in the United States when 300,000 southerners, Caribbeans and others migrated north looking for work in the 1930's. Hubbard and Monaghan wrote that the Savoy "capitalized on the special qualities of this mixed community." The dancing was enhanced through the variety of styles as older dance forms "alternated with the development of new ones and even the celebration of other communities' dance fads," which in turn drew a diverse crowd.[33] The dance was basically social and recreational, but the elite dancers such as the 400 Club and Whitey's Lindy Hoppers lent an air of professionalism. They often won Harvest Moon Ball competitions, an amateur, though highly regarded, contest sponsored by the *Daily News*, danced in feature films and stage shows, but still returned to where their artistic prowess "was infused back into the general mix,"[34] charging the atmosphere with self-respect and pride.[35]

There were other clubs in New York, but none racially integrated except the Savoy and a little basement club named Smalls Paradise which opened in 1925 and chose to accept both Black and white clients *and* Black and white employees. There was a small dance area, occasional music by Fletcher Henderson and James P. Johnson, no door charge, and low meal prices, catering to a socially and economically diverse client base. Notably there was a small staff of dancing waiters managed by Herbert "Whitey" White, the founder of Whitey's Lindy Hoppers. Smalls success may have helped Gale and Buchanan determine it was "more financially profitable to admit patrons of every color, race, provenance, and financial standing," a rare egalitarian policy which made national headlines.[36]

Dancers and Teachers

Known as "Whitey" because of the streak of white in his hair, **Herbert White** (1901–50) was a former prize fighter, a bouncer at the Alhambra, and the headmaster of the Lindy Hoppers at the Savoy. An interesting character, he founded and led the Jolly Fellows, a Harlem street gang, and several of its members were the dancing stars of the Savoy, including Shorty George and Leon James; he also insisted on absolutely courteous behavior toward women, and personal cleanliness.[37] The Lindy had spurred fierce competition, dancers wouldn't dare enter certain sections of the Track, the nickname for the main dance floor, unless they believed themselves to be among the elite, and Whitey kept an eye on all of them. In the early 1930s as "requests came from downtown socialites who wanted to have the Lindy Hoppers perform at their lavish parties," he had a good eye for talent, and like a good coach, he knew how to nurture it. He was able to hand-pick exciting dancers and send them to gigs with the admonition, "Remember, ain't nobody better than you."[38] Though he was not regarded as a great dancer Mura wrote that he was the first Savoy jazz choreographer:

> Whitey, a great creator and organizer. He took the most gifted youngsters, interchanged their inventions and styles, and created the new classic routines: The Tranky-Doo, California, Big Apple. Every afternoon in the Ballroom, Whitey conducts rehearsals with the discipline of a ballet-master. They work on speed, rhythm, surprise, but most of all to retain the brilliance of spontaneity in set routines. . . . The Thursday nights present a breath-taking performance by professionals. Whitey's Lindy Hoppers are sent around the world, creating a sensation.[39]

He began booking his dancers at public and private venues, and by late 1936 employed more than seventy swing dancers. Some worked a six-month engagement at the Cotton Club under the name Whitey's Hopping Maniacs, and another performed under the name Whitey's Lindy Hoppers.[40] He was known to skim from the members who won the Lindy Hop Division at the Harvest Moon Ball competitions and from their professional gigs, but was able to translate their "success into an international tour that took them to Broadway and the Moulin Rouge in Paris," the 1939 World's Fair in Flushing, New York, and led to film appearances, such as the Marx Brothers' *A Day at the Races*. "The troupe's appearance in the movie *Hellzapoppin'* introduced the Lindy hop to the masses and touched off a global dance sensation."[41] Creativity and individualism fueled their moves as the foremost Whitey's Hoppers were social dancers and improvisors even after they had learned choreographed routines and been paid in professionals gigs. They, like the musicians at the Savoy, could perform tight arrangements yet still perform "completely original jazz improvisations night after night."[42] Though the Hoppers mostly disbanded in 1942 after many of the male members were drafted into the Second World War, Whitey trained dancers until he died in 1950.

Mattie Purnell and her partner **"Shorty George" Snowden** (1904–82) were probably responsible for the creation of the Lindy hop. He was instrumental in its spread through the US in the 1930s, and paved the way for the next generation of Savoy Lindy Hoppers and the hundreds of thousands of people that dance it today.[43] Born in lower Manhattan, he moved to Harlem with his strict Episcopalian mother in 1910, was told after breaking both ankles ice-skating he would never dance again, and by 1920 he was in a "reform school."[44] He joined the local Jolly Fellows social club, run by Herbert "Whitey" White, and despite his injuries became an exceptional Charleston dancer.[45] Snowden and Purnell, couple number 7, represented the Jolly Fellows in a marathon at Rockland Palace in 1928. Snowden lost his grip of his partner's hand but managed to reach and pull her back in, veiling the mistake with fancy steps. They garnered a $15 gold prize for a new dance called the Lindbergh Hop, named after Charles Lindbergh's flight across the Atlantic. The following September, when appearing in Harlem's Lincoln Theatre, he rechristened it The Lindy Hop. Two months later Snowden was the first to have his company on a Broadway stage, and three of the couples went on to dance in the short film *After Seben*.[46]

To Dehn, Snowden's routines were Savoy classics, she wrote: "His spur of the moment innovations seemed inexhaustible. This little man held sway over the roughest crowds, commanding the respect and attention due a master which led to him being described as 'King of the Savoy'. One of his later partners, Big Bea, who was twice his size, would throw him up in the air, down on the floor, pick him up and throw him down again."[47] Snowden won Lindy hop championships with different partners, at the Roseland Ballroom in 1930 and the Savoy Ballroom in 1931. Paul Whiteman's Orchestra recruited his dancers in 1932, and they took the dance to many different parts of the United States. In 1937 Shorty and Big Bea appeared in *Ask Uncle Sol* and were a major success at the Cotton Club, where everyone was dancing. The Shorty George becoming one of the few Savoy dancers to have a step named after them. Snowden later taught the Lindy at Dehn's Academy of Swing. Terry Monaghan wrote that he concluded his career modestly, "opened a dance studio for a while in Harlem, . . . spent time in Queens dancing socially where he continued to be in great demand as a partner and went dancing with Big Bea whenever he could."[48]

Dehn's third major influence from the Savoy, **Alfred T. Leagins** (1912–99) was born in South Carolina. His parents died when he was four, and he passed through the care of various family members before landing in New York, where he was raised by an organist for the Metropolitan Baptist Church. "He was a devout churchgoer, and Gospel rhythm deeply influenced his dancing."[49] Despite strict non-dancing orders from the minister, he began attending the Savoy shortly after it opened in 1926, taking part in the parties for kids on Saturday afternoons. Leagins learned to dance before the Lindy was developed, his dancing had an easy, relaxed ballroom feel, and he was noticed by Shorty George. However, when Snowden and his company started playing with acrobatics and air-step routines, Leagins stayed on the floor. At one time the floor manager, Whitey, directed his petty-gangster associates to "beat up Alfred for refusing to join the new company."[50] He stayed away until Whitey found other dancers, but returned later, and major artists, such as Arthur Fiedler, who came to the Savoy thanked him for his "valuable hints." Tallulah Bankhead, Billie Holiday, Ethel Waters, and Ethel Merman looked to him for dance instruction and other advice.[51]

His student, Roger Pryor Dodge, introduced Leagins to Mura, who called him "the Prince of Rhythm, a bouncing, jumping, jazz Harlequin." In her manuscript she noted his advice: "Learn neatly and with artistry, then originate through yourself.[52] She further observed that his posture was perfect, then suddenly he would break into a slide-sweep with his body down to his knees and up in a cascade of rhythms and African arm movements, like ribbons in the air. Comparing dancing to driving a car, he said: "You have to watch out for other people, and you have to know how to lead your partner. Then you can relax and have a good time." When sitting at her kitchen table with him in the movie *In a Jazz Way*, Dehn giggled, "you only have one or two good partners in your lifetime, just like one or two good husbands."[53] Monaghan wrote: "Dance was far more than therapy though for him. It was about identity and empowerment which he demonstrated throughout his life."[54] On his business card was printed: "PSYCHOLOGY *or* HAPPINESS POISE DANCING."[55]

In May 1942 Leagins entered the armed forces, and emerged as a sergeant, changed by the war. He worked various jobs in drugstores, as a messenger, and a building superintendent, and began attending lectures by Professor Charles C. Seifert, a self-taught historian who had assembled one of the largest book artifact collections on African culture in Harlem. He assisted Seifert's widow in preserving the collection following Seifert's death in 1949 and became the curator of the collection when she passed away. In the 1980s he taught several workshops for the New York Swing Dance Society.[56] He and Mura remained close throughout their lives, and danced together in the film *In a Jazz Way*.

The music was continuous at the Savoy, and the next band was always ready when the previous one ended. The big bands needed space on stage, and during the Depression ballrooms could afford them.[57] The number of people attending nightly provided a steady, substantial income, funded the renovations, and helped to maintain low prices for the working-class. The Track was spring-loaded, no smokers were allowed near it, and the dance floor's long, unobstructed design allowed the dancers and musicians to fully realize the swing potential of energetic dance styles such as the Lindy hop.[58] The Hop may not have been born there, but it was developed and became famous there for its exuberance, creativity, and as an uncensored release."[59] The dance and music were distinctively American, the foremost form of cultural expression of and by African Americans, and provided the terrain for ethnic inclusiveness on a scale unprecedented up to that point in American history. Despite that and the efforts by the borough president to save it, the Savoy and the nearby Cotton Club closed permanently in October 1958, demolished for the construction of a housing complex. Count Basie was quoted in *Harlem World Magazine*, saying, "With the passing of the Savoy Ballroom, a part of show business is gone. I feel about the same way I did when someone told me the news that Bill [Bojangles] Robinson was dead."[60] It was there that the first originators of jazz dance created and practiced their social art form and Mura began her documentation of America's first folk dance. She had developed her love for folk dance in Russia because it was the only true form of expression for the everyday person; she realized that what she had lost in Russian folk dances was available here in the form of Black social dance. She understood that the performers at the Savoy were not "joining an existent movement but setting national trends; this was not the dance of the academicians, but of vaudeville, nightclubs and even the streets":

> I came to the Savoy and I saw the purity, the innocence, the directness, the nature like quality of the dance, you know. That was a revelation that it can be easy, you see, and that everything that we looked for in theatrical form was there naturally, the humor and the exaggeration and the tremendous, what shall I say, dexterity of technique which came from rhythm. You see, rhythm made it possible to do the impossible.[61]

Early Concerts on New York Stages

One of the first people Mura collaborated with in New York was **Roger Pryor Dodge** (1898–1974). They met when each presented stylized compositions in the 1930 Billy Rose variety show *Sweet and Low*. Dehn stated that their pieces were "A daring jump into the modern grotesque, a first such experiment in a commercial musical."[62] Dodge continued to work with the Billy Rose show for several years, though Dehn argued with the director and was not hired back. As a dancer, choreographer, and music critic, Dodge brought a unique perspective to his work, which, like Dehn, concerned the survival and future of jazz dance. Roger moved to Paris and studied ballet with Legat and Yegorova, then moved back to New York to study with Michel Fokine and at the Dalcroze School.[63] While in Paris he realized that Vaslav Nijinsky, the brilliant ballet star whose life was cut drastically short, had never been filmed, so set on a quest to retrieve every photograph he could find to memorialize his career. Notably that collection was donated to the New York Public Library and was largely used for Lincoln Kirstein's 1975 book *Nijinsky Dancing*. Dodge danced in the corps de ballet of the New York Metropolitan Opera from 1921 to 1928 while choreographing and performing with the Marx Brothers, Michio Ito, and Adolph Bolm, among others. His admiration for and collaboration with Bubber Miley, Duke Ellington's lead trumpeter, led him to choreograph to jazz music which he performed in New York and Paris and later filmed.[64] One of these works, *East St. Louis Toodle-Doo* was created in 1930; he and Mura filmed it in 1937, and at the time of writing of this book it was available on YouTube.[65]

Dehn and Dodge formed a professional partnership, frequented the Savoy, performed in each other's dances, and had lively discussions about jazz, art, and dance. Roger's style, like that of Mura in the 1930's was unique, angular, and geometric, very unlike the dancing at the Savoy. A 2020 review of *East St. Louis Toodle-Doo* reads: "this is a mesmerizing piece of jazz dance from 1937 by partners Roger Pryor Dodge and Mura Dehn, angularly Expressionist, the entrance is almost a Nosferatu moment." The European, modern dance and Dada-ist influences that each brought to their work are immediately evident when watching the film. Warren goes on to say:

> Jazz dance by white Greenwich Village intellectuals might, I suppose, be nowadays damned as an insulting cultural appropriation, but Dodge does not imitate Black dancers of the time, let alone parody them. His approach

is sympathetic to their art and deeply understanding of it, but his Modernist costume and choreography are essentially original, things in themselves.⁶⁶

Dehn and Dodge worked together through 1938; he retired from dancing in 1940 to concentrate on writing about jazz music and dance. Like Dehn he insisted the relationship and partnership of jazz music and the dance was absolute. One of his first articles, "Negro Jazz" in 1929, was a response to Gershwin's *Rhapsody in Blue*. He wrote that the rhapsody was far from the ideal of jazz, most likely because it lacked the main ingredient of improvisation.⁶⁷ Also, like Dehn, Dodge's work is sometimes taken out of context and critiqued for particular language. His son would argue that anyone who knew Dodge understood that "if anything he was a champion of the form, protecting and respecting jazz and the artists at all times."⁶⁸ Dodge may well have influenced Mura to create her films.

The year 1932 was an important one for Dehn. She performed at the Guild Theater, the Young Men's Hebrew Association (YMHA) Dance Center, the Paramount Theater in Boston, and became a US citizen.⁶⁹ One of the concerts often asserted as her New York debut was on April 10 at Steinway Hall, where she collaborated with Zora Neale Hurston, whom she considered a foremost authority on African American folklore and one of her mentors. Hurston's Negro Chanters accompanied Dehn, who created and performed *The Wise and Foolish Virgins*. This concert also saw a Dehn duet with Jane Dudley, and Roger Dodge's first wife, Anne, played the piano. In addition, Dehn performed a Russian folk dance. The program for the concert indicates that it was a benefit for the Kentucky Miners.⁷⁰

Zora Neale Hurston (1891–1960) was an anthropologist, writer, and choreographer who trained in ethnographic research at Barnard College and Columbia University. She wrote over fifty short stories, plays, and essays about contemporary issues of the Black diaspora, racial division, and struggles of African American women. Lillian Morrison described Hurston as among those who, like Dehn, went against the grain, and Hurston sadly died unrecognized and in poverty.⁷¹ Her literary work was somewhat obscure until 1975, when an article by Alice Walker, published in *Ms.* magazine, renewed interest in her writing. Anthea Kraut later wrote about and brought recognition to her choreographic works.⁷² Hurston lived in Harlem during its Renaissance, addressing racial inequity through writing and dance, and like Dehn was friends with poets Langston Hughes and Countee Cullen.

Dehn often credited Hurston with guidance through her investigations into Black folk arts. When reading Dehn's work, especially segments such as

Journey Through the South, one can feel Hurston's influence in her copious notes recording the words of African Americans, where they lived, worked, and danced. She also, like Hurston, told tales of the "people and folks" whom she met on collecting trips, thereby making her notebooks rich with nuance, epistemological recordings of life at various intersections in America. Dehn wrote: "Zora Hurston the great expert on [Negro] folklore spirituals has said that a spiritual is created by a group bent on the expression of feeling."[73] An early Black performance scholar, Hurston identified a number of characteristics of Negro expression and noted the predominance of action words in African American English. She felt that the dance elements which stood out the most clearly were rhythms, accents, continuous fast weight transferences, continuous use of motion, and a feeling of liveliness.[74]

The Wise and Foolish Virgins generated some controversy. Dehn had only been in the United States off and on for two years, and she was struggling to find her place in the New York dance scene. She lamented that prominent dance artists such as Helen Tamiris would never use her, and like most dancers during the Depression, she was barely surviving.[75] She admired, befriended, and learned from Hurston, using her advice in her own enquiries, and using her name in the publicity for the concert. One complaint was that while Dehn's thirteen white female dancers were onstage, Hurston's Chanters were offstage, leaving the singers to only "punctuate and accent" the choreography.[76] Dehn could have unwittingly contributed to the African American artists being invisibilized, which in hindsight would be an unacceptable practice, but it is doubtful she would have deliberately added racialized dynamics to obscure Hurston's influence. Dehn wrote about Hurston with adulation, never with disrespect.

Virgins also had mixed reviews. Mary Watkins wrote a scathing editorial in the *Arts Weekly*, declaring it should be "avoided as the plague."[77] *New York Times* dance critic John Martin, however, wrote: "by introducing a flavor of satire so strong as to be classified as caricature . . . it is not pretty or even invariably pleasant, but its biting humor draws forth even unwilling laughter."[78] Adolf Dehn, in defense of his wife, wrote a letter to *Arts Weekly* answering Watkin's review:

> If I am a distinguished artist, as she says I am, I want you to know that I am distinguished for the same kind of things that she damns Mrs. Dehn. Our approach and methods of working in our respective fields are the same, to give a specific example Mrs. Dehn's ballet, the *Wise and Foolish Virgins* was first prompted by a drawing of mine, which Miss Watkins must have seen reproduced

on the announcement for the recital, if she will examine it, she will find that the spirit of this drawing not only the spirit matter, but the rhythm and composition as well is the same with only one difference, that the drawing is more revolting by a long shot.[79]

It is not clear that either Watkins or Martin saw the full concert, as both also reviewed another performance the same night and may have come into the recital during intermission. Adolf questioned how "the critic in the supposedly enlightened city could be shocked by dances based on early Greek vases and Negro primitives. . . . After all a work of art stands by its form and style, even though an unaccustomed eye may not recognize its 'ancient heritage,' and be shocked by its novelty."[80] A viewing of Mura in Dodge's *Toodle-Doo* described above reveals an angular, sharp, rough movement approach, probably a first for Watkins and Martin, and very likely new, so controversial, for any audience. Yet Hurston, herself wrote to her patron, Charlotte Mason, that the concert went very well and that Dehn "has more talent than most dancers, and for that reason she will not be so easily understood. Her African primitive number was exceedingly fine."[81]

Dehn's curriculum vitae states that on September 6 she was at the Woodstock Maverick Theatre in an *Evening of Dance by Mura Dehn and Sophia Delza*, and on September 27 in the Manhattan Varieties at the Cosmopolitan Theater, again with Jane Dudley, who later joined the Martha Graham Company.[82] In this vaudeville-type revue, the Dehn/Dudley duet *Greek Meets Greek* was described as a "whimsical, sharp, and biting farce on the art of the ancients. Gesticulating in a grotesque fashion, striking unique poses, the young women were duly accorded." The duet prompted responses such as "a first act highlight" and a "show stopping act," and another critic wrote: "then there are Mura Dehn and Jane Dudley in a travesty on classical Terpsichore, which rocked the house. Their burlesque will fit into any big-time menu." On October 20 Dehn and Dudley performed a dance titled *Left Bank,* a musical comedy, the "high spot" being the "burlesque classical dance of Mura Dehn and Jane Dudley."[83] Dehn was incorporating her European avant-garde art style, Duncan-esque technique, and new explorations, though she was transitioning toward the jazz she was witnessing in the dance halls.

When Dehn returned to Paris later that year, Pierre Sandrini asked her to stage *La Grimace*, and she was on the covers of *Voilà Magazine* and the Paris Music Hall program. We know from her letters to Adolf that work was inconsistent and money very tight, but she choreographed and starred in a revue of can-can dancers at the famed Bal Tabarin, a revue which consisted of song and dance numbers by scantily and provocatively clad young women, as was typical of the era in Paris.[84] (Some of her letters to Adolf were written on Tabarin letterhead.) Also in her collection are pictures of her on the May cover of *Paris Magazine*, photographed by Ergy Landau in a white can-can skirt, though it is impossible to know whether those pictures were taken that year or taken earlier and later made it to the magazine covers.

Dancing on the Left

The Great Depression (1929–39) was particularly hard for dancers and gave rise to leftist organizations striving to support unemployed artists such as The Federal Theater Project (FTP), the Federal Dance Project (FDP), the Workers Dance League (WDL), and the New Dance Group.[85] The latter created group dances to encourage social protest on the plight of the working class and sponsored concerts in trade union halls.[86] Elizabeth McPherson wrote that the "social, political, and economic upheaval and instability of the US in the 1930s" influenced artists to "feel a personal responsibility to be agents of change."[87] The arts-related projects were established under the Works Progress Administration during President Roosevelt's first term; the leadership of Helen Tamiris, and lobbying by New York City dancers was instrumental in dance being included.

The FTP/FDP and the WDL operated from 1936 to 1939. Having spent her twenties among the progressive, anti-bourgeoisie art world in Paris, it seemed a good fit for Dehn, but she had mixed feelings about her involvement. On one hand it was "a magnificent adventure that showed that culture can be brought to the masses and to the places where it never reached them before," and it was also educational. Dehn was very much into the political movement, and participated in the picketing, marching, and letter writing. "And then we staged protests and occupied the Workers' Alliance premises. And they were afraid of us and they simply gave in . . . we sat there in either that courthouse or jail on 10th Street and Sixth Avenue, screaming and threatening to break the windows."[88] However, the dance units of the FTP were mostly geared toward the more acknowledged/trained modern dancers to the exclusion of anyone outside their norm or style. Dehn did not think of herself as a typical modern dancer, her quality was different than Tamiris' or Anna Sokolow's. Jazz dancers like herself were not considered for roles within the units, and she was paid to sit six hours a day in the theater. "Then I was assigned to Anna's company for *Sing for Your*

Supper, and there was no place for me there at all. I stuck out like a sore thumb because they all had a certain manner. First of all, they were all small."[89] She did, however, participate in at least two FTP-sponsored events: the 1936 National Dance Congress and the Young Choreographers' Laboratory in the sculpture court of the Brooklyn Museum Dance Center. The first event was held in May at the Theresa L. Kaufmann Auditorium, at Lexington Avenue and 92nd Street. The intention of the congress was to encourage a firmer relationship between art and society, and between dancer and audience, with the objective to alert as many people as possible to the economic situation and the need of a dancers' organization on a nationwide scale. The joint committee of eighty-three dancers included Mura Dehn and Roger Dodge. It was attended by 1,400 people, and 200 dancers performed in the Variety and Theater Program.[90]

Included in the congress' proceedings were thoughtful examinations of the status of dance, including several specifically concerned with African Americans: *A Few Words about Jazz Dancing* by Dehn, *Negro Jazz as Folk Material for Our Modern Dance* given by Dodge, and *A Few Aspects of Negro Dancing* by Leonore Cox.[91] Dehn had already begun to recognize the significance of jazz dance as both high art and folk art, and was sensitive to and appreciative of grassroots contributions. In her address she said there was a clear tendency to regard jazz dancing as something unfit for an "artist" of the dance. "Jazz dance is the dance of the people today. It is danced in the cities, the villages, dance halls, popular theaters, and in movies all over the world and in every stratum of society":

> It has touched some very vital sense of dance, rhythm and movement in contemporary peoples. . . . That popular dance expression prefers jazz is to be expected since jazz is born out of our time, our costume, our gesture, and out of the speed and rhythm of society today. . . . The average person has never seen modern dancing, nor understood the kind of music that induces it. But the people of a modern city do fall naturally into the sometimes jerky, sometimes gay, sometimes blue jazz movement which permits them a round back, negligent throw of arms, collapsed knees and quick toe movements. Jazz rhythm revives the worn-out, nerve-strained city person.[92]

Dodge, like Dehn, spoke about the survival and future of the form, with the philosophical similarities obvious:

> Probably every critic, grudgingly or otherwise has acknowledged folk art as a source of the more extended forms now known as fine art and classical art, but it is not always clear from their writings exactly how contributory they believe the

folk to be—or how necessary.... [Negro] jazz has so infused all our popular music and dancing that in some degree, this entire generation exercises itself in it.[93]

Cox talked of aspects of Negro dancing such as economics, technical training, and the career of Hemsley Winfield. She was concerned for the "art" of the people, and that the dance of the Africans and African Americans be given thoughtful reflection by the dance community. Dodge and Dehn were among the only whites striving to make the voice of the disenfranchised African American folk artists heard contiguous to Cox, and Hurston, who was the supervisor of the Negro Unit of the Federal Writers' Project. Cullen and Hughes also were participants at the congress.

The congress may have been hurriedly put together, but managed some success and offered a full week of performances. "Whatever their specific failures and shortcomings, they have made it possible to visualize for the first time some kind of collective action in the dance field," according to Martin.[94] Ten days later the same dance critic wrote that the congress did not meet expectations of being a national event and was rather a rallying call for the political left, who must accept responsibility for its ineffectualness. "After an eight-day session of performances and conferences, it is incumbent to speak a few polite but sorrowful words," he wrote, adding that it was hastily organized, offered a series futile exhibitions, and in the last two or three days, "quite literally talked itself to death."[95] Dehn's criticism was more about the difficult nature of the FTP:

> The promise came that would make it possible, and then along with it came conditions that would make it impossible.... You know, that is a very, very special quality I find in American cultural support of arts. They give it to you and they strangle you at the same time. You can do just enough not to be quite hung but never fulfilled.[96]

Regardless, Martin's review also stated that the evening folk dances (in which Dehn performed) came off well. Among those were a boogie-woogie danced by Dodge accompanied by his first wife, Anne Dodge, *Get on Board Lil Chillun* by Edna Guy, *Tiger Rag* danced by Dehn and the Bahaman Dancers, *Lindy Hop* by Shorty Snowden and his group, plus Hungarian, German, and Yemenite folk songs, and a tango danced by Anita Avila and Jack Nilo.[97] The Negro unit of the FTP produced Momodu Johnson's *Bassa Moona*, but besides that and *What Direction Shall the Negro Dance Take?* performed by Hemsley Winfield and the Negro Ballet, Black dancers and dance were virtually absent from the FDP; though many white members of the FTP/FDP were regulars at the Harlem ballrooms.

Grant Code, Director of the Dance Center at the Brooklyn Museum, offered its facilities to the FDP, leading to the organization of a unit entitled the Young Choreographers' Laboratory. The unit was to "give talented newcomers the opportunity to design and stage their own productions" and to provide a "forum for experimentation in choreography."[98] In the first performance on January 16, 1937, Mura danced two solos, *Dance of Plenty* and *Sixteenth Century Venus*, both accompanied by Anne Dodge. She wore a gold necklace and a costume constructed by Dora Kaminsky based on an African costume in the museum's collection. Mr. Code "opened the vaults and told them to use the costumes jewelry and the instruments." *Dance of Plenty* had a "wonderful mask and breasts," enabling her to dance in an "authentic costume although the dance was not authentic dance at all. It was just my interpretation of the sculpture and it was solo African dancing." Code thought for the most part the programs had a great deal to commend them, but the sentiments were not shared by other administrators and the unit was disbanded the same year. Importantly, however, he later gave Mura regular access to use the dance studio at the museum from noon to 3 p.m. every day,[99] which was a coup considering the prohibitive costs of renting studio space. Dehn then had a place to rehearse and create.

Funding for the FTP and related government-supported organizations halted abruptly in 1939, due in part to their socialist disposition and in part to government funds being channeled elsewhere. Financially and emotionally the United States was preparing for the Second World War, but the artists Dehn met during its run, such as Momodu Johnson, and acquiring studio space for rehearsals set her up for the next phase of her journey:

> we became very good friends. So I got together with them, I had a studio ... first we went to some kind of a market to buy things to fashion drums. They made six drums and they would come many times a week to my studio in the evening and drum to their heart's content and dance African dances. .... I got imbued with the motion, with the rhythms, with the whole richness of the performance.[100]

In January 1938 Dehn and Dodge performed *King of the Zulus* in their final concert together, *Dance Recital of Concert Jazz*, accompanied by master of swing music and symphonic jazz Herman Bueller. From this point on Dodge would dedicate himself to writing about music and dance. In the same year at Times Hall Dehn presented *Primitive and Concert Jazz* with Winifred Widener, Faith Dane, Trumpeter Frankie Newton, Pianist Ray Parker, and the Nigerian Drum Quartet Effom Odok, John Antiga, Thomas Udo, and Etem Offiong.[101] A picture in her collection that year also shows her in a piece called *Birds of Prey* with

Asadata Dafora and Coker, in traditional African dress. This is one of the first representations with Dafora, and their partnership over the next eight years would produce concerts, lectures, and a school for jazz dance.

The Academy of Swing

John Warner "Asadata Dafora" Horton (1890–1965) was born in Freetown, Sierra Leone, a colony founded by British abolitionists in 1787 to resettle freed slaves. John Perpener wrote that Asadata, interested in those outside of his Westernized environment, would "leave home without permission to explore the countryside and observe the rituals and festivals of villagers who maintained older traditions."[102] He learned seventeen distinct African dialects, continued to explore indigenous cultures, and immersed himself in the music, dance, and folklore of different ethnic groups. His family moved to Europe in 1910, where he studied at Milan's La Scala Opera House.[103] The tenor first supported himself by singing when he moved to in Harlem in 1929, his free time was spent creating authentic African dances, and he soon began producing a series of dance-dramas employing African and African American dancers.[104] His productions, *Zunguru* (1940) and *Batanga* (1941), introduced African dance and music to audiences in New York, which were often staged by the African Academy of Arts and Research (AAAR), founded by Kingsley Ozuombo Mbadiwe, with the intention to show American audiences that the folklore of Western African nations constituted worthy artistic contributions.[105] His childhood memories of the dances were incorporated with detailed accuracy into performances which further refined the purity of the dance. A stunning example of this is *Ostrich*, set to African drumming and flute by Carl Riley. With elegant movements, torso rippling, and resplendent struts, the dancer articulates the nature of a majestic bird; *Ostrich* remains in the repertory of the Alvin Ailey American Dance Theater to this day. His first full-length opera, *Zoonga*, met with moderate success in Harlem, however, it was the staging of *Kyunkor* ("The Witch Woman") which established him as an artist who presented the "cultural gifts of Africa to the world."[106] While there were some mixed reviews, John Martin's led to the production being moved from the small, semi-professional Unity Theater to the larger Chanin Theater on Broadway, where the dance-opera became the season's box office hit:

> Mr. Horton has woven a wisp of a story of African life just strong enough to hang a wealth of folk rituals upon. A bridegroom comes to an "African Maiden

Village" to choose a bride. When he has made a choice, he becomes the victim of evil magic directed toward him by a disappointed candidate for his affections, and it requires the services of a witch doctor to revive him. That is all the plot to the "opera," but the amazing songs and dances it entails, more than compensate for its slightness.

Three drummers on the side of the stage beat "hypnotic rhythms sometimes of extraordinary composition. Against this background the beautiful voices of the singers rise from time to time, but more often the terrific vitality of the dancers vents itself." Martin continued that the performances were superb and it was one of the "most exciting dance performances of the season."[107] Overall critics were "amazed by the propulsive energy of the dancing, overwhelmed by the polyrhythmic power of the drummers," and his staging of authentic African art.[108] Dafora also performed *Kykunkor* in a festival at Jacob's Pillow in 1942. The program stated that the piece "not only shattered many myths concerning the potential of Black ethnic material as themes for concert dance, [but it also] proved Black dancers could be successful on the American concert stage." His work influenced the development of later generations of Black dance artists with a "humanity which had not been seen by America in the thirties."[109]

Most likely Dehn met Dafora through the AAAR, where she had already met Momodu, and the Nigerian drummer Prince Effom Odok; or they met at the FTP, as the company he formed, Shogolo Oloba, was sometimes known as the Federal Theater African Dance Troupe. Both concerned with folklore, they began to work together, she on what she saw developing in the dance halls and he on Western African dance, respectively vowing they were worthy artistic contributions. They founded the academy to do that work; however, like her experience with Momodu, Mura told Wickre:

> he taught us, also cautiously, also withholding. He did not give us as much as he gave to his black pupils who were his company and I only found it out when we performed. I saw the poverty of our vocabulary in African and the richness of theirs, but he gave us a lot even so. The thing was overflowing, you see, and we had drummers that were magnificent. And the Academy of Swing was terrific with two of the best drummers, Coker and Simba playing for us.[110]

Regardless of his reservations, their partnership produced concerts, a school, and lecture demonstrations. In 1940 they presented *African and Swing Dance* at the Charles Weidman Theater in Manhattan; in 1943 they established the Academy of Swing, first at the Gellendre Studios, then later at 5 West 52nd Street, known as "Swing Lane."[111] There is some confusion about the name, as she called it the "Academy of Swing," though it is referred to as the "Academy of Jazz" by some journalists. *PIC Magazine* wrote that while most "American youngsters learn jitterbug dancing by spontaneous combustion . . . an atmosphere anything but scholastic . . . at the Academy of Jazz it is treated as a serious art form and a significant contribution to our native culture." In order to trace the roots, Dafora gave a course in African dancing where one could compare "step by step the movements of American jazz and the African original." Their special course in improvisation became the most exciting where some of the best material for their concerts was created.[112] The aim was to assemble and classify the jazz vocabulary, and they hoped to form a pool of professional dancers in the pure folk technique for concert stages. Dafora taught African dance, Dehn taught jazz dance, and at different intervals Whitey, Shorty George, and Al Leagins taught Lindy.

The academy was an attempt to define the form and rhythm of jazz dance. Dehn thought that a jazz movement is never simple or single, there are always several rhythms going on simultaneously. At the base of every movement was a constant pulsating bounce, which is as important in jazz as the pulsating reflex of the torso is in African dancing. Eighty years later Rennie Harris explained the pulse of the torso moving the same way, each bounce keeping the beat or time.[113] Dehn said: "On top of the bounce there is an accent what one may call a syncopation or off beat." Another important aspect was the pause, "a suppressed or choked movement so to say, under the skin [that] manifests itself in a pressure of muscles, a hesitation, a stop." A pause gives jazz its contagious power, she explained, it is not an empty waiting for time, but a stop charged with withheld rhythm and energy.[114]

The Academy offered three courses to guide the serious student through research in the classical form of jazz dance: *Origins of Swing*, which comprised native African or any other Negro primitive dancing of African origin; *Jazz Vocabulary*, divided into two courses: *Early Jazz* and *Current Swing*; and *Concert Jazz*, a summing up and development of the two above-mentioned courses.[115] When first established, neither knew exactly if jazz was African or American in origin; they actually found South and Latin American rhythms to be closer to African roots than those rhythms found in jazz. They reasoned that the dominant Protestant culture in the southern parts of the United States during slaveocracy feared the drums of the enslaved West Africans and banned them. They may have recognized their communicative abilities, but looked down upon them, and the accompanying dance, as barbaric. In contrast, in Latin America Africans were frequently allowed to retain some semblance of their instruments and religions, hence African retentions were much more apparent in the rhythms of samba and rhumba than those found in the jazz of the United States.

A 1943 *Academy of Swing* concert program at the Humphrey Weidman Studio Theatre included *Tiger* by Dehn, *African Dances* by Dafora, and *Harlem Routine* by Randolph Scott. African Drums were provided by Norman Kocar; the Boogie Woogie Angels were Edith Kapell, Corinne Malkin, and Sonya Searle. Dora Kaminsky made the mask, and costumes for Dehn's solo *Birds of Prey* were by Sara Ripault.[116] In May of that year a newspaper photo of *Unity through Dance* included Dehn, Dafora, Scott, and an assemblage of folk dancers at the New School for Social Research. In June 1944 she again performed *Tiger* with Randolph Scott and a group of dancers from *Carmen Jones* at the Humphrey-Weidman studio and at Times Hall.[117] *Tiger* prompted Martin to write: "Miss Dehn's definition of jazz is a singularly inclusive one, ranging all the way from African drumming and ceremonial dances, through the conventional blues, to a kind of Sino-Malaysian Bird of Paradise and a little kitsch burlesque called Venus and Eros." He seemed a bit confused about the "amorphous nature" of the concert, but finished by saying the audience was of good size and most appreciative.[118]

Mura was also in Lake Placid, New York that year, again dancing *Tiger* and *Babalu* accompanied by Anne Dodge. An August article described some of the work Dehn and Dafora were doing at the Academy of Swing. It briefly mentions Dehn's theory that jazz dance was the first folk form to be born in the United States. Dehn meant that most cultures have long histories and have not been witness to their ancestry. They are born into and are the heirs to the statements of their country's folklore. Children learn it from parents and grandparents at festivals, commemorative events, and in daily living. "It is a people's testament of their national character." Yet, Dehn said: "because the Africans were brought unwillingly to this country and not allowed to continue with their own cultural practices, their new folklore was being created daily," at a dynamically different rate than experienced by other cultures.[119]

A 1946 benefit concert titled *African Indian American Concert* for the AAAR featured La Meri, Josephine Premice doing *Haitian Dance*, Asadata Dafora performing *West African Dance*, and Juana in *Indian Dance*. It received a tremendous response from the audience, being called extremely instructive and enjoyable. The reviewer wrote: "what is technically known as 'killer-diller' came from Miss Mura Dehn, who interprets varied phases of American life . . . when waving her highly expressive derriere to a moaning blues, she gives one the impression that this is exactly what the blues-writers were talking about."

Her last number, called *Ad Lib*, was done with Alfred Leagins and Leon James. Beginning with a classic routine, the dance evolved into a "jitterbug dance designed to make a Savoy habitue positively green with envy.[120]

The Academy of Swing and Asadata Dafora pushed Dehn to articulate and write about jazz dance theory. She was moving from creating impressionistic pieces based on what she observed to performing and presenting what was actually being done in the dance halls, and toward documentation in the forms of writing; the latter would continue, but also segue into filmmaking. Jazz musicians from that point on were integral to her work, and Dehn collaborated with some of New York's finest, the above-mentioned included, and with Art Hodes, Frankie Newton, Cecil Scott, Hot Lips Page, and Wilbur and Sidney de Paris.[121] In a 1947 letter to *Jazz Record* she and the Savoy Swingsters asked would there be any jazz music if not for the dancers? Later, in a 1948 article for *Dance Magazine*, she argued both jazz dancers and musicians receive their impetus and feel the emotion from rhythm- both start from the "beating of the hand on a drum."[122]

It is hard to imagine how Mura supported herself after relief from the FTP ended in 1939, though she must have procured some money from the articles, concerts, the academy, and teaching dance classes. In the mid-1940s she met Herman "Dutch" Thomas, a captain in the Merchant Marines, and probably married him in 1947. A picture that year from her father has the inscription, "To you my dear darling Mura and Dutch, my love and best wishes for a long life of happiness."[123] Dutch was often at sea during the first half of their marriage; he enabled Mura's nomadic and artistic lifestyle by supporting her financially, yet providing her with an inestimable freedom in her pursuits. Mura Dehn was unable to have children; without dependents but with a dependable income, she continued to travel and pursue her research.

4

Swingsters, Masters, and Champions

[In the 1930s] Black and white dancers were working closely together . . . then whites took all they could from the Negroes and the Negroes were not hired . . . the white artist was the lucky one . . . and my work was to give recognition and to show who is the initiator and the great creator of this American style of entertainment.

Mura Dehn[1]

The Dance Hall Takes the Stage

The Harvest Moon Ball (HMB) competitions propelled both the Lindy to global popularity, as well the careers of the Savoy champion dancers. Some went on to perform across the United States, Europe, Brazil, Australia, Broadway, and Hollywood. Mura Dehn was dedicated to these ballroom artists with whom she danced, and increasingly chose dance hall-style vocabulary, musicians, and dancers for her performances, including one February 1947 at the Norlyst Art Gallery. Titled *Jam Session* with the Savoy Swingsters, the concert featured Baby Dodds on drums, Pops Foster on bass, and Cecil Scott on clarinet and saxophone. On April 13, in a concert at the Local Auditorium titled *Masters of Jazz*, the assisting artists were Sandra Givens (Sandra Gibson), Esther Washington, Tiny Crawford, Helen Daniels, Leon James, Albert Minns, and Willie Posey, this time with noted pianist Art Hodes and Scott, Dodds, and Foster. The program listed the Charleston, Big Apple, Snake Hips, Trucking, and Shim Sham. On November 30 Dafora, Dehn, and Franziska Boas performed at the Solidarity House in a benefit for the Youth Fund. The following year Mura Dehn's Jazz Dancers did the sugar foot stomp at the Stuyvesant Casino.[2]

An entry in Dehn's unpublished manuscript alludes to difficulties working with the dancers.[3] Whitey's group fell apart after the Second World War, when the dancers realized how much money he made, and how little he paid them. She approached the elite members of his company, who were eager to start on a new venture, though she had nothing to offer them "except my enthusiasm to present Jazz dance in its pure non-commercial forms and the determination to find new possibilities."[4] The dancers were not happy; while they may not have articulated why, everything they felt showed in their actions, and Dehn was puzzled on the depth of their blues. Most of them had been on nationwide or international tours with astounding success (if low-paid), yet after the war the opportunities waned. They would not let her into their ecosphere, even if they wanted or needed the gigs. Dehn believed that the creators of jazz thought they could achieve recognition through its power; if the movement was allowed to mediate, it would bring a mutual understanding and respect between Blacks and whites; the dance and music would be the evidence and proof of their humanity. She commented on the underlying temperament of the changes: "After WW II appears a new generation of Black artists. They are in a different mood. They feel betrayed. They understood that the unity and equality so much hoped for by the jazz generation was never realized, never will be given of a free will by whites."[5]

Though frustrated, with customary tenaciousness Mura carried on. Critics who insist Dehn could not possibly understand the former champions because she was white and classically trained ignore the fact that she danced with these same artists at the Savoy multiple times a week for two decades. She interviewed dozens of Black artists and valued and recorded their words. Dehn did emit an air of authority; however, a complete analysis of her collection reveals she never promoted white hierarchy. In fact, she championed the Black artists at the expense of the dominant white narrative that since Paris had revealed itself to her as fixed and unprogressive. Others assumed that because she was white she was wealthy, and like the impresarios before her would take advantage of and profit off their talents. By every account, Dehn's life was financially modest, and she assumed all the expenses for rehearsals and musicians. Profits would be divided among the dancers.[6]

It is difficult to line up some of her reminiscences with notices in the *New York Times* and the programs in her collection as her manuscript was composed at least two decades after the first concert with the Savoy dancers. She recalls the recital being at Cooper Union, but most likely she was referring to the concert at the Local Auditorium (sometime that year it changed its name to Tammany Hall, furthering confusing the details). Her strength and perseverance were evident, even as she admits despondency. She was dealing with habitués of the Savoy who rehearsed routines, created new steps, and competed with "speed and brilliance and glory." She found that working with them was quite different from the pleasure of watching them on the dance floor. She wrote:

> A few weeks before the performance I called a meeting to say that we had our first chance to appear in [sic] Cooper Union. There was no pay, but it was good publicity and a "public audition for agents." The answer was oblique.... The hats went down deeper on their noses. Side glances were exchanged. Records put on and without further reference to the concert, dancing started. They tried out novelty steps just for themselves—in a captivating elusive manner.[7]

Demand for the professional Lindy teams was almost zero after the war, and she thought they would like the opportunity to dance with a great orchestra and possible recognition as concert artists. However, the first meeting was spent settling beefs among themselves, jokes at times, and hostile sullenness at others. The only even-handed member was respected dancer Pepsi Bethel, who wrote very favorably of Dehn and these rehearsals in his memoir, and was "trying out for himself in the concert field and was obviously disgusted with the bunch."[8] They reluctantly agreed to the concert, yet only four of fifteen appeared at the first rehearsal, did not want to practice, and repeatedly asked for more money, which she did not have. She felt like she was inside an "Alice in Wonderland Croquet Party." Though Pepsi and Leon James reassured her not to worry, she felt lonely and friendless, having to run about on the day of the show rounding up dancers and rearranging the musicians' line-up. Fifteen minutes before the opening the program had to be reorganized as only six of the original fifteen showed up. Regardless, she assured the performers they were "good enough for any goddamn show" and ultimately thought the show a "triumph," leading James to say: "Always you worry for nothing." She realized improvisation was a most forceful aspect of their art. "They were very professional—Whitey had them trained enormously although it was all based on what they did at the Savoy.... It was all assembled . . . but within the routines they would improvise, just like the jazz musicians who improvise upon any music they play which is already composed."[9]

The Masters of Jazz

The dancers listed in the *Masters of Jazz* performance who would go on to work with Dehn were Sandra Gibson, Esther Washington, Leon James, Albert Minns, and Pepsi Bethel. As one objective of this monograph is to pay homage, with ink, to those innovators, I attempt to acknowledge them with deepest respect, admitting the tributes are uneven depending on the length of their involvement with dance and what could be found in books or on the internet. Since the 1980s revival of swing dance extensive attention has been paid to the original Lindy Hoppers still living, and thankfully many swing websites contain biographies and film clips of their heroes. The websites are predictably varied in academic intentions, quickly arise and disappear, but are considered when appropriate herein. Of the other dancers in the 1947 *Masters of Jazz* gig, extensive searches turned up nothing on Tiny Crawford. Helen Daniels was a finalist in the 1945 HMB and later danced with Frankie Manning's Congaroo Dancers during one of their annual summer-long gigs in Atlantic City.[10] Willie Posey was among the third generation of Savoy dancers who, had a "series of decisive victories for the Savoy";[11] he was a finalist with Janie Hansford in 1948 and 1949, and Sugar Sullivan in 1950.[12] The *Village Voice* wrote that Posey asked Barbara Billups to enter the last HMB in 1958. Apparently he was a wild dancer and had difficulty finding another partner. Even after Billups protested, saying, "You know I can't dance!" Posey insisted, and the couple ended up placing third.[13] Billups went on to dance with Sonny Allen and the Rockets; Posey helped to cement the Savoy's dominance in the HMB right before the Savoy doors were closed forever.

The other Savoy masters are well known in the Lindy universe, most were second-generation Lindy Hoppers, featured in magazine articles about Dehn and Dafora's *Academy of Swing*, and appeared in the first volume of Dehn's *The Spirit Moves*. **Esther Washington** was a good dancer who could partner anyone.[14] It is possible to see her at the time of this writing in multiple video clips on YouTube, though an exhaustive search could not locate a birth or death date, or any other biographical information. What is known is that she danced at the Savoy and joined Whitey's Lindy Hoppers by 1938. In the spring of that year, during a three-week engagement at the Roxy Theater, they were spotted by producer Harry Howard, who hired them as two of the only eight Black dancers to tour New Zealand and Australia in the *Hollywood Hotel Revue*. The group was billed as The 8 Big Apple Dancers, and performed in Melbourne at the Princess Theatre from January to March in 1939.[15] When the orchestra's tempo sped up and filled the theater with a "frenetic, loud, toe-tapping, ear-bleeding swing number," eight dancers seem to spontaneously form a circle and began to dance so fast they blurred the colors of their costumes. One reviewer wrote: "the eight apple dancers work up to a startling climax of color and speed, creating a magnificent spectacle seldom witnessed on stage or screen." The finale recreated a Mississippi show boat act.[16]

Returning to the United States, Esther and Billy Ricker partnered in the HMB in 1939, where they did "grab the pants and pull-back" and were credited with creating a swing-out followed by continuous air-steps called "mutiny."[17] In the 1940 HMB she placed second with Ricker.[18] She was one of the Hoppers to appear in the 1941 *Air Mail Special* and in the 1947 *Boy What a Girl*.[19] Also that year she actually danced a Charleston with Mura Dehn and James in the aforementioned *Masters of Jazz* concert. In April 15, 1951, she appeared in the presentation by Mura Dehn titled *Panorama of Jazz* dancing the cakewalk with Al Minns and Leon James, *Hip-Cat Blues* with Teddy Brown, and jive with James.[20] In *The Spirit Moves* (*TSM*) she performs several dances, including the *Tranky Doo* with Minns and James.

Esther's biggest fan was **Sandra Gibson** (née Mildred Pollard, 1919–?). Born in Atlanta her blues dancing in *TSM* was strong, sexy, and silken. She first met Al Minns as a child when her family moved to New York City, where her father was a minister and she often sang in church. When she was eighteen they began going to the Savoy, participating in the Saturday night contests,[21] and she was soon recruited into the Lindy Hoppers, playing the Apollo Theatre and touring to California in 1937–8, where she appeared in RKO's *Radio City Revels*. In the *Revels* Mildred was afraid to do aerials but was quite strong, so picked up her partner at the end of the dance.[22] After the tour Whitey paired her with Al Minns, "combining a male who could play with partnering techniques ranging from strong leads to submissive follows, with a female who possessed a similar range of abilities."[23] It was Pollard and Al Minns who invented the famous "shake-the-change" step Al performs in *Hellzapoppin'*, where the follower holds the man upside down while he shakes his legs.[24] Pollard, nicknamed "Boogie" for her boogie-woogie wiggle which she did "very low down and funky," and Minns, named "Rubberlegs" for his sensuous limbs, won first prize in the 1938 HMB.[25] She and Al went to work at the Cotton Club alongside Cab Calloway, the Nicholas Brothers, and the Berry Brothers from September 1938 to February 1939, taking "them to a new level as the demand for ace Lindy Hoppers continued to intensify."[26] Later, with Minns in *Hot Mikado* on Broadway, she performed an erotic shake dance in a skin-colored leotard with strategically placed flowers, foreshadowing her second life as an exotic blues dancer.[27] Al and Millie also found time to fit in a week at the Apollo in 1938 and danced together into 1940. When *Hot Mikado* finished, Mildred decided to break with Whitey's operation and turn solo. She met Albert "Gip" Gibson of the Chocolateers at a party thrown by Mura Dehn; they married and she became Sandra Gibson. After her time with Whitey, she continued in show business performing exotic dance and stand-up comedy; she and Gip later had a show called The Mad Gibsons. In 1988 Sandra had a part in the documentary *The Call of the Jitterbug*.[28] Her husband (profiled in Chapter 7, Section I) worked for nearly a decade with Dehn and the Traditional Jazz Dance Company.

Al Minns and Leon James met Mura Dehn at the Savoy in the late 1930s, danced in her concerts in the 1940s, and films in the early 1950s. They are among the most well-known of the *Masters of Jazz* company, enjoyed individual success on Broadway and Hollywood films, and danced as a duet on and off for over twenty-five years. **Alfred "Al" Minns** (1920–5) was born in Virginia, grew up in Harlem, learning to sing at church (where his family held hopes for him to lead a ministerial life,) and dancing on street corners with other neighborhood children to make money. His daughter, Denise Minns Harris, described him as "a renaissance man" and one who broke barriers. Minns began by learning the Charleston and the snake hips eventually becoming an expert in the Lindy hop.[29] He said: "My father played the twelve-string guitar, and when I was six, he'd take me along to rent parties, and I'd sing and dance." The entrance fee for the parties was twenty-five cents, and there was homemade whiskey, food, and dancing to piano and guitar music.[30] Later Al went with friends to the Savoy, which became a "second home. He would go after school, do his homework there, practice dance steps, go home for dinner, and return."[31] Al was invited into the Hoppers, where Whitey coached and helped each dancer develop an individual style, making them "do one chorus for five hours, tearing it apart. No two fellows kicked out alike; no two girls twisted the same."[32] When Whitey paired Al, then eighteen years old with lightning speed, with the powerful Mildred Pollard (Sandra Gibson), they won the Lindy division of the HMB on their first attempt in 1938. The couple received the most applause when they appeared in the victor's performance at Loew's State hosted by Ed Sullivan, who was a columnist for the *New York Daily News* and had made it a practice to feature HMB champions in his variety shows every year.[33] In 1939 they worked the Cotton Club and the Apollo and performed in eighty-five performances of *Hot Mikado*. Through all of this, demand for the elite Hoppers intensified. When Pollard turned to a solo career, Whitey sent Minns, with new partner Willamae Ricker, on a tour through the Midwest.[34] In 1941 they danced in *Hot Chocolate* with Whitey's Harlem Congaroos, were among the four couples dancing in *Hellzapoppin'* and one of three of the film's couples who went on to a successful engagement at the Rio De Janeiro Casino in Brazil.[35] Many years later, when Minns and author/swing dancer Robert Crease went to the street where the Savoy once stood, he related that the Savoy held the happiest memories of his life. "It was a beautiful place," he said. "Black people and white people and, oh! everyone dressed in suits and furs. You had to act like you had class. No loud talking and no cursing, or they'd throw you out. You kept your jacket on, and by the end of the evening your jacket would be black with sweat."[36] Minns was drafted in 1943, served with a detached regiment in Europe, and entertained Black troops in a revue called *The Harlem Express*. "When I left Harlem," he said, "it was jumping. When I came back, it was limping."[37]

Minns' longtime partner, one of the most well-known Savoy dancers, **Leon James** (1913–70), was born in New York. In clips available online at the time of this writing, he is recognizable by his constantly moving legs and hands and flashing eyes. "My parents thought that if you study too much, you'd crack up, so when I was a teen-ager they urged me to go dancing."[38] He was shy but able to create steps, slides, spins, and knocking knee movements alone in front of the band at the Alhambra Ballroom. At first the others thought he was snob and also called him "rubber legs" (seemingly a common nickname of dancers of the time). Eventually some girls came over and asked him to dance, and he soon found himself at the Savoy.[39] James told Stearns: "Nobody (at the Savoy) copied anybody else or copied anyone's specialty ... I could never do steps like the other guys anyway; I'd just wiggle my legs and it came out different—Clock Clock they called it or sometimes legomania."[40] In 1935 James was a building superintendent, and a member of the Jolly Fellows, the dancing arm of Whitey's gang. Remembering how the Lindy Hoppers were chosen and developed, James said: "Whitey, wasn't a dancer, but he had an imaginative eye. He took charge of the best dancers and supervised them and he'd get us work.[41] Whitey had entered the dancers in the first HMB, though they did not think they could win "because we were black, and also because they had a lot of rules, such as you couldn't break away from your partner. Whitey insisted they break all the rules, they kept telling the band to 'Pick it up! Pick it up!' and we did the freeze for an encore—we'd dance and then all of a sudden stop."[42] He and Edith Matthews won the HMB in 1935. James' talent and innovation were motivated by the music. "Every time [Gillespie] played a crazy lick, we cut a crazy step to go with it, he dug us and blew an even crazier lick," and that game challenged all of the dancers and musicians to continuously create.[43]

In 1940 Leon became a national figure when he and his dance partner Willamae Ricker were featured in a photo essay in the August 23, 1943 issue of *Life* magazine. That year he was also in the MGM musical *Cabin in the Sky* with Lena Horne, Duke Ellington, and Louis Armstrong. Due to his poor eyesight James was one of the few Lindy dancers not drafted into the army during the Second

World War, allowing him to continue his career teaching and performing. In 1947 Dehn approached Minns, who was working in a paint factory, and arranged for him, James, and a few other Black jazz dancers to give performances, the first one took place in the aforementioned Norlyst Art Gallery.

Minns, James, Washington, Gibson, and Bethel demonstrated the dances of the Savoy in Dehn's concert-style lecture-performances, and were in many of the photos that were used for promotion and her magazine articles. She continued writing in 1947 through 1948, performed in Mexico in 1949, then recruited all of them for her epic film *The Spirit Moves*, parts of which were shot inside the Savoy. Al and Leon met Marshall Stearns when he became involved in Mura Dehn's live productions. Whereas Mura focused on dance, Marshall also took an interest in their vocal expressions.[44] In 1952 they danced and spoke with Stearns in the Lenox Music Inn series. In 1954 they were recruited to inject some "authenticity" into *Jazz Dance*, Roger Tilton's film of the "then mid-town student jazz scene."[45] They appeared with Dehn at the YMHA in her American Jazz Dance Company in 1957 and 1960. In 1958 they performed in *An American Dance Concert* at the YMHA with Stearns and were participants in Rhode Island's *Newport Jazz Festival*, where they attracted an audience of 400. According to John Wilson, they "stole the spotlight from the major programs of the festival." The two men were partners in the "Lindy Hop segment and even perform[ed] an aerial routine together."[46]

Minns and James joined Stearns at the New School in a November 1960 lecture-demonstration, *History of the Jazz Dance—from Cakewalk to Cool*,[47] then appeared with him in 1961 in the TV specials *The Dupont Show of the Week* and *The Playboy Club*.[48] From December 1960 through October 1961 they were also advertising in *Dance Magazine* monthly, calling themselves "The Jazz Dancers" and "Specialists in the History of Authentic Jazz Dance."[49] They were in the TV special *Chicago and All That Jazz* directed by Bernard Green in 1962, followed that May by *Jazz Showcase and Dance* at the Woodstock Hotel, calling it a "promising step toward the revitalization of jazz as dance music."[50] They had planned to continue with similar presentations on a weekly basis, though there is no evidence that happened.

When Marshall Stearns' health began to decline around 1965 he retired to Florida to write, and passed away in 1966. His wife published his epic book *Jazz Dance: The Story of American Vernacular Dance* in 1968, prompting Minns and James to perform a tribute to him at the Town Hall in January 1969, again finding receptive audiences. This time they used records as accompaniment and blended "authenticity with the atmosphere of a vaudeville show."[51] Crease also commented: "These occasional appearances were well and good," but the dancers were barely able to support themselves with menial jobs. "Furthermore, [Minns] was embittered by the fact that younger blacks viewed his generation of black entertainers as Uncle Toms, content with bit parts while whites held the lead roles" (for example, Minns played a busboy in *Hellzapoppin'*). After the death of James in 1970, Minns turned to excessive drinking and stopped performing.

A decade later, a 1981 news clip depicts Minns coming out of retirement at age sixty-one with a new company at the Theater of Riverside Church.[52] That year he attended a reunion of Savoy dancers thrown by Mama Lou Parks. Larry Schulz, a jazz enthusiast and a news writer for a television station in New York City, spotted him there and persuaded him to teach at the dance studio run by his wife, Sandra Cameron, where Minns met Crease, who wrote:[53] "He taught classes but had infinite patience with us, and our wooden hips," and "didn't seem to care that all of his students were white . . . as he threw himself into the kind of dancing he loved, agile and limber as a teenager."[54] Soon after, the Swedish Swing Society brought him to Europe, where he participated in the revival of the Lindy hop by teaching several hours a day, five days a week. He gave up drinking, his classes were touted on the radio and in newspapers, and they attracted hundreds of people. Minns danced as if "the entire sixty-four years of his life had been nothing but joy."[55] In July of 1982 he appeared on US TV with Sugar Sullivan in *In The Circle: Stories from the Savoy* for the *Riverside Dance Festival*. In 1984 Norma Miller reunited Al, Frankie Manning, and Billy Ricker, the three surviving male dancers from *Hellzapoppin'*, during her production at the Village Gate. Minns had been a great contributor to the swing dance revival in both Europe and New York; when his poor state of health finally caught up with him after returning to New York, he died in April 1985.[56]

When I had the privilege to interview another of Dehn's *Masters of Jazz*, **Alfred "Pepsi" Bethel** (1918–2002) in February 1996, he was still a "dapper, genial presence," who had an embodied knowledge of the roots of authentic jazz dance.[57] He was a slight man with a cap of gray hair and a body that could be described as "near-Cubist—all edges, angles and indentation," certainly a man in love with what he did.[58] Pepsi was born in Greensboro, North Carolina, was raised by his grandmother, who gave him the nickname under which he performed throughout his career.[59] He was self-taught and learned dancing "from the streets and from the ballrooms, I came to it with tennis shoes on, eight or nine years old."[60] Before reaching his teens, a reunion with his father led to regular visits to New York City, where he discovered the Savoy. In North Carolina he organized his first ensemble, The Southland 400, importing the ballroom's standards of performance, dress, and appearance. Without monetary rewards, they performed with joy during the intermissions at many of the big band shows within a fifty-mile radius of Greensboro. Unable to resist the allure of the Savoy, Pepsi returned to New York and came to the attention of Eunice Callen, one of Whitey's Lindy Hoppers, who found him roles in the *Basin Street Revue* at Broadway's Roxy Theatre.[61]

At the Savoy Bethel had gravitated toward the Tuesday night 400-Club sessions, where he and Al Minns helped get the Lindy hop off the ground. He explained that Lindy was basically the same dance as the jitterbug, except that "in Harlem, at the Savoy, nobody'd dare call it the Jitterbug." The major differences were the frantic tempo and the astonishing air-steps.[62] His charm and grace are evidenced in his 1990 memoir *Authentic Jazz Dance: A Retrospective*, in which he wrote that he and his partner, Audrey Armstrong, competed successfully in the HMB in 1942. The following year he was cast with Whitey's Jitterbugs in a Bill "Bojangles" Robinson revue, *Born Happy*, in the film *Crazy Horse* with the Count Basie Orchestra, and danced with the Jivadeers around Los Angeles before returning home. The HMB brought Pepsi back to New York in 1946, where he took second place with Leona Jones. He wrote: "It was during this period of my life, when I made the acquaintance of a truly remarkable person, Miss Mura Dehn. A dedicated jazz enthusiast, she made it possible for me to rehearse dance steps with two most extraordinary dancers, Al Minns and Leon James." Throughout his book he credits Dehn with having an impressive career as a dancer, introducing him to jazz legends James Berry and Avon Long, and creating stimulating atmospheres in hours-long studio rehearsals.[63] Bethel was in Dehn's *Masters* concert in 1947, and in 1950 Dehn filmed him demonstrating various dance styles from the cakewalk to the Jersey bounce at the Savoy, a project that led to his involvement in a series of Dehn's lecture/demonstrations in the 1950s and 1960s.[64]

In 1954 Pepsi's growing reputation helped him win a scholarship at New York's Adelphi College under Hanya Holm, where he studied ballet and modern dance for two years. "The jazz I can never lose because I've lived it. But I've got the other side of the fence—the ballet and modern side—too. Other raw dancers like me, they just have the jazz side. And they don't go for any training for performance, they don't warm up or nothing. You better not say warmup, that's an insult to them."[65] He settled in New York in 1961, danced in Dehn's *Carnegie Recital Hall Concert* with James Berry and Georgia Peach, and the following year, took a role on Broadway in the Tony Award-winning *Kwamina*, choreographed by Agnes de Mille.[66] In the 1960s and 1970s he taught at the

Alvin Ailey Dance School, reminiscing: "We had the Roseland Ballroom, the Savoy Ballroom, we had the Palladium—and each one had a different thing. The Palladium had the Cha Cha and all that; the Roseland had the Peabody, the Shag; and the Savoy had the Lindy Hop." He recalled that the most exciting thing was when Ed Sullivan would host the HMB at Madison Square Garden. "Everybody waited for that particular moment because you had five, six and eight teams on the floor at the same time, in tempo, doing air steps. . . . I mean it was a show!"[67]

In 1969 Pepsi was featured in Dehn's tour of Africa. Hubbard wrote that Bethel acknowledged Dehn as an artistic mentor and performance coach, who maintained a watchful eye over his artistic development.[68] Dehn in return learned from him, and in a 1969 interview Bethel proclaimed the characteristic of individuality. He told her: "Jazz is individual. This is what makes jazz so important. . . . In my opinion there are no two jazz dancers alike." He went on, "In jazz the flexibility of the whole body is an answer to what is happening in the feet, and the rhythm. You have no particular form of the body in jazz to stick to. It may bend, it may be straight, it may twist at any given time."[69] After touring Africa and Europe and teaching in Amsterdam, Pepsi continued to teach at the Ailey school, and the Clark Center for Performing Arts, where he offered a "unique approach to teaching, featuring a rhythmic delivery, an emphasis on individual expressiveness, live music, and combinations derived from authentic jazz dance movement vocabulary."[70] There he met Thelma Hill, who encouraged him to form *The Authentic Jazz Dance Company* in 1972. This extraordinary venture, continued Monaghan, went against the "current African American cultural tide, which gave a largely Africanist interpretation to Black consciousness." Influenced by Dehn, he insisted on an accurate representation on the vernacular styles from the minstrels of the nineteenth century to the Lindy hop in the 1930s and 1940s, highlighting the importance of previously dismissed dance forms. Pepsi was often asked to teach, but was skeptical of the modern jazz dance in college dance programs where the students looked "for too much too quick. They want everything like instant coffee. Nothing works like that, not your mind, not your body, nothing."[71]

In 1980 Pepsi was honored as a choreographer in *Celebration of Men in Dance* at the Thelma Hill Performing Arts Center in Brooklyn. His company's success led to staging the revue *An Evening with Charles Cook and Friends* in 1984 at Aaron Davis Hall.[72] In 1986 he taught and choreographed for Monaghan's company in London, The Jiving Lindy Hoppers, in a production called *That's It!*, a tough but immensely rewarding experience that enabled that company to turn professional the following year.[73] He was choreographer and consultant on revues conceived and directed by Vernel Bagneris, including two productions of *One Mo' Time*, a jazz revue set amidst the black vaudeville circuit of 1920s New Orleans, and the 1987 *Staggerlee*. That year he was also a production consultant for *Sing Hallelujah!*, a gospel musical, and later for the 1994 *Jelly Roll*. In 1997 a disastrous fire at his apartment destroyed many of Pepsi's belongings, after which he became a recluse. His former pupil, Eddie Robinson, cared for him until he passed one day shy of his eighty-fourth birthday.[74]

Despite the aforementioned trouble with the dancers, Dehn's insight into the form grew and she became even more passionate about jazz. The intensity of her mission to preserve the dance she witnessed at the Savoy is revealed in a 1940s letter to Marshall Stearns. A portion of the letter reads:

> The mass of people where [jazz] really lived doesn't need it anymore—it has to go to some other channels. . . . Jazz dancing needs now the support of the academic world. It would be very tragic if it were only to survive in the ballets of [Jerome] Robbins, through the lofty incorporation of it by modern dancers or through the scholarly castrations of it by Katherine Dunham or even through self-discovery. . . . This is what I think is needed and what I think you could help us realize . . . jazz is a one-legged proposition without dancing . . . Negro art without dancing is unthinkable . . . so it really is your business as much as mine . . . because they really need us.[75]

Dehn was earnest trying to convince academics of the seriousness of her mission (Stearns as a Harvard graduate and a professor at Hunter College). While "because they really need us" ignites images of the "White Knight" rushing in to save the victim, even if when victim is not asking to be saved,[76] Dehn's beliefs and her mission were sincere. She positioned the Black social dancers as equal to the most noted artists of the day, such as Jerome Robbins and Katherine Dunham, and her confidence enabled her to do her work with a magnificent obsession.

5

Jazz Profound

Mura Dehn has the distinction of being the only artist in the jazz field who has analyzed, classified, and assembled the essential material of jazz dance and thus has made it possible to present a panorama of the entire art.[1]

Ethnography, Inquiry, and Analysis

The quote above was penned by Marshall Stearns, probably in connection with the lecture demonstrations they worked on together in the early 1950s. From other clues in Dehn's writings, it is apparent that she knew Stearns from as early as the mid-1940s. The letter goes to say: "In her work, Miss Dehn's first achievement was to discover dancers who employed the greatest form. She then helped to guide them toward the finest and richest qualities in jazz dancing." "Above all," he continued, "Miss Dehn is admirably equipped with the intelligence to analyze the nature of the art she is presenting, as well as the artistic ability to create the dance itself in person—a rare and fine combination. Her goal is a Jazz Ballet based on this rich but neglected folk art."[2]

The 1950s ushered in a productive phase in Dehn's efforts to document jazz dance, she added films and lecture demonstrations to her schedule of talks, concerts, and writing articles. She lectured on Jazz Dance in the Educational Program at the YMHA, whose faculty also included Doris Humphrey (Modern Dance), Bonnie Bird (Tap), Walter Terry (Dance Criticism), and Richard Kraus (Dance History). The October 10, 1951 *Y Bulletin* announced that beginning on October 17 Dehn would offer a class in American jazz, stressing the Charleston, Lindy hop, Big Apple, and Savoy routines. Beginning on November 7 she traced the development of jazz dance through lecture demonstrations on twelve Wednesday evenings with Asadata Dafora, "who has done pioneer field work with the outstanding leaders of American Negro, folk, and jazz idioms." Lecture material in Dehn's Folder 228 was prologued by this note:

> The unprecedented renaissance of American jazz dancing, a "Dance Craze," invaded and conquered this country and Europe and lasted for twenty-five years. It reached its peak first in the 20's during the Charleston and Flapper Era and in the middle 30's in the Lindy and Jitterbug. The recent postwar period marks a period of quiescence; there is a definite decline in general dance interest and participation; and it may be that we are witnessing the disappearance of one of the most virile expressions in American Dance History— a unique folk-dance period which since, as one writer puts it, has become the property of the world.[3]

Dehn goes on to suggest that semester courses be taught in universities, that films be made to document jazz dance, that lecture courses be given on tour to colleges and dance programs, and that books be written to explore the folk idiom. Interestingly, this was just before Stearns began the long research on jazz dance which culminated in his well-known books, and decades before others began writing about the dance. Dehn aligned her work with standard ethnographic practice by attending conferences with Gitel Pozmanski, a lecturer in Anthropology at Hunter College to help integrate the conceptual framework of the study. She also received encouragement and sponsorship from George Amberg, curator of Dance Archives at the Museum of Modern Art, Allen Porter, assistant secretary of the Museum of Modern Art, and from Paul Magriel, an editor of *Dance Index*, who reassured her of the validity of her approach to the field research. Dehn recorded the voices of many jazz dancers in their communities, seeking to interpret their origins and meanings, resulting in a polyphonic description of the folk form.

Unapologetically appreciative of Black social dance, Dehn thought it a crucial element in the cultural design of America that served both the Black community and the world community at large.[4] Dehn, and her text and artifacts, cannot be reduced to one dimension, but rather reveal an industrious, courageous woman who used her dancer, choreographer, researcher, anthropologist, writer, and film maker experiences and knowledge. She considered the who, what, and why of African American vernacular dances in relation to their cultural significance, their symbolization, and their embodied politicized responses. She was received at times with some skepticism, but her passion, her direct involvement with the dance forms, and her collaborations with Black dance artists motivated her to continue. Without formal training at a university or in any social sciences, she was still a dedicated and meticulous student who wrote from what she observed. Her work and intuitive methods were well respected and supported by the scholars Stearns and Alan Lomax.

Journey through the South

Wanting a clearer understanding of the evolution of jazz, Dehn boldly traveled to the segregated Southern states of Alabama, Florida, Georgia, Louisiana, and South Carolina[5] during a time of deep racial division where few white women would venture:

> I made a journey through the south to get a deeper insight into jazz dance. . . . I visited churches, dance halls, night clubs, spoke to people young and old in the markets, small villages, universities, towns, and outskirts of towns. I am sure it is easier to penetrate the secret societies in Africa than as a white woman to be admitted to the other side of the tracks. But once the obstacle was removed the cooperation was perfect by both whites and by Negroes. I found the Blacks in the south more open and sincere in talking about what moves them and what pains them. The word used most often was the word "spirit." Spirit moves me, Spirit leave me, Spirit touch. I went away with deep respect for that spirit: indomitable, resourceful, and immensely creative.[6]

Henry Louis Gates wrote in 2021 that the Black church was "formed out of fragments of faith that our ancestors brought to this continent 500 years ago," and was the first site for the development of many African American aesthetic forms. The church afforded room for both spiritual and secular expression to be practiced at the same time. Spirit stirred creative and liberating energies through expressive bodies, connecting communities through felt experiences.[7] Dehn was moved by the spirit she witnessed, and felt the jazz mood was one of upliftedness, despite the underpinning of trying to overcome oppression. "During this journey," Dehn observed:

> What seemed to me a peculiar quality of Americans: not to acknowledge tragedy. Tragedy was a mistake, a shame, to dismiss from our conscience. But the Southern Negro had to face tragedy. There was no way for him to escape it. . . . And in spite of the pain the art forms espoused a tremendous, contagious, uplifting vitality. Even the blues (which was essentially meant for self-consumption) became the most popular Black lore, acclaimed for its sensuous drive.[8]

Dehn believed the mood of the dance, along with the steps, the styles and associated meanings, changed over time as a continuous reflection of each era, a belief she learned from her informants, not only the dancers of the Savoy, but also the Black folk she met in the Southern states. Langston Hughes gave her the name of a friend who was a reverend of the Christian African Methodist Church in Savannah, Georgia. Her observations that their dance is inseparably connected with life and only by speaking about life could they convey the meaning of the dance came from Reverend Guilbert, who told her: "Negros know no textbooks on the history of their lives." She reflected, "and maybe it is better. Everything is still fluid, the past and the present are still simultaneous and everyone sees it in his own way":[9]

> it is the ability to communicate with spirit. That is the great gift of Afro-Americans. That was their protection against destruction. Now after 350 years of being suppressed, of being forgotten, (of being ashamed of) the African quality takes over. Not only the Black and white Americans but the whole world. It is the creative spirit of Africa finally made use of by everyone, thanks to the American blacks.[10]

Dehn began to understand what Black Americans had endured through an examination of one of their most poignant semiotic systems of expression and communication. Dance is embodied commentary, a kinesthetic response to a given event or idea. According to Dehn, jazz reflected social attitudes on current events, trends, and conditions. In discussing the social aspects of dance, she did not dislodge the form from the people, but rather strove to understand the movement in relation to its context. "I tried to record the statements of the dancers as accurately as possible, even if it sounds repetitious. The choice of words, the manner, even the mistakes reveal the undercurrent feeling of life and dance. It often reveals something they don't want to say outright."[11]

In her effort to record a chronicle of a folklore-in-the-making, Dehn unwittingly produced a homage to America embracing the contribution of its largest ethnic minority. She wrote that the "song and dances of a people reveal the essence of their being. In dancing, people express their own character through using their bodies in a manner designed to provide personal satisfaction."[12] Cultural relativity, what cultural artifacts mean to the people, is a principle of anthropology. Her questions were: Is there a definite pattern to the dances? Was the African heritage conveyed secretly? When did the church dance originate? Is speaking in tongues African memory? A summary of her journey was published in *Le Jazz Hot* in Paris in 1952:

> [Reverend] Gilbert said to me: "Blacks only aspire to be happy. And we comes to church to enjoy ourselves. This is how we say I came to enjoy the Sermon." . . . [He told her] "everyone confesses publicly, out loud, encouraged by the crowd of participants." Whether those present are seated or standing, their bodies begin to move, little by little everyone dances on the spot. The atmosphere soon reaches

its paroxysm, the blacks are then truly happy, until the women are seized with convulsions and fall unconscious. Being happy therefore consists of reaching this state of grace, this moment of ecstasy where, from the depths of their being, Black people have communicated rhythmically. . . . Dance is part of religious ecstasy.[13]

Folk Arts as Creative Resistance: Black Awareness in Art

Dehn experienced pushback during a visit to a Baptist church in New York. The account of the first time she was in an African American church in Harlem is telling. The parishioners "got the spirit" and were allowed to partake, but when she became involved, one of the "angels" of the church told her to stop:

> All my dancing in the States I learned from the Negro people [she told the angel, who] thundered back: "There are no Negroes here, there are colored folks." I was confused, Negro is a Spanish word, maybe she did not know that it meant dark black. She looked at me with great emphasis: "I know what it means better than you can ever teach me" and went away.[14]

Dehn refers to "getting the spirit," "speaking in tongues," and "Voodoo" celebrations in her manuscript, and realized that deep religious spirit could manifest itself in dance in and outside of the church. She may not have known the parishioners' diasporic connections, or that they were probably involved in a deeper ritual of actualizing a deity—not merely dancing but embodying the spirit. That metaphysical lineage, traced in Ventura's article "Hear That Long Snake Moan" and later by Gottschild and Carl Paris,[15] was enculturated by the African American church congregation, but would not have been obvious to those outside of it. Even if Dehn could not share the religious service with the congregation on that level at that time, she came to comprehend its powerful significance, and the "Spirit" underscores much of her writing.

She was also interested in gospel singing, prompted by friendship with the renowned Georgia Peach. Ms. Peach performed with Dehn's company at Carnegie Hall when James Berry made his return to the stage. She also wrote two articles on Peach for *Le Jazz Hot* (1952 and 1962),[16] and interestingly enough, it was her former partner, Roger Dodge, who produced Peach's first album. In spite of the rejection at the Baptist church, which would have been typical at that time in a country torn by racial conflicts, she persisted with her investigation of the Negro church as a repository, and the place in which the folk forms were born. "I should explain that for Blacks, the church is not an austere, pious place, but rather the opposite, it is the place where they exult in an absolute freedom, where they let themselves go, where they open themselves to God in their quest for ecstasy." [17] The sanctuary of the church offered a place for free expression—out of sight and hearing distance from the oppressive and dangerous Euro-American culture. Dehn, as usual, was interested in the voice of the churchgoers themselves, asking how they saw their experience and the birth of their lore. Just as rhythm was the foundation of Dehn's definition of jazz dance, it was also the reason, she believed, why the folklore developed as it did. Dehn theorized that when Africans were brought to the United States, European Americans could not conceive that there was an African culture and did not acknowledge their gifts of dance and rhythm. African dance horrified the whites, who saw it as "hideous, an abomination and bestial sensuality."[18] The spontaneous, full-body, rhythmically complex movements of the Africans must have seemed extraordinary to a culture whose folk dances had traditionally consisted of a controlled movement style, dictated by a straight, centered spine.[19] Dance and music were an assimilation mechanism, and the slave holders were also aware that the forms were a method of social interaction and political expression.[20] The dances of the enslaved Africans were soon forbidden, and they were encouraged to reject them. From the start, thought Dehn, the "most precious gifts of Africa were misunderstood and defiled." "Tom-toms" frightened the white masters, and African drumming brought a liberating energy that was too dangerous a weapon to leave in the hands of the slaves. The drums were destroyed and forbidden.[21]

Hazzard-Gordon wrote: "From the moment of capture, the slaves were under siege. The Europeans attempted to destroy their past and to crush their world view, particularly their religious beliefs, which held the key to culture and personality."[22] The captors introduced their own doctrines, expecting to convert the enslaved. But, Dehn wrote, "paradoxical as history is, the Black church, entrusted to divorce the black people from their heritage, became the repository of their national character, their African memory and their life experience in this country."[23] She elucidated:

> Although the African tradition worshipped deity through dance, the black American church put a ban on dancing. But the religious feeling of the blacks had to express itself through rhythmic motion and the "holy" dance had to be incorporated into the Black church. Even the forbidden drums reappeared first in the church and the shout (of African origin) became a part of the Christian worship.[24]

So even as a dominant culture tried to impose its own views of piety and civility onto the enslaved people, the dance and rhythm that were so essential in Africa remained as vital ingredients among the enslaved. Consequently, the rhythmic cadence—in sound and motion—which had once accompanied their lives as a collective reflex, remained. Dehn believed that within the church the cadence found a breeding ground, and worship and celebration developed within new boundaries, but with a familiar response of the body. The church became a vessel of Negro sound and motion; the great spirituals which would fuel future generations of gospel singers, and the accompanying movement, which would mix with social dance of the white culture to become jazz dance, were kindled and nurtured.

Nor was the rhythmic cadence squelched completely in other aspects of life. Dehn observed that "there came into being the work song and its body accents, even on the chain gangs, on railroads, when loading the ships or in the fields." Admittedly, Dehn recognized that "All hard-working people of the world help themselves with a rhythmic chant: the Volga boatmen, the hoeing peasants, the marching soldiers, the seamen chanteys." With the Blacks, she argued, the rhythm catapulted the chants into something else, "[they] became a re-creation of life into art," folk art.[25] "The only avenue they had to realize themselves was through music and dance." Dehn lamented: "God knows how people preserved the ability to create under the inhuman pressure of toil and disapproval."[26] Adaptive crutches, movement and music were powerful tools of resilience, perseverance, vitality and were celebrated. "Afro-American creativity [was] an answer and a guide to the problems of the moment,"[27] and dance became an opportunity to resist white domination.

Oppression was dealt with and creatively termed "Creative Black Resistance" by Mary Jane Aldrich Moodie.[28] Her paper on the Savoy Ballroom, asserts that there was a clear discrepancy between Black social dance as it was understood by its Harlem originators and as it was subsequently represented and reproduced by the dominant white culture. The difference defined itself in self-expression, especially in relation to the imbalance in their relative social and economic realities. She based her thesis predominantly on Dehn's films and written materials found when she served as archivist and cataloguer for the New York Public Library Dance Collection; "Creative Black Resistance" was what Dehn often referred to as "Black Awareness Through Art," the dance and music were sacred to the African Americans, and their artistry was political. Proactive and reactive at the same time—at once expression that could not be controlled by the dominant culture, a vehicle for comment on the same authoritative culture, and also, perhaps, a way to be recognized. "From the time the first Africans were brought to this country, until after World War II, the main effort of Black Americans was given to overcome the segregation imposed upon them, because of their African origin. With all the force of their spirit they fought to integrate completely; to become an inalienable part of this country."[29] Dehn rued that "The constant condemnation made them feel they had to prove themselves worthy of this recognition. The only avenue open to realize themselves without obstruction—was through their folk art in music and dance. Here they show their ability, their insight, their contribution.[30] Ann Douglas echoed the sentiment when she said: "The younger generation of Harlem artists turned their backs on the struggle for economic and political opportunity undertaken by their predecessors, Black Manhattan put its money on culture, not politics; Negroes were to write and sing their way out of oppression."[31]

The artistic endeavor was a daily enterprise interwoven into the very fabric of the culture. On the back of a piece of paper in Folder 131 Dehn had scribbled this thought: "Today we [whites] respond to events and to life around us through media, through a general intellectual awareness. This awareness of the contemporary pulse of life as transformed among Black Americans is reflected directly into folk art." The culture valued creativity and invention in dance and music, and consequently the forms were a consistent and prominent aspect of daily life. Daily encounter with music and movement facilitated the enculturation of the forms, which were absorbed kinesthetically as well as consciously. This was a partial explanation for the dancers resisting the idea of forming a school to teach the technique. "They are burning with the desire to be famous, not to organize a school; . . . they don't need it, the great stream of folk creation is constant among them, they do it at home." One of her more poetic explanations of this phenomenon reads: "The American Black is not born into his folklore. He does not inherit it. He does not embody its national character. He *is* the body out of which it is made. Before he comes it does not exist."[32]

The body and the dance were important, and jazz became the culminating expression of their understanding of American life, and a proof of identity with it; an expectation that through their "own resurrection in talent and spirit they gained an equal place in this land which they helped to build, which became their own."[33] Her feelings about the "jazz people" were mirrored by others who wrote of the Harlem Renaissance as the first systematic attempt to generate a cultural movement by Black Americans. The poet James Weldon Johnson wrote: "great art and literature made the world regard a people as great and would do so for the [Negro]."³⁴ Unfortunately, the status of jazz as a "lower" art form did not help the attempt to elevate the condition of African Americans.

Dehn felt that after the Second World War bebop was created by intellectual, revolutionary musicians who abolished the spirit of early jazz: "they don't want to please and don't want to be accepted, they are an elite."³⁵ What Dehn felt undergirded the form was a rebuttal, intentionally disconnected and incoherent, intended to alienate the uninitiated. She observed that the bop dancers in a cerebral and emotional revolt proclaimed themselves "Africans" and "Primitives," and believed the beginning of the "Back to the Roots" movement of the next decade began with disappointment among the artists, a stigma that influenced the art and the psychological ethos of the time. She wrote: "Only when hostility and misunderstanding really disappear will the Negro be able to develop with pride as a native son. Until then the double quality of audacious insight and banal preference will be intertwined in the psyche on the Negro artist. . . . The dancers don't smile—they avert their faces even from admiration. They don't compromise because they don't need to be accepted."³⁶ The bebop dance (and hence the bebop body) created and reflected, communicating a political impulse that the Eurocentric culture could only partially comprehend. Additionally, bebop was primarily designed for African American appeal; gone was straddling the line of wanting to assimilate and retain distinction. The dialogic body absorbed information from the environment and transmitted an opinion through movement. Dehn felt the creative energy of the Black artists and the attitudes of each era could be read on their dancing bodies. In her manuscript she said the *New York Times* described the postwar era as "cool," then analyzed the new psychology of the young and found bebop a perfect expression of "emotionally withdrawn, unastonished, cynical and critical of everything except the inner self."³⁷ However, unlike the rhythm of the swing era, argued Dehn, the rhythm of the beboppers was not a steady bounce with a plethora of off-beats; the rhythm instead was disjointed and the mood angry. "This period can be summed up as an alienation from white dance forms. A dismissal of white paternalism—a deliberate choice of orphanage in this civilization. . . . It brought Africa closer. The bop generation discarded fear."³⁸

A pause is necessary here, and a repeat. Dehn's response to what she saw and heard was, "*God knows how people preserved the ability to create under the inhuman pressure.*" Work songs, blues, jazz dance and music, bebop, and hip-hop were political expressions attempting to create personal narratives for survival. In an interview in 2020 Bob Boross asked me: "What you would like to tell people about Mura Dehn?" My answer: "Read her work."³⁹ Dehn was constantly querying Black artists to explain their motivations and inspirations, through which she was able to feel their struggles and vexation. Her investigations and journey through the South enabled Dehn, a white, Jewish, Russian woman, to recognize the frustration of Black Americans, *which is yet ongoing and unresolved*. The Black Lives Matter movement which exploded in 2020 was voicing exasperation and weariness over the same issues. After centuries of struggle their efforts still have not been fully realized. How long will it take to afford equality and value regardless of skin tone and shade? A reading of her documentation first gives an understanding of this history and, as Christi Wells wrote, "the complex and fluid web of social dynamics and power relations African Americans have had to endure and negotiate"; and second how their arts were created to negotiate them.[40] A grasp of history is imperative to empathize and understand the present; in turn the present is advanced by consideration of, and responsiveness to, the past.

Le Jazz Hot

Marshall Stearns spoke at the beginning of the April 1951 *The Panorama of Jazz: From Cakewalk to Mambo* concert in which Mura danced with Bethel, Washington, Leagins, Minns, and James.[41] Presented at the Kaufman Theatre, the presentation also included Milton Kamen and Theresa Mason—the latter a winner of both the 1942 HMB with Paul Chadwell, and the 1950 HMB with Ambrose Hall.[42] Killer Joe, and The Stuyvesant Casino All-Star Band were guest artists. On July 22 of that year Dehn danced the Hucklebuck, Apple Jack, Black Bottom, Lindy, and Big Apple at Carnegie Hall with the Savoy Champions while Buster Bailey's Rhythm Busters played the top tunes from three decades: "In other words, thirty years of Jazz and dance in one jam-packed night" at the air-conditioned Interplayers Theatre.[43] She also wrote a film proposal, "Epic of Negro Dance," and created the first part of *The Spirit Moves* with Herbert Matter.[44]

It is unclear where Dehn met Matter, but he was originally a painter then photographer who lived in Geneva and Paris at the same time as Mura and Adolf. He emigrated to New York in 1936, where his illustrations, like Adolf's, appeared in *Vogue* and *Harper's Bazaar*.[45] In 1952 the first section of Dehn's and Matter's documentary, covering jazz, bebop and mambo, was completed. She was invited by Henry Langlois of the Cinémathèque Française in Paris to present the (then silent) film to a select audience, "among whom were such visual artists or filmmakers as Cocteau, Pierre and Jacque Prevert, Rossolini, and Franju."[46]

An unedited version was presented, assisted by author and jazz expert Charles Delaunay, the founder of *Le Jazz Hot* magazine. The best music was selected, and with two record players running simultaneously, Dehn was able to change the records according to the dances on the film while providing live commentary.[47]

The screening was a tremendous success, newspapers gave rave accounts and the Académie de Cinéma organized a tour of a several venues, including Le Sciences Antropologiques et Ethnologiques, Comité fu Film Ethnographique, and the Musée du Cinéma in Paris. Many times, at the end of a showing the audience requested an encore, confirmed by a French newspaper clipping titled "*L'esprit Bouge*" ("The Mind Moves").[48] "Of the reels that we experience, it is undoubtedly the first dedicated to the 'hot' dance which is the most interesting, so much so that the public demanded an encore," even as "it was projected in its raw state, without cutting and without sound," making *The Spirit Moves* "one of the most brilliant documents to be placed in the jazz history file." The Paris newspaper *Les Actualités des Arts* called it Un film sensationnel de Harlem."[49]

At this point Mura was fifty years of age. She had performed almost continuously over thirty years, she graced the covers of magazines, lived in four countries, and published four articles in the United States before venturing into film work. While in Paris Dehn wrote the first three of seven articles for Delaunay's magazine *Le Jazz Hot* (which was among the first magazines in the world covering jazz). *Issue 59, Les Noirs et la danse par Mura Dehn*, was published in October 1951 and issue 60, *Jazz Musique/Jazz Danse par Mura Dehn*, in November. *Les Noirs* recounted some of her research. The introduction to the article by Delaunay said that during her visit to France he had the opportunity to meet and speak with Mura, "a choreographer, [who] has devoted herself to Black dance for twenty years. She traveled throughout the southern United States to trace the origin of all the folk dances which constitute the rich past of this art." She had organized and presented "in public a troupe of black dancers recruited from among the best specialists in the US, let's hope we have the pleasure of hosting them one day in Europe."[50]

The preface of the second article (translated here) read: "Several readers having kindly informed us of the interest they had in Ms. Mura Dehn's article 'Black People and Dance' published in our last issue, we thought we could respond to their desire by publishing below a second article by the same author." Here Dehn wrote the ABC's of jazz included the essential aspect of rhythm; while comparing jazz to ballet she wrote: "A ballet step is a succession of precise positions animated and organized by rhythm. In contrast, the jazz step is the interrupted movement of a human mobile, stopped by the pause resulting from a surplus of rhythm charged with potential energy." She talked about the birth of a folk art occurring only "when the old means of expression have become inadequate" and jazz was born out of a need for new energy. "The old folk dances of Europe placed dignity, pride, grace above all else; in other words, they took themselves very seriously. Jazz is essentially ironic and humor . . . the jazz artist is creative at every moment . . . jazz whose means are surprise and whose goal is freedom . . . never mechanic, never deliberate, [improvisation] appears irresistibly necessary."[51] A third article, published in October 1952, was titled *Introduction au "Gospel Singing" par Mura Dehn, and* the other four were penned in the 1960s and 1970s.

During her two years in Europe while touring with her film and writing for Delaunay she was also visiting her brother Boris in Lausanne. The first page of the chapter "Artists of the Theater," one of several versions of her manuscript includes that she stayed in Europe for personal reasons, then:

> Upon my return to the U.S. during 1954 I realized that the important era of Strut and its high-hat and cane dances needed to be presented by the professional virtuosos of "high society" style. I felt that the professional performers of the Black popular theatre, stylists, comedians, mimes and tap dancers had to be included into the documentary film to give a more comprehensive picture of Black dance contribution. In other words, the old timers of carnival shows, night clubs, vaudeville and musical comedy had to be searched out. I decided to contact the Berry Brothers, whose act of cane and high-hat strut was of the purest style and virtuosity.[52]

By 1954 she had returned to the United States and met James Berry, and together they created the first rendition of her performing jazz dance company. When asked what he valued in dancers, Berry spoke about individuality and possessing something acknowledged to be a profound presentation, presenting themselves from the depth "they throw off the ethics (rules) they go against the rule because they know they come out right, more than right."[53] **James Berry** (1915–1969), born in New Orleans to Ananias and Redna Berry, was first known as the child actor Bubbles.[54] The family, including older brother Ananias (Nyas), moved to Chicago, where the boys recited poems by Paul Laurence Dunbar. The young elocutionists followed the church circuit to Denver, where the duo performed at carnivals and younger brother Warren was born in 1922.[55] Their father, who was a religious man, at first did not approve of their performance aspirations, but eventually relented and taught them the cakewalk and the prancing strut. They were in Hollywood by 1925, where Bubbles had a job in the *Our Gang* comedies, and they entertained luminaries such as Mary Pickford and Douglas Fairbanks in their homes. James had parts in ten short silent films.[56] The two older brothers went on to an apprenticeship on the black vaudeville circuit the Theatre Owners' Booking Association (TOBA), leading them to New York City, where they received their only formal lessons from eccentric dancer Henry Wessels. There the teenagers developed their unique dance style, opening for Duke Ellington in 1929 at the Cotton Club, which for five years was their home base, though they also played the Apollo Theatre and traveled abroad. They rivaled the Nicholas Brothers, at one time upping them in an informal contest at the Cotton Club.[57] Their father had always insisted they have clauses in their contracts to ensure they were treated fairly, and they fought against racial discrimination. They were the first Black act at the Copacabana in 1929, and later that year they performed with Whitey's Lindy Hoppers at the Moulin Rouge. The duo danced with Ethel Waters in Broadway productions of *Blackbirds of 1930* and *Rhapsody in Black* (1931), and they were one of the opening acts at Radio City Music Hall on December 27, 1932.[58]

Nyas left the act for four years, and Warren stepped into his place. Later, when Nyas returned, the Berry Brothers turned into a trio that is considered one of the finest class acts of the time, known for their strut number *Papa De Da Da* throughout the world.[59] They combined the steps they learned from their father, mixing cakewalk and strut with soft-shoe, jazz dance, and acrobatics. Fortunately, they can be seen in various clips on YouTube doing the routine that propelled their fame in nightclubs, stage, and film and remained the same through the end of James' career.[60] They were elegant and extremely physical, using high kicks, multiple turns, splits from jumps, back handsprings, and lifting and spinning each other. They looked like they were tap dancing but never wore taps, using their top hats and canes with sensational effect while appearing in the Hollywood films *Lady Be Good* (1941), *Panama Hattie* (1942), and *Boarding House Blues* (1948.) In 1943, with Ella Fitzgerald and Don Redman's Orchestra, they Opened the Cafe Zanzibar, which allowed integrated audiences.[61] In 1951 Ananias tragically died of a heart attack at the age of thirty-nine; Warren performed with James that year in a revival of *Shuffle Along*, then retired.

Mura saw their unforgettable performance at Radio City Music Hall, describing them as flying through the air with "gaiety and brilliance."[62] Until then she had worked with only the dancers of the ballroom, without choreographed stage acts. She had realized that the era of the "Ritz" as important to jazz dance was yet not represented in her films and sought them out, finding James retired and living with his younger brother. He "condescended to dance for Dehn, Matter and Langston Hughes, which began their long and tumultuous relationship."

They became partners in 1954, and co-founded the James Berry-Mura Dehn Dancers, filmed two additional sections of *The Spirit Moves*, and saw each other almost daily over the next decade except when Dehn traveled to Europe. Their first company contract was for six months, with Berry receiving 60 percent to Dehn's 40 percent after all expenses had being paid, including the salaries of the dancers.[63]

"The world-famous Berry Brothers, one of the most fabulous Negro dance teams in show business, last weekend emerged from the shadows of retirement to score a smashing comeback at Wingdale Lodge" read a news release from 1955. It went on to proclaim: "if the roaring applause which greeted their guest appearance at New York's most popular interracial summer spot was any indication the Berrys' four-year absence has only made the hearts of their faithful fans grow fonder." Jimmy and Warren sent the "interracial audience to stompin' its feet and pounding its palms." They sang phrases of "I'm Gonna Live 'Til I Die" to each other, showing that time had "dimmed little of the old Berry magic." Interviewed after the show, the brothers said: "You know we've always fought against segregation wherever we played. More places like Wingdale Lodge and old Jim Crow will really go!" The Berrys had always argued for full citizenship, and James recounted that when he was making the celebrated *Our Gang* silents, his father would not let him be seen in any "picture that was insulting to the Negro people."[64] Their precedent-shattering victories included being the only Black act in the opening of Radio City, they were in the first interracial show in Miami, at Alan Gale's Celebrity Club, and followed that by becoming the first Negro act to play in Tampa, Florida. They told the interviewer they would "never perform in a place where they were not accepted as equals." The lodge provided a place to entertain and vacation in "the kind of atmosphere that really hits Jim Crow where it hurts the most."

Mura's manuscript is an unfinished narrative of African American social dance comprised of the voices of many artists, including James'. "James opened the memory chest, not hiding the black roots—the 'race' as he called it. And little by little this folklore (past and present) was opening itself to me."[65] He told her that the essence of jazz was being rhythmically conjured, caught in the spell. "Like being enraptured. They were possessed in a sense." He called it "Jazz Profound," a feeling that "lifts your spirit" and "Makes you have a good outlook on life." She saw this spirit come alive every time he danced or even spoke about dancing, and it was evident in the films they made and concerts they produced. John Wilson of the *New York Times* wrote that the midnight performance of *The Spirit Moves Me* at the Carnegie Recital Hall, with James Berry as solo artist, had "elements of an exciting program, but only able to sputter with fitful gleams of brilliance." Apparently there were compelling performances inside a "loose and rambling production." The Savoy couples included Zizi Richards and Pepsi Bethel, Thomas and Montoya King, and Teddy Brown and Vicki. Georgia Peach sang and Rex Stewart played trumpet with Milton Hinton's Jazz Quartet.[66] Bethel wrote about Berry in his book, saying that in rehearsals Dehn was ably assisted by the great master of jazz dance. Through Berry's patient demonstrations he conquered the difficult art of "strutting," to experience the emotional aspect of the dance and to move in a dynamic but graceful way. He described:

> As I watched James Berry, he would bring his leg up to his ear and then go into his strut. I have also watched other dancers bring the leg up to the ear but that was all it was, a leg up to the ear. With Mr. Berry, the movement was always expressed with style. Another thing that Mr. Berry did, and this never failed to intrigue me, centered around his spins or turns. They came off with such grace and smoothness, I never could detect the point at which his turns began.[67]

Mura often visited James in the apartment he shared with his poodle Clue while interviewing him about his days in the TOBA and his knowledge of minstrelsy. Of the TOBA he recollected they worked with such greats as Bessie Smith and King Joe Oliver in the days when Louis Armstrong was just a side man in the band that toured with them, and Cab Calloway was operating the spotlights and doing an occasional stint as an MC. He often sprang into impromptu performances and improvisations; "part of the day was spent in bed, legs on the wall, scheming unimaginable schemes to the constant sound of the radio." When the apartment was demolished he moved into the 1, 2, 3 Hotel on 43rd Street, "a dark, single room with a TV set." Many of his professional friends would visit, watch TV, and compare "the new stars with their own triumphs of yesterday, remember[ing] the elegant suites in other hotels, the extravagant homes that used to be theirs, the gambling and pranks and jokes and money rolling in and spent without a thought." The most frequent visitors who would later dance with them were Baby Laurence, Big Stump (James) Cross of Stump and Stumpy, and Chuck Green.[68]

In 1958 Berry and Dehn teamed with Leo Hurwitz and Herbert Matter to create *Artists of Jazz: Dancing, James Berry*, a seventeen-minute documentary on 16 mm film with musicians Wilbur DeParis, Buck Clayton, Milton Hinton, and Moe Wechsler.[69] Hurwitz was a progressive artist whose work was denounced during the political repression of the 1950s, yet he continued to produce, and his contributions were central to the birth of film as social commentary. His estate donated a copy of the film to the Eastman Museum in New York.[70] The video begins with a solo version of *Papa Dee* with Berry in top hat and tails doing high kicks, cane in hand through characteristic juxtapositions of slow, sultry steps with whipping high-speed turns and falls into splits that are jaw-dropping. The museum's version is introduced by William Ferguson II, who says: "Mr. Berry's artistry was demonstrated with absolute control, especially in the use of split screen in 'I'm Gonna Live 'til I Die,' the effective use of the improvisation in the jazz video defines the intelligence of Mr. Berry's artistic expression ... What an amazing treasure."[71]

By the early 1960s a hybrid of jazz dance was moving away from the motivation of the rhythm, individuality, and improvisation that was in Berry's flash acts and the swing Mura experienced at the Savoy—aspects that Dodge and Dehn had felt were important became secondary considerations. Dehn persevered. Under the auspices of the James Weldon Johnson Community Center, Inc., she was invited to create a show titled *Jazz, Our American Heritage*, presented at the East Harlem Plaza.[72] This group was called the Razzle Dazzle Scintillators, with stars of the "Cotton Club Jazz Era." Noble Sissle, best known as the lyricist and playwright for the 1921 *Shuffle Along*, was the master of ceremonies. The cast, performers from vaudeville through rock 'n' roll, included the Berry Brothers, Baby Laurence, Buster Brown, Albert Gibson, Chuck Green, Elaine Johnson, Danny Barker, Fred Moore, Taft Jordan, Skinny Brown, and David Martin, and the first five would later dance with Dehn in the Traditional Jazz Dance Company. The press release states that the show was "created by the entire cast to blend with the initial vision of Mura Dehn under the guidance of Bert Gibson" and took place in the "open plaza around a fountain like the Italian Commedia dell'arte of the 16th century." She also invited a group of neighborhood youngsters to participate in the rock 'n' roll section, as Black social dance was segueing into its next stage.[73]

Much of what Mura heard from James, memorialized in her manuscripts, was also published in *Dance Magazine* in 1961 and *Dance Scope* in 1977.[74] Though her friends felt she was "often saddled with Berry, he got into trouble and she got him out of it," Dehn never spoke ill of him; she talked only of Berry's talents.[75] She affectionately referred to the clownery and theater mastery he inherited from minstrels, from carnival shows, and from traveling circuses. She believed that he carried a bag of tricks that went back as far as sixteenth-century harlequins, "harlequins who were black-faced, mysterious, triumphant and elusive.[76] Still he progressively sank lower into alcoholism, "the drinking, the 609 house ... finally this room became hell's paradise. I became his 'dance treasure' and he trusted me

... and we fought constantly." She described his room as full of smoke and drink and dreams which at times became a stage:

> They were inspired. I looked on surprised, admiring, encouraging and somehow these people and I became the We. We were going to show it to them, This will be the 609 Story, in the room. The old timers, the professionals staged their show. It will start with rhythm. Out of the dark all of them beating some makeshift instruments. James in red-flannel shirt and naked legs, hat and cane.[77]

Dehn and Berry were always hoping for a big break; meanwhile one or two concerts a year in Little Carnegie, the Cooper Union, Bob Maltz's Jazz Club, East Harlem Plaza, and wherever possible kept the group together. Berry assisted Dehn's courses in jazz dance history at the New School of Social Research, at the YMHA, and at Nadia Chilkovsky's Academy of Dance in Philadelphia.[78] Berry's drinking, however, became increasingly problematic, until he was finally hospitalized. In his condition Dehn continued to support him and take him out of a sanitorium to her home on weekends where he would comment on all of her "domestications" while continuing with his jazz antics. For years her studio apartment was a home for James:

> He came with a bottle of Scrap Iron (cheap, cherry wine) and made himself comfortable in an easy chair. . . . Many peaceful hours were spent in "family life"—he watching and improving my domestic chores. . . . James received a hundred dollars for a television show; the hundred dollars turned into two hundred bottles of Scrap Iron. James was taken to the Hospital, gravely ill.[79]

When the James Berry-Mura Dehn Dance Company finally acquired an engagement under the auspices of the Smithsonian Institution at the 1968 Mexico Olympics, James was too sick to take part. He passed away on January 28, 1969, and the next summer they went to Africa without him.[80] A verse in Dehn's anthology *Lion Tamer* reads:

> James
> I lost myself
> The many years on 308 15th
> belong to someone else.
> . . .
> He settled in our kitchen
> in tales and talks
> and jumping up
> to show what it was all about
> inspired unrepeatable scrap performances.

In her 1957 article "The ABC's of Jazz Dance" for *Dance Notation Record* Dehn discussed with the Berry Brothers how Labanotation could be applied to jazz dance, as they had expressed interest in the system. Warren Berry, who was also a choreographer, wanted to know whether this method of transcribing dance could be "up to the task of recording the fluid motion through the body, with its occasional rhythmic accents, which may occur in the hip, the shoulders, or the head, while the step maintains its own precise rhythm." He wondered if notation could "render the sensuous beauty of the movement . . . and the need for detailing the interrelation of different rhythmic patterns of several dancers moving in counterpoint," mentioning that improvisation during a pause is a necessary ingredient of a jazz.[81] Due to hip injuries and subsequent surgeries Warren performed as a vocalist in several of the Berry-Dehn concerts, worked on sound for one of her films, then worked for fifteen years as a film editor for Screen Gems. He, the last Berry Brother, died on August 12, 1996.

6

The Spirit Moves
A Life's Mission

> *Jazz dance, like jazz music, is one of America's major contributions to world culture, and if you haven't seen the film, then you have been cheated of your own dance history.*[1]
>
> Sally Sommer

An Epic of Negro Dance

Film lovers were invited to a showing February of 1959 in the University Auditorium, St. Peter's Square, Geneva, urging those interested in seeing the "triumphal film" to get tickets right away as Mura Dehn would only be in the Switzerland for a few days. According to a jazz reporter David Millwood,[2] Dehn was in Geneva to visit her brother; she was back in the United States when her father, who had been living with her since 1947, died in 1960.[3] She continued to work tirelessly on her films through the Berry epoch as she met new entertainers and incorporated their expertise. She also continued to write prolifically: in addition to the 1957 "The ABC's of Jazz Dance" in *Dance Notation Record*, she penned "Negro Dance and Puritanism" in *Jazz Monthly* in 1961, "New Spirit in an Ancient Dance: World's Fair" for *Dance Magazine* in 1964, and "Jazz Dance" in *Sound & Fury* in 1966, in which the editor's note read:

> At a time when many readers of S & F were yet unborn, Mura Dehn was already paying her dues in jazz dance. Russian-born, Paris-reared, with a sound training in classical ballet, Mura underwent a spiritual rebirth when the jazz virus took possession of her; like a lot of other white people with strong esthetic sensibilities, she dropped everything, as it were, to enter the jazz world. She has been in it ever since: organizing ballets, films, fighting for "her" dancers, writing

in her not quite perfect but very eloquent English, passionately sure that the Jazz Dance is the human art form par excellence, a one-woman Crusade. We give you herewith a sampling of her sincerity, and her fierce and selfless devotion to her idea.[4]

Performances also continued, though the names of the group changed. February 9 and November 18 saw the Mura Dehn Jazz Dance Theatre at Cooper Union, while June of that year it was *Living Jazz, The Making of Folk Lore* at the Great Hall.[5] Lectures also continued, and in 1963 Billie Mahoney wrote in the Dance Notation Bureau's *Library News* that as jazz dance classes were still new, the DNB sponsored a forum "What Is Jazz" inviting Mura, Matt Mattox, and Billy Taylor to speak.[6] The March 1964 *Down Beat Magazine* announced that Dehn's lecture-demonstration course Authentic Jazz Dance was assisted by James Berry and Teddy Brown. In 1965 she taught a survey course on jazz dance during spring semester at the New School,[7] and *African American Folklore and the Church* was presented on November 18, 1966. Seemingly tireless, she continued her mission.

Dehn's plans for the film, originally titled "The Epic of Negro Dance," began in 1946 after she had organized the first concert of Swingsters.[8] The name, *The Spirit Moves*, was chosen because it is "an expression constantly used among Black people, especially the rural and working people of the South," in relation to all aspects of life but especially to the Black dance. Her aim was to "show the history and development of jazz, its meaning in the contemporary world for Negroes, for Whites, for America and for Europe." At that time half the research and a third of the writing had been completed for what she termed a "Jazz Dance Visual Manual" which would include illustrations and still photographs of the artists with news reels, film montages, and feature motion pictures. The manual would be geared primarily to dance education and be a document of American dance history. She called her new field of research a "reconnaissance" study as she feared a decline in interest and participation, possibly the disappearance of a unique folk dance. The plan's outline included "The 1920s Charleston and Flapper Era, "The 1930s Lindy Hop Era," "The Second Generation of Lindy Hoppers," "The 1940s Reaction," "A Twenty-Five Year Vocabulary of Dance Steps," and "The Social Function of American Jazz Dance." The last section, an indication of her depth of inquiry, was comprised of "In Status of the Individual," "In Therapeutic Value," "In Race-Relations," "As an Established Folk Dance," and its "Influence on the Emergent Jazz Academy." Her passion for the project is revealed in her proposal: "The [Negro] people of the United states created it. The white Americans supplied the passive material of their cultural inheritance and the mechanical tempo of the new civilization. The [Negroes] transformed it into an organic rhythm, joined to it the spirit and life of today." In the culture of the old and the new world the magic of African rhythms was "reconciled and reborn," she continued, "We find ourselves in it renewed and transformed. Jazz becomes the mirror of ourselves; that is why it is of such universal importance today."[9]

Dehn deserves unequivocal gratitude for her passion and work. *The Spirit Moves* is one of the most important films made of the chronology of jazz dance in her time. While all of the elements of the "Visual Manual" plan did not make into the film, it is literally used by hundreds of scholars and artists to understand the form. When seemingly no one else was paying attention she forged ahead, creating a lasting tribute to the artists. "Everyone interested in the history of modern dance and in Black creative history owes a debt to Mura Dehn for the fine work she has done in documenting this tradition, while it was at its peak of vigor and beauty," wrote Alan Lomax, director of the Cantometrics Project at the Department of Anthropology, Columbia University:

> The dance steps invented by these largely unknown and unappreciated geniuses influenced the popular dance everywhere and have left their mark on modern choreography, especially that of the popular theatre. In a sense American Blacks invented the first *internationally accepted* dance language. Mura Dehn was among the first to take a serious interest in these developments. We are lucky that she, instead of writing about it or incorporating it in her own dancing, decided to film these dances and film them systematically. She researched the field and became a close friend and a sophisticated and critical observer of the work of many of the most important Black dancers. Working with a well-trained cameraman she filmed not excerpts, but entire dances, and, in some cases, the whole of the occasions in which the dances took place. The camera work was not fancy or creative, but straightforward and reporter-like, so that nothing interferes between ourselves and the dancers, who in most cases are the finest performers of, or the actual creators of, the material filmed.[10]

There are actually seventeen films or videos listed in the New York Public Library Dehn Collection. Two shorts, *In a Jazz Way: A Portrait of Mura Dehn* (two copies) and *Glances at the Past: Documentation of Jazz Dance* are about Dehn as a film maker and ethnographer. Two other films in the collection focus on Dehn as a dancer, one in a solo concert and one with Roger Dodge, both filmed in the 1930s. James Berry, Pepsi Bethel, Vicente Escudero (two films), and a Harvest Moon Ball are recorded in separate films. The remaining seven items in the collection comprise the four volumes of *The Spirit Moves*, and with the exception of number three, all volumes consist of two parts.[11] Dehn's dear friend Lillian Morrison convinced her to donate a copy of several sections to the New York Public Library. Swing dancer and International Lindy Hop Championship co-founder Sylvia Sykes heard of the films in March 1986 at a swing dance event organized by Terry Monaghan and Robert Crease held at The Cat Club. Sykes contacted Dehn's lawyer Mark Scherzer, who arranged a meeting at which Mura told Sykes she thought people were secretly copying the films at the New York Public Library and distributing them. She sold Sylvia a copy for $3,000 with the instructions that Sykes could "show her students and other swing dancers but not charge for viewing."[12] Except for receiving a fee for a print in a film festival, this is the only evidence this researcher could find of Dehn monetizing her films. Dehn left copies of the movies and the majority of her work to Eiko and Koma, who then gave a full, further edited, copy to the New York Public Library.[13] Eiko sold a version to the publishing house Dancetime Publications, from which clips were cut and copied and now can be found on multiple swing dance websites.[14] At this writing parts of the film could be found (and had been viewed tens of thousands of times) on YouTube and used DVDs were for sale on Amazon.com.

Widely popular as a historical resource, *TSM* has generated some differing responses, from rich description to skew-whiff critiques, though the latter are mostly narrowly focused and lose potency when the gestalt is examined. For instance, in one critique the film is acknowledged as "unequal in its scope," but it contends that Dehn thought of her dancers as "underclass" (a word not found in her archives).[15] Rather, she wrote: "The jitterbug[ger] should be treated more seriously and with more respect. At the time of his devotion to jazz he spends five to six hours a day, practicing, polishing, improvising. He is his own pupil and instructor. He is not only an excellent technician and executor, but also a constant creator."[16] Another asserts that Dehn romanticized jazz, but does not acknowledge her sixty years of experience with the form, often dancing nightly at the Savoy with Leagins, Minns, and Shorty George, or her promotion of jazz dance concerts through the 1970s. She worked without monetizing or profit and immersed herself in researching and recording the voices of ordinary folk and professional artists, proclaiming jazz to be one of America's most important cultural artifacts. Scherzer, her lawyer, remarked: "I was always amazed she could continue to work as this bohemian artist for decades while making no money."[17] Nor did Dehn ally herself with the intellectual artistic community; more often she found herself outside, unable to penetrate it, writing: "The great new dance era that jazz brought along is ignored by the academic and purist dance world."[18]

Of course, no person of consequence is without controversy. Dehn had some off-putting personality traits, but she did not degrade or disrespect the artists in word or action; empathy, tenacity, and determination drove her work. She wrote: "Although conceived by Black Americans. . . . Jazz dance enriched the Caucasian dance culture," which she tried to portray in her films.[19] Dehn remarked in *TSM* that the dancers didn't fully realize the connections to Africa, which does not align with current theories of Black cultural retention, but she learned this from the dancers themselves. They weren't cognizant with the evolution of the steps they were doing; they were handed down through the diasporic body, not textbooks,[20] and together they discovered links to dances of different countries in Africa during their 1969 tour. When Mura asked dancer Willie Ray where his movement came from, he told her: "My movement is the expression of my race. It comes naturally. I don't know where it comes from. I copy to a certain extent James Brown, but listening is more important. . . . the music and drum tell me what to do. . . . I get ideas from just walking on the street to music."[21] Concerning the aesthetics of the filming, some decry the dance being taken out of its organic locale and filmed in a studio rather than the dance hall, not acknowledging Dehn's struggles to film on site. Nor is the input of film maker Herbert Matter credited, whose visual work was both manipulative and imaginative; both he and Dehn were aligned with modern, avant-garde art.

Regarding the views of some dancers, Robert White wrote that some, "like George Sullivan, were suspicious that Mura's interest was exploitive and refused to take part in her project (but his wife did); Frankie Manning did a little filming but decided that was enough" (Manning's expertise would not have been useful or needed in any other section); and Judy Pritchett (who used Mura's films in her own work) recalled Norma Miller putting her feelings bluntly: "That woman was crazy" (which probably holds a thread of truth).[22] Nonetheless, the dancers are immortalized in the film.

Others comment that Dehn did see the "societal forces shaping the dance," that "jazz was a dance of hope," and *TSM*'s range enabled the "spectator to see a century's worth of dance in quick succession."[23] *New York Times* dance critic Claudia La Rocco wrote: "*The Spirit Moves*, Mura Dehn's miraculous history of Black social dance . . . possess[es] a certain compelling messiness or strangeness, spontaneity (often as a metaphor for freedom) and the celebration of individuality within a larger group."[24] Terry Monaghan defended Dehn, saying she "developed through her life's work a pronounced awareness of the true classic stature and resilience of the African retention and how the dancers embodied it in their movement and vocabulary."[25] Giltrecia Head remarked that Dehn's "cinematic historical collection of African American dance movement proved beneficial in capturing the spirit of dances and dancers. . . . *The Spirit Moves* is a significant addition to Black social dance scholarship."[26] Dehn met Charlie Dorkins at the Savoy, where he was employed as a photographer's technician, developing the pictures taken of patrons, which patrons could then buy. They remained friends and colleagues through the 1980s. He told me of the numerous times he spent with Dehn, Berry, and others driving to Jones Beach on Long Island for the afternoon, or other outings, and the strongheadedness Dehn consistently showed in every aspect of her life. When working together on films, Dorkins recounted arguing with Dehn over many issues, including her selection of music, the method of filming, the content of the narration for the films, and others. "She did it all wrong," he said, "but I guess we should be glad she did it at all."[27]

Black American Folk-social Dance 1920–80 on Film

Below is a brief description of Dehn's documentary with the names of the dancers. The films, recorded between 1950 and 1984, are not ordered in the actual chronology of the dances, but rather in the sequence in which they were conceived; James Berry, who was filmed in the late 1950s, was edited into the 1970s films *Artists of the Theater*. The first mention of National Endowment for the Arts grants in her collection are *circa* 1970–71, so the opening credit must have been attached during later editing. It is important to note that certain clips found on the internet, those packaged by Dancetime, do not align with the original complete version in Dehn's Collection. Details of each section of the film, a total of 224 minutes, can be found in the New York Public Library Legacy catalog. All but Volume 4 were filmed by Herbert Matter, though he was joined at times by John Cohn (Volumes 2 and 3) and Joey Eysman (Volume 2), and the fourth volume was co-produced by Henry Chalfant with Martin Moore, editing by Cathy Weis and Burleigh Wartes, sound by Rick Patterson, and consultant Peter Kovac. James' brother, Warren Berry, was sound editor for Volume 1.

Volume 1, Part I, *Jazz Dance from the Turn of the Century 'Til 1950*, consists of studio demonstrations of ragtime, blues, Savoy routines, and postwar trends by artists of the Savoy Ballroom: Pepsi Bethel, Al Minns, Leon James, Esther Washington, James Berry, Sandra Gibson, Teddy Brown, Willa Mae Ricker,

Frankie Manning, Thomas King, and Scoby Strohman. The studio floor and walls are mostly white, the dancing exuberant and joyful, and at times Matter plays with tempo and lighting. Each dancer is, as Sally Sommer described, "silky and sexy.... The mark of the Savoy dancer was the splendor of his individual style."[28] Volume 1, Part II, *Savoy Ballroom of Harlem, 1950s*, is one of the finest in the series and was actually filmed inside the Savoy. Dehn asked for years, and finally was the only person manager Charles Buchanan ever allowed to film on the Track. Skeptical of her intentions, he insisted she put the camera in one position and did not interfere with the dancers.[29] The general public were filmed on a ladies' free night but, the film also includes a line routine, led by Leon James, a Charleston solo by Al Minns, and a rehearsal for the Harvest Moon Ball. Here the syncopations slide one step into the next, and even the line dancers execute individual style and vitality; timing, finesse, and improvisation are at a premium. (When watching this section, it is easy to understand why Dorkins and Bethel thought that the jazz that followed the Golden Era was "commercial, and merely cheap imitations."[30]) Volume 1, Parts I and II were filmed in 1950 and 1951.

Volume 2, Part I, *Postwar Era, 1950–1975*, was also filmed at the Savoy and other ballrooms of Harlem. *Flying Home* is performed by Teddy Brown with Sugar Sullivan, and *Bebop Time*, a sequence of solo concert dance improvisations, is performed by Jeff Asquiew, Leroy Appins, (Oaky) Milton Hayse, and (Scoby) Clarence Strohman. Here one can clearly see the disconnectedness, plethora of off-beats, and disjointed rhythms in bebop as Dehn described. A mambo/apple jack challenge is danced by the general public at Public School (PS) 28. *Dancers of the Palladium Ballroom* records Tandaleo and Jackie, Dottie Adams, A. Vasquez, Teddy Brown, Cuban Pete, and Millie Donni (Donay), whose Latino steps and sensuality are evident. Volume 2, Part II, *Postwar Era, 1950–1975*, is performed by Louise (Mama Lou) Parks and the Dance Company: Gloria Thompson, Gigi Brown, Arnold Gregory, Edward Johnson, Deborah Youngblood, Micky Wall, David Butts, Dickie Harris, and guest artist Willy Ray. This was filmed at the Savoy Manor in the Bronx in 1971 and includes rock 'n' roll step vocabulary such as the twist, pony, jerk, funky chicken and the boogaloo by the Harvest Moon Ball Champions.

Volume 3, *Artists of the Theatre*, includes a jazz minstrels dance by the Berry Brothers; comedy skits by Pigmeat Markham, Baby Seals, and Sandra Gibson, and *Jazz Comes Home* danced by the company. Highlights are Berry's elegant strut *Papa Dee Da Da* and *Gonna Live 'Till I Die*, Markham's *Here Comes the Judge*, and the Charleston, danced by James Berry and the Savoy Ballroom Dancers. Dehn dubbed this section *Old Timers* and filmed it in 1973. Volume

4, Part I, *Artists of the Street*, was produced and directed by Dehn and Henry Chalfant, a visual anthropologist who made documentary films about urban popular culture. Here a *Break-boogie Workout* features Lorenzo Harris, Gilbert Kennedy, and Steve Glavin of The Magnificent Force company directed by Julie Fraad. Dehn speaks briefly about the history and importance of breakdancing in Volume 4, Part II, *Breaks & Boogie*, followed by improvisations by Steffen Clemente, George Pabon, Gilbert Kennedy, Steve Glavin, and Lorenzo Harris. Filmed in the early 1980s, The Force demonstrates the waving, locking, popping, and floor work of hip-hop done on the streets of Spanish Harlem and the Bronx.

The Cast of *The Spirit Moves*

Though Dehn wrote copiously about jazz, she was neither a meticulous editor nor linguist, and *TSM* credits are laden with typos and a few off-putting word choices. The typos made researching her collection and her dancers tricky. For instance, "Tranky-Doo" is misspelled as "Trunky-doo," and Part I of *TSM* lists the California Lindy danced by William and Franky Manning, who were most certainly Willa Mae Ricker and Frankie Manning as they often partnered and *TSM* is listed by both as a film credit; Millie Donni was actually Donay. Robert White told this author he and Gloria Thompson, Sonny Allen, and Sugar Sullivan identified "Big Nick" Nicholson and Lee Moates as dancers in Volume 1, Part II, but as they were not in the credits please see more about them on his wonderful website *Swungover*.[31] Some of *TSM* dancers were profiled previously, and those who continued with Dehn appear later in this text; information that was available at this writing follows, in order of their appearances in the film. Most at one time were Savoy, Harvest Moon Ball, or Palladium champions, and the following mini-bio-scripts aim to memorialize these amazing artists for posterity.

Volume 1

The dancers in Volume 1 not covered in previous chapters include **Theophilus "Teddy" Brown** (1932–?). Sonny and Sugar told Robert White that Teddy was a "great Latin/mambo dancer who attended the Palladium ballroom regularly."[32] Brown perfectly illustrates Dehn's description of the "pause," captured energy, vitality, and joy in jazz dance. The silhouette of him dancing and the footage of him and Sugar Sullivan doing *Flying Home Harlem Style* in *TSM* are exceptional examples of fast feet, loose knees, and the sinuous torsos of the Savoy dancers. He was as a finalist in 1951 and won the 1952 HMB with Elizabeth Stewart. That night 18,000 people witnessed the eighteenth annual event at Madison Square Garden, and Ed Sullivan, of *Toast of the Town* served as master of ceremonies.[33] Dehn wrote in her manuscript that at age eighteen Teddy was the calypso star of the Savoy: "His body vibrates from the shock of his lacquered hair to his heels. Legs sent backwards in a double step, slide from under, soles fly out." He was "slick, humorous, elegant" as he faced his partner, who ducked her head and shook her the shoulders with a "teasing accent." They both floated on the "Calypso wave."[34] Brown also performed a mambo (an offshoot of bebop with an African-West Indian rhythm) in *The Spirit Moves Me* concert at the Carnegie Recital Hall in May 1960. Sadly, that is all that could be found on Mr. Brown, but fortunately we have *TSM* to remind us of his prowess.

Due to her roles in the movies and in magazines, **Willa Mae Ricker** (née Briggs, 1910–78) is the one most often seen in pictures and clips of the early Lindy Hoppers on the internet. She in grew up in Harlem, Frankie Manning was one of her best friends, and they began going to the Savoy and dancing for Whitey at the same time.[35] Ricker toured extensively and appeared in *A Day at the Races*, *Hellzapoppin'* in 1941, the 1941 soundie *Hot Chocolate (Cottontail)*, and the short tongue-in-cheek documentary *Outline of Jitterbug History*. She was featured in two *Life* photo essays on the Lindy hop: in 1936 with George Greenidge and in 1943 with Leon James.[36] Willa Mae's marriage to childhood sweetheart Billy Ricker, also a dancer, began in 1934, though they rarely danced together. In *Hellzapoppin'*, for instance, Willa Mae partnered Al Minns and Billy partnered Norma Miller. *Hellzapoppin'* was also a successful Broadway stage show, still one of the top 100 shows of all time, and readers are encouraged to watch a clip online as it is one of the most iconic Lindy scenes ever to be put on film or stage. Riki Panganiban wrote that it is important to remember the film was a product of the racism of the time:

> The dance scene is completely superfluous to the rest of the film. The dancers appear in no other scenes. In fact, there is only one tiny sequence where a Black person and white person appear in the same shot, for a throwaway joke about the standing bass. That segregation is intentional and was common practice in Hollywood at that time. Black people performing or speaking in scenes was still controversial or even scandalous to certain white audiences, particularly in the

American south. So those scenes were shot in such a way that they could easily be omitted in certain theaters. I think of Frankie and his teammates and what they must have known when they came together to shoot this scene—how they were going to be depicted in the film, how it might never be shown in parts of America. And yet they decided it was worth it to get their art out to the wider world.[37]

Willa Mae was known for her height—she was as tall as most of her partners—and her balance and physical strength allowed her to lift her partners; she is the one seen holding Minns upside down in the film. She was also a skilled producer, known for her business acumen and dependability. During the Second World War, when so many Lindy Hoppers were serving in the armed forces, she managed Whitey's Harlem Congaroos. Notably she is remembered as standing up to Whitey and demanding equal pay for woman.[38] She acted as manager for his Lindy Hoppers when the group was on the road, and thanks to her managerial abilities, Willa Mae often served as group captain when on tour. Known for her sophistication of style, after the Congaroos disbanded she had a successful career as a fashion model.[39]

Willa Mae's friend **Frankie Manning** (1914–2009) was born in Florida and arrived in Harlem when he was three years old.[40] He also trained at the Savoy, and soon became a lead dancer and choreographer for Whitey, appearing in *Radio City Revels* 1937 and *Hellzapoppin'* in 1941, and touring with Count Basie, Cab Calloway, Ella Fitzgerald, Duke Ellington, and Bill "Bojangles" Robinson. While in London in 1937 he gave a command performance for King George VI; in 1941 "Musclehead" Manning's acrobatic brand of Lindy was featured in a *Life* magazine article. In 1946, after serving in the Second World War, he took over management of the Congaroo Dancers, touring again and appearing on Milton Berle's and Ed Sullivan's TV shows. Though he continued to dance socially, as with many Hoppers when he could no longer find work as an entertainer he took a day job (with the US Postal Service), married, and raised a family. Rediscovered by swing enthusiasts in 1986, he began teaching and touring again. In 1989 he was featured on the *20/20* television series and received a Tony Award that same year for his choreography in *Black and Blue*. Among his many honors are the City Lore People's Hall of Fame (1993), an NEA Choreographers' Fellowship Grant (1994), a National Endowment of the Arts National Heritage Fellowship Award (2000), and a Flo-Bert Award for Lifetime Achievement in Tap Artistry (2004).

The Frankie Manning Foundation (FMF) was formed to carry on the culture and joy of Lindy hop; it focuses on ensuring that the stories of Manning and the Savoy are preserved, "building, connecting, and supporting the Lindy hop community." It is sponsored by Beantown Camp, Herrang Dance Camp, and the International Lindy Hop Championships. The largest swing dance event of the modern day took place in New York City on May 2014 and brought together over 2,000 dancers from forty-seven countries to honor Manning's 100th birthday. All of the above data can be found on the FMF website with additional biographical information, descriptions of ongoing programs, resources on the Lindy and for Lindy dancers, and dancer profiles by Robert Crease.[41]

Also a third-generation Lindy Hopper, **Thomas King** (birth and death dates unknown) placed in the HMB in 1946 with Jean Morgan, in 1952 with Beatrice "Bea" Pierce (in which he can be seen doing his signature sliding movement), and in 1953 with Montoya Borden.[42] The lack of information about the rest of his life is unfortunate, but serendipitously, led to a piece by Robert White on his website *Swungover*. It bears repeating here. White is among the swing historians, with Riki Panganiban and Peter Loggins, who take great care to pay homage to Black artists with every entry on their sites. The following is particularly potent as Mura often referred to the joyful vitality of the jazz dancers. Experiencing an ecstatic realm while dancing is transformative, which Dehn often referred to as "spirit." White puts that in context of the HMB: "there is a difference between the *fun* spirit most of the HMB White dancers exude verses the *joyful* spirit of the Black American dancers. The Harlem tradition was not just about 'having fun,' but as Dehn often said about personal and cultural expression." Revealing their "incredible skill honed by thousands of hours of practice, in a competitive cultural environment [was a] joyful defiance to the oppressive society they were within":

> That resulting joy has an edge. It is a joy that includes fierceness, wryness, and power—emotions that the young white dancers of the same city seem too often interpret as fun, goofy, showy.... Several dominant cultures created the concept of race within the last five hundred years, and in doing so, made those who fit into the category of "Black" as significantly different.... It is only natural that the culture surviving that ordeal develops ways of expressing themselves, their excellence, and their joy, as a positive and necessary means of defiance. And it is only natural that those not living that ordeal, and not seeking to understand it, don't get the complex difference between "fun" and "Black joy."[43]

Volume 2

Remarkably, at the time of this writing **Sugar Sullivan** (1930–) was scheduled to teach at Beantown Dance Camp in the summer of 2024 at ninety-two years old.[44] Born as Ruth Guillory in Harlem, she began dancing when she was four, studying ballet, singing, and predominantly tap. Her mother was a "shake dancer who had a rooming house near Harlem's Apollo Theatre, which accommodated many comedians and tap dancers."[45] She fell in love with Lindy after seeing *Hellzapoppin'*, entered a HMB contest in 1946 through the Roseland Ballroom preliminaries, and began to train at the Savoy as soon as she turned eighteen. "I went every day and night until it closed in 1958 except when I was pregnant."[46] She missed only two years of the HMB, the years she had her children, and after each she returned to practicing as soon as possible. She told White that many dancers were able to train and raise families as they brought their children to play with others at the Savoy when they were rehearsing. "The ballroom left their large windows open, allowing for breeze in the un-airconditioned, 2nd story ballroom. The kids would suck on ice from the ice machine, and the adults would have to constantly pull them down from the windowsills."[47]

Sugar and her husband George Sullivan won the HMB in 1955, were crowned the Jitterbug Jive Champions and danced, as tradition had it, on the *Ed Sullivan Show* on TV.[48] She was then invited to join Sonny Allen & the Rockets training six hours a day for eight months before they opened at Smalls Paradise, boasting "We could do push-ups on our knuckles!"[49] Their show toured the United States and Canada for thirteen years. When the Rockets folded, Sullivan took off a couple of years, brought up her two children, but rarely missed an opportunity to dance herself. In 1980 agent Larry Schultz asked her to dance with Al Minns, who had already been rediscovered by Lindy enthusiasts, and they performed at the Savoy Manor (which opened after the ballroom closed) and Smalls Paradise. After Al's passing she found herself involved with a new generation of Lindy revivalists, and today she is one of "very few dancers from the old-school generation still passing on the Harlem dance traditions to new dancers all over the planet."[50] Peter Loggins asked her what "Savoy Style Lindy Hop means to you?" She thought for second and said: "Speed, what makes the Savoy dancers different is they can dance so much faster than any other dancers. It's natural, it is what we worked on . . . and we had the bands to do it."[51] Latasha Brown asked her how she felt about the idea that white revivalists stole the Lindy from the Black people as Norma Miller had accused. She replied: "It was never stolen, the music changed, the ballrooms went away, there was no longer partner dancing." She said Lindy was rediscovered: "it was rescued in a sense because it was gone from Harlem . . . it was just the changing of the times." When asked how to get more African American youths interested in the dance, now largely done by white folk, the answer was in education, schools, and through the teaching of history. "This is our dance; they should know that."[52] Sugar Sullivan is in the International Lindy Hop Hall of Fame.

Drummer, jazz dancer, and poet **Clarence "Scoby" Strohman** (1940–96) was born in Brooklyn, began performing as a tap dancer when he was five, and soon after began playing the drums. Described by John Wilson as "a brilliantly vital and imaginative drummer," Strohman performed a combination of poetry and drumming he called "drummetry."[53] He performed live throughout the country and in Canada, Europe, and Africa in concerts, documentary films, and festivals, and recorded with his teacher Max Roach. He also performed with Langston Hughes, was a sand dancer, a scat dancer, and like James Berry, a soft-shoe rhythm-dancer. In 1981, saxophonist Johnny Griffin and his quartet performed with scat dancers Scoby and Jafar Abdullah in *An Evening of Jazz and Dance* at the *American Dance Festival* in North Carolina. The bebop program was improvisational and featured music by African American classical composers. Strohman and Abdullah developed their dance techniques alongside great jazz musicians.[54] When Strohman was twenty he helped form a bebop quartet with Jeff Asquiew, Leroy Appins, and (Oaky) Milton Hayse, who performed the solo concert dance improvisations in Volume 2, Part I of *TSM*. Strohman is listed as an author of *Social Dancing: At the Cotton Club and the Savoy*, a 1985 video recording housed at the New York Public Library. *Social Dancing* explores "the role of dance as a means of expression in the Black community in which Strohman demonstrates the Applejack and scat dancing in the style of Earl Snake Hips Tucker."[55]

Other than Asquiew performing in several of Dehn's concerts, a search found no more information concerning him, Appins, Hayse, A. Vasquez, Tandaleo, or Jackie other than that they appeared in *TSM*, Part III. Dottie Adams is listed on the website Palladium-Mambo.com and in the credits of *Dance and Immigration: The Mambo, a New York Story*, produced in 1993 and housed at the New York Public Library. The catalog entry states that the "panelists in the video recording discuss salsa and the mambo craze that flourished in New York from the late 1940s to the 1960s; its emphasis on its appeal to dancers of different ethnic groups and classes and the Palladium Ballroom." The mambo's origins as a musical form in Cuba are also described, as are Killer Joe Piro's mambo lessons.[56]

Considered the "Maestro of the Mambo," **Pedro Aguilar y Trujillo ("Cuban Pete")** (1927–2009) was born in Puerto Rico and was also called *el cuchillo* ("the knife"). After the breakup of his parents' marriage, he grew up in a succession of orphanages and foster homes in New York's Spanish Harlem. He reconciled with his mother, Nellie Trujillo Masdeu, when he was teenager, after which she taught him Latin dance steps, and later studied for two years with Katherine Dunham.[57] Some believe his quick foot movements are due to his training as a boxer. "He had an exquisite sense of timing, an impeccable rhythm," said Barbara Craddock, a decade-long dance partner. He was called "King of the Latin Beat" and "Prince of the Palladium"; in 1954 *Life* magazine proclaimed him "the greatest mambo dancer" ever. A weekly performer at the Palladium, his "blindingly quick footwork and swivel-hipped gyrations" were praised along with his "innovative steps." Aguilar said he invented the signature movements the Porpoise, the Shimmy Shimmy, and the Prayer. When Pete partnered with an Italian teenager named Millie Donay, the interracial duo sparked controversy with a duet called *Love for Sale*.[58]

Cuban Pete appeared on TV and is the only Latin dancer recognized in the Latin Jazz exhibit at the Smithsonian Institution. He won numerous prizes with Donay, danced at the White House for Presidents Eisenhower and Johnson, and appeared at a Royal Command Performance before Queen Elizabeth II. Aguilar was a consultant on the 1992 film *The Mambo Kings*, collaborated with Edward Villella of the Miami City Ballet, and was featured in the 2002 documentary *The Lucky Man*.[59] Aguilar and Craddock were both inducted into the International Latin Music Hall of Fame and were the recipients of the 2007/2008 Latin Jazz USA Lifetime Achievement Awards.[60]

Pete's first wife, **Millie (Donni) Donay** (1934–2007), born Carmela Dante Di Stefano, grew up watching her ballroom dancing sisters and became very good at the Lindy.[61] Cuban Pete asked her to compete with him at the Palladium when she was fifteen years old, and they won $12.50. They soon began doing exhibitions, which enabled them to hone their skills, later were married, and had one daughter. Soon they became the resident dance team at the Waldemere Hotel in the Catskills, New York State. She appeared in many TV variety shows with her husband, and they were the featured dancers in 1955 movie short *Mambo Madness* with the Tito Rodriguez Band. Between 1950 and 1956 they appeared at the Palladium, the Waldorf Astoria, Carnegie Hall with Tito Puente, the Apollo Theater with The Platters, and in Madison Square Garden, and taught Latin dances to Arthur Murray Dance Studios teachers. Alan Feuerstein wrote: "They met dancing—were born to dance. When they danced, those who watched held their breath, quickly swept into the spell created on stage. Their dancing set them apart, and they set the standard for beauty, movement, and sensuality in Latin Dance." After their breakup Donay danced side by side with Marilyn Winters for two years, then as a soloist in Las Vegas for two years before returning to the Palladium. She retired after a second marriage and second child. Feuerstein said there could "never be a discussion about mambo without talking about what Millie and Cuban Pete did for the dance."[62]

Volume 2, Part II

Johnson and Youngblood are the Louise Parks dancers from Volume 2, Part II that are covered here, the others are covered later in Chapter 7 as they continued to dance with Dehn until the mid-1970s. During the 1950s and 1960s **Edward "Roe" Johnson** (birth and death dates unknown) was part of the new generation of Lindy Hoppers that arose from the coaches trained by Mama Lou Parks (also profiled later).[63] Johnson danced in the 1988 *Call of the Jitterbug*, a 35-minute documentary by Green Room Productions which includes clips of *The Spirit Moves*. *Call of the Jitterbug* also included TSM dancers Gibson, Parks, Sullivan, and Deborah Youngblood.[64] The latter, **Deborah (Debra) Youngblood** (1940–) is still a prominent Lindy hop and jazz dancer. She was born Debra May Boyd, the second of six children. After her family moved from Georgia to Harlem she was stricken with rheumatic fever, yet still had dreams of becoming a dancer, so followed her mother, to the Central Ballroom on 125th street. There she encountered big bands, was overwhelmed by the aerial Lindy Hoppers, and joined the dancers at Ms. Parks' afterschool program at the PS 68. When she was eighteen she joined Mama Lu Parks and Her Savoy Lindy Hoppers and performed with them through 1990.[65] Youngblood actually led the dance troupe with David Butts Cairns when Parks was not present. She became known as the daredevil of the group for her tenacious attitude, quick timing toward attempting and executing air-steps with her dance partners, and even performing fire-eating on tour.[66]

The Parkettes were often labeled as "Twist dancers," and "Go-Go dancers," and toured and performed with Joe Frazier, Chubby Checker, The Harlem Blues and Jazz Band, James Brown, Lionel Hampton, B.B. King, Cab Calloway, and her husband, Lonnie Youngblood.[67] Deborah and David won the HMB in 1980 and were dance partners for over fifteen years.[68] Her film credits include *Cotton Comes to Harlem* (1970), *The Call of the Jitterbug* (1988), and the *Twist* (1992). As a founding member of the Parkettes, she was part of their impact on social dance, and she continues to play an important role in keeping Lindy hop and jazz dance alive.

James Brown impersonator **Willie "Ray" Raynor**, (birth and death dates not known) was born in North Carolina but he received most of his early training singing and dancing in New York City.[69] An article in *Ballroom Dancemagazine* (November 1960) has a picture of Ray in "Behind the Scenes and 'Out Front' at the 26th Annual Harvest Moon Ball." The caption reads: "When Jitterbug opponents Willie Raynor and Eunice Wall broke a wishbone, it showed Willie would win. He did—with partner Patricia Williams, and as tradition were featured on the *Ed Sullivan Show*. They were trained by Lou Parks at a community center."[70] Ray danced at the Apollo Theater with Otis Redding, Smokey Robinson, Fats Domino, and Bo Diddley, and established a James Brown tribute act "that far surpasses that of any other Brown impressionist." He spent time in Montreal working at the Peel Pub, Studio Montreal, and headlined at the Jello Bar for the Millennium Celebration on New Year's Eve 2000.[71] In 2010 Willie Ray performed as James Brown during the 10th Annual Celebrity Impersonators Convention at the Stratosphere Hotel and Casino. The convention is an opportunity for "tribute artists, lookalikes and soundalikes to network and impress agents and producers during their showcase performances."[72] A Facebook post in 2017 located him at the Plate Bar and Grill, Sunrise Manor, Las Vegas, and another in 2018 states: "This is Willie Ray. The man is in his 70s and he was ripping it up on the floor at Boulder City Swings."[73]

Volume 3

Sandra Gibson and James Berry were covered previously, and Pigmeat Markham and Baby Seals are covered later, in Chapter 8.

Volume 4

The "Artists of the Street" were **The Magnificent Force**, one of the very first successful breakdance companies. Dehn saw their dancing as a continuation of what she witnessed at the Savoy, in bebop, and in rock 'n' roll. It was "dance as life"—an expression of resistance, a way of encountering, defying, and commenting on their lives. At this time New York City was in a depressive state and hopes of the Civil Rights movement diminished. Failing budgets slashed school funding, basic services, and job training, and drugs and crime "haunted the streets." DeFrantz wrote that the original hip-hop (break) dancing was an outlet for working-class young people of color responding to rising tides of economic inequities to speak truth to power.[74] Yet again the energy of young dancers created new ways of responding, moving, and dancing. The term "breakin'" was used several ways: as a title of the dance forms, or as a response to an insult or reprimand: for example, "Why are you breakin' on me?!" A break was also an aggressive, percussive section of music where the dancers reacted with their most impressive steps and moves.[75] Lillian Morrison recalled that she and Mura (both approaching eighty years old) would often go to the Bronx and Spanish Harlem to watch the dancers on the streets. Through Henry Chalfant, Dehn met and invited The Force to appear in the fourth section of her film. (This section was not included in the versions acquired by Sykes and Dancetime Publications, clips are not found on public sources, and they remain exclusively in the New York Public Library archives.) Several of The Magnificent Force went on to become the leaders in their field.

The Force's director, **Julie Fraad** (*c*. 1948–), is listed with Steve Glavin, Gilbert Kennedy, George Pabon, Steffan Clemente, and Lorenzo Harris as the dancers. In an interview she clarified that what the group did in *TSM* was "Electric Boogie, and Pop-Locking." Fraad was a "top professional dancer, choreographer and leading force in the breakdance movement" according to a 1985 *Learning Annex Newsletter*, where she said: "Breakdancing is a folk art, the kids themselves created it. There are no schools to teach it."[76] At that writing she had been dancing for fifteen years, performing with Twyla Tharp and other modern companies in New York and Wisconsin, but the "break" was what she had been seeking. Sally Banes wrote: "The professionalization of breakdancing had begun, downtown choreographer Julie Fraad organized The Magnificent Force and gave their performances a narrative structure."[77] Fraad was the director/manager of the ensemble, which morphed and changed over time. She conceived some of the theatrical material and organized concerts and a tour of Europe.

Fraad is also listed in the credits for *Style Wars*, a film about the subculture of hip-hop which focused on graffiti art and breakdancing.[78] In 1984 she staged the dance scenes for The Force in *Beat Street*, and directed The Force in the *Black Dance America Festival* in Brooklyn (Mura Dehn spoke at the same event).[79] She performed in *Fresh Faust, a "Rap Opera" in Progress* at the Whitney Museum in

1987,[80] and in *Dancing Hands* (1988), performed by Magnificent Force dancers Steve "Wiggles" Clemente and Gilbert "Shalimar" Kennedy. *Hands* was filmed in The Vault under the Brooklyn Bridge.[81] Following that event she went back to school, became first a high school teacher, then a principal, and later an adjunct at New York City Technical College in Brooklyn. She is retired and lives in upstate New York.[82]

Born in Spanish Harlem, **Steffan "Mr. Wiggles" Clemente** (1965–) was raised in the Bronx, "rocking" many aspects of hip-hop and street culture. "Rockin'" could describe actions such as "one could rock the mic [microphone], rock the dance floor, or rock some fly gear [dress impressively]." He earned his crafts on the harsh streets of New York, and his stripes battle by battle.[83] Mr. Wiggles is a dancer, actor, choreographer, teacher, music producer, and graffiti artist. He is a member of The Rock Steady Crew, The Electric Boogaloos, and the graffiti crew TC5. TC5 is known for writing (graffiti) rockin' (a freestyle dance done by many Latinos in the 1970s), breakin'/b-boyin' (footwork and freezes), MC-ing (crowd pleasing, echo chamber, and what is now known as ra), popping (a funk dance created in Fresno, California by The Electric Boogaloos), and locking (a dance style created in Los Angeles and made popular on *Soul Train*). On his website he states that his longevity is based on the fact that he was versatile, so "I just mixed everything and I was able to blow up and I think what keeps me motivated now is the fact that it got me out of the Bronx and once I got my first plane ticket I turned that one plane ticket into a million man, I just kept flying."[84] Battling throughout the streets of New York City eventually led to stage performances in Europe, South America, Asia, the Middle East, Canada, and on Broadway. Wiggles was in two movies: 1983's *Wild Style* and Harry Belafonte's 1984 *Beat Street*. In addition he has appeared at the Apollo Theater and the Kennedy Center, working with Graciela Daniele, Bill Irwin, and Ann Marie DeAngelo and in music videos with Missy Elliot, Usher, Madonna, and Limp Bizkit, among others.

On the same site we learn that Mr. Wiggles and The Rock Steady Crew collectively won a 1992 New York Dance and Performance "Bessie" Award for Best Choreography for the production of *So! What Happens Now*. Wiggles along with the members of the Rock Steady Crew was acclaimed at the first VH-1 Hip Hop Honors in 2004 and was one of the first to teach hip-hop at New York's Broadway Dance Center. He urges dancers to embrace technology to take their art to the next level and showcase it to the world. He distributes his music, dance videos, and clothing wear through his website and says he is still "learning his crafts till this day and will remain a true student of the culture till the day he dies, teaching the lifestyle and spreading the joy of all the elements to the youth."[85]

Mr. Wiggles met and became Popmaster Fabel's dancing and tagging (creating graffiti) partner at the New York High School of Art and Design when they were fourteen years old.[86] **(George) Jorge "PopMaster Fabel" Pabon** (1965–) was also born in Spanish Harlem and is known for his unique "pop and lock" dance moves. He and his twin brother were raised with their two older sisters by a single mother. He credits his "old-school Puerto Rican mom" with keeping him on the right track. "Dance, nature and nurture converged on him when his sisters introduced him to salsa music and James Brown, at which time he *had* to dance."[87] Fabel wrote on the *PhysicalGraffitti* website that the unnamed culture known today as hip-hop was forming in the early 1970s in New York City's ghettos. Interestingly, like Dehn with jazz dance forty years earlier, he determined that The common pulse which gave life to all these elements is rhythm" and is revealed by "the beats the DJ selected, the dancers' movements, the MCs' rhyme patterns and the writer's name or message painted [in graffiti] in a flowing, stylized fashion."[88] Pabon told *Rolling Stone* magazine that if it weren't for the violent street gangs like Savage Samurais that laid claim to Harlem's streets, he might never have become a professional dancer. The "gang on my block . . . [n]one of them were Japanese. They were all Puerto Rican and Black. They wore patches like bikers, but none of them had motorcycles. These guys were notorious but were amazing dancers."[89]

Popmaster became a member of The Rock Steady Crew, The Electric Boogaloos, and co-founder of GhettOriginal Productions Inc. Popmaster met Dehn through Henry Chalfant, toured internationally with The Magnificent Force, was in the film *Beat Street*, and later was Chalfant's consultant for his 2006 film *From Mambo to Hip-Hop: A South Bronx Tale*. As a dancer, said Chalfant, "Fabel was always on the beat, and he could flow."[90] With GhettOriginal Fabel co-authored, co-directed, and co-choreographed the first two hip-hop musicals, *So! What Happens Now* (1991) and *Jam on the Groove* (1995).[91] Wanting to highlight the DJ again, Fabel and Christie Z created park jams. "So-called hip-hop was hijacked by the recording industry," he says. "The dancing, the aerosol art, even the DJs, at one point, were kicked to the curb." Their goal was to reunite its four pillars, something Fabel has lectured on since 1999, when he became an adjunct professor at New York University's Tisch School of the Arts, where he also teaches movement and history and participates in outreach programs and conferences internationally.[92] He is a reviewer for the National YoungArts Foundation and was important to the *[R]Evolution of Hip-Hop* exhibit in the Bronx and the *50th Anniversary of Hip-Hop* in August 2023. Concerning breakdance in the 2024 Olympics, he said, "He wants everyone to understand it is a cultural phenomenon, a dance that gives one a sense of purpose ... an exceptional b-boy or b-girl is the combination of musicality, and individual character, a freeze, physical punctuation and swag and direct relationship to the rhythm and music." And he hopes there will be some trickle-down benefit to the youth of the inner city.[93]

Steve Glavin popped up in several, barely visible hip-hop video clips of The Magnificent Force from the 1980s, and apart from *Dancing Hands* the only other item found on "Shalimar" Kennedy was his picture in the same newsletter advertising Fraad's course.[94] Also pictured in that newsletter is Rennie Harris. **Lorenzo Rennie Harris** (1964–), a.k.a. Prince Scarecrow and Prince, was born and began "stepping" in North Philadelphia. Notably, while still in high school he was paid by the Smithsonian Institution to go into local schools and perform stepping in an effort to help preserve the transient "urban folkdance."[95] As a teenager in the late 1970s he moved to New York City and began dancing in the ranks of the b-boy elite as "Prince Scarecrow" and later "Prince." Harris was offered a spot in the crew of Magnificent Force, danced in the *TSM* led by Fraad, then toured the world with top rap acts like Run DMC and Kurtis Blow.[96] After many dance twists and life turns, in the 1980s Harris formed the first, and now longest-running, hip-hop dance touring company, Rennie Harris Puremovement (RHPM) in 1992. RHPM has toured the world, and Harris has created works for many of the world's leading dance companies and presented workshops across the United States. At a February 2024 lecture demonstration for Dance NJ he insisted what he did was a street dance.[97] He has been a professor and guest artist for fifteen years at the University of Colorado in Boulder, yet continually tours and performs with his company. Harris has received two honorary doctorate degrees, one from Bates College in Lewiston, ME in 2010 and another from Chicago's Columbia College in 2013. His list of accomplishments, performances, and acknowledgements far exceeds the space available here, hence the reader is urged to peruse the RHPM website for a fuller account of his impressive career.

Interestingly, Harris and Mura Dehn had some similar aspirations: to bring their social dances to the concert stage, to establish an academy to train dancers in both the execution and history of their forms, and to understand the spirituality of the mission. It is remarkable to hear him say what Dehn said over eighty years ago, though he managed to do what Mura only dreamed of, bridging his popular and folk form with dance as art, while staying true to the foundations of hip-hop and pleasing audiences from both sides. Harris has collected the stories and movements of the pioneers and brought them together in concert to preserve the vernacular form. He was introduced to West African dance by

Reginald Yates, and toured with Chuck Davis' Dance Africa, which gave him new motivation to contribute to the African heritage dance movement.[98] Like Dehn, who saw the Academy of Swing as an enterprise "to form a pool for professional dancers in the pure folk jazz technique, for both the theatrical and concert field" and teach not only the steps of jazz but its links to Africa,[99] Harris has developed a curriculum to establish a strong foundation for all street dance forms, or styles, "fostering technically proficient teachers who are cultural ambassadors of the rich history and cultural lineage of the forms."[100]

In the 2024 Dance NJ lecture demonstration and a 2017 interview Harris stated that the three laws of hip-hop were innovation, creation, and individuality. Likewise, Dehn felt that no jazz dance step was an end unto itself, rather every vibration was a potential for a new formation; the forum for the inventions was the dance hall, where the exchange of innovations among dancers was constant. Improvisation gave the dancer an opportunity to develop a personal style. "Every artist tries to find a style of his own. He wishes to be recognized for it—this is his pride, his own indisputable contribution." In the Lindy the dancer was on their own to "dig back" from a break with their partner—a license for individuality and creativity and inventiveness of the dancer was encouraged.[101] Harris said the same thing, noting that every hip-hop artist is an original and reinvents himself everyday with innovation developing an individual style. Harris, however, found a way to assemble and preserve this material; he said hip-hop "adapts to its environment and situation . . . so of course it fits in the theater."[102]

Rennie Harris changed the possibilities of dance on stage, making him among the most important choreographers of the first decades of the twenty-first century, "an artistic giant" who received the Herb Alpert Award in the Arts, a Governor's Arts Award, and a United States Artist Fellowship.[103] The London *Times* wrote of Harris that he is "the Basquiat of the U.S. contemporary dance scene."[104] He also, like Dehn, recognized the "spirit" in African American dance, saying: "I'm coming from a hip-hop place but it's the spiritualism within the dance of it, which is really about our need for the culture of freedom. Our new secular culture and religion called freedom; you know what I mean?"[105]

It is incredible that *The Spirit Moves* includes some of the most important Black dancers—the best class acts, masters of the Savoy, Latin/mambo kings and queens, Harvest Moon Ball champions, and the most acclaimed hip-hop artists of our time. The swing revivalists, through Minns, Sykes, and pirate copies, discovered *TSM*, and for the last forty years it has been seen by literally tens of thousands of enthusiasts and scholars around the world. It is a primary resource for many interested in learning steps, Lindy hop and the history of

Black American social and vernacular dance. In December of 2020 Mark Hikara wrote on his website *Swing It Seattle*:

> Though her name might not be familiar to you, her influence and contributions are massively important to Lindy Hop & jazz dance. Mura Dehn produced "The Spirit Moves." This series provides some of the best and most notable footage we have of jazz dance in this era. Without question, [*The Spirit Moves*] is a hugely influential piece of work. Dancers like myself have spent countless hours watching and rewatching this material. It has achieved something of biblical status amongst Lindy hoppers around the world.[106]

7

Rag to Rock, Section I

The Program and Cast

Rag to Rock, is a survey of Afro-American dance creations in this century covering the Rag, Jazz, Swing, and Rock 'N' Roll periods.[1]

A Panorama of Company Names

In 1967 the *Village Voice* listed an announcement that Mura Dehn's Dance Theatre would present a free program, *Afro-American Folklore*, at Cooper Union.[2] From the time jazz became her focus in 1926, the titles of Dehn's concerts and presentations changed numerous times. Jazz or "swing" appeared in most headings of early performances, in the 1940s titles contained the words "Savoy Dancers," "Masters," and "Ballroom Champions," and early in the 1950s turned to the "Panorama" of jazz dance over four decades. She and Berry founded the James Berry-Mura Dehn Dancers, which lasted several years, and as the Civil Rights movement was beginning the company changed its billing to *Black Social Dance, Afro-American Folklore*, then *Afro-American Dance Show*. A handwritten contract from the Smithsonian Institution lists Black American Jazz Dance Theatre. Dehn began negotiations with the US State Department as Mura Dehn's Jazz Dance Theatre, but the dancers and musicians signed contracts as Afro-American Folk Dance Theater.[3] Finally, in the early 1970s the Traditional Jazz Dance Theatre, Inc. (later the TJD Company, TJDC) was created. These shifting monikers are indicative of what she was presenting, who she was presenting with, and the ethos of the time when they were presented.

In 1968 Professor Henrietta Yurchenco asked her student **Allen Blitz** (1947–) if he would manage Mura Dehn's upcoming performance at the City College of New York (CCNY). A tall, generous man, Blitz was born in a tough working-class neighborhood in the Bronx. He was just nineteen when Yurchenco introduced him to Dehn. Majoring in sociology, he was active in the Department of Student Life, which presented different types of cultural events; Yurchenco was an ethnomusicologist at CCNY who also hosted a radio show on WNYC and knew the New York City folk music scene well. She was a friend of both Alan Lomax and Mura Dehn, and was instrumental in bringing Dehn to campus for a "showcase performance." Blitz ended up overseeing that performance and "jumped at the chance" to become Dehn's company manager from 1968 until 1973. He and his wife Dorie then moved to North Carolina, where they both supported political causes, and he worked in public housing for almost a decade. When they returned to New York City in the early 1980s they re-established contact with Dehn and Yurchenco and continued their friendships. When I met Blitz in May of 2022 he said: "I had been in her kitchen so many times, I remember her voice." He told me that in her Russian accent she would always start with, "Oh darling, it was not like that," and Dehn clearly "had an impact" on his life. Allen contacted me, eager to share what he knew about Mura, after hearing my interview with Bob Boross on the Jazz and Tap Dance Life YouTube channel.[4] Blitz credits Yurchenco and Dehn for the path his life took, saying: "You have to get to this level of maturity to know the value of our predecessors. Mura introduced me to the vibrancy of the Black culture; she also turned me into a mensch." In 1968 Allen and Dorie moved in very avant-garde circles; they lived in an artists' community in Brooklyn, packed with political activists, where "close friends of ours were famous writers, some in the Living Theater, and so much at that time was happening intellectually."[5]

Blitz is quoted in *The Campus* (the newspaper of CCNY) announcing the *Afro-American Dance Show*: "There is no center or school to carry on the traditions of the American folk culture which is why it is disappearing." He explained, "Much of the dance is improvisation and has to be learned first-hand from the artists themselves that originated them." Headliners for this event were Johnny Hudgins, Cook and Brown, Buster Brown, Mabel Lee, Chuck Green, and Albert Gibson. The Savoy Swingsters and The Lou Parks Dancers also performed; the band was directed by Milton Hinton. Blitz, who was Chairman of the Finley Center Program Agency, invited the students to the *Afro-American Folk Dance Theater*: "the program entitled from *Rag to Rock*, is a survey of Afro-American dance creations in this century covering the Rag, Jazz, Swing, and Rock 'N' Roll periods."[6] This was a time when Civil Rights and Black Rights struggles were widespread. On the day of the concert Martin Luther King Jr. was assassinated and social unrest spread through Harlem Heights. Out of respect, the show was postponed until April 30.

A stage had to be built to host the event, and the entire student body was invited. Blitz wondered if the comedy acts, especially those from the vaudevillian era, would be perceived as Uncle Tom-ish. For instance, headliner Johnny Hudgins, in his seventies, had sometimes performed in blackface early in his career, and many in the Black Power movement, believing that was demeaning, wanted to distance themselves from those kinds of representations. However, the concert was warmly received, Hudgins did an excellent dance mime, and the show flowed from one epic of Black dance to another and was highly appreciated for its historical relevance and artistry.[7] *Rag to Rock* became the template for performances over the next six years; intermittently it was perceived as having racial overtones, though most of the reviews were outstanding and the shows understood for their attempt to document a rich history of Black arts.

State-sponsored Engagements

The 1960s had seen a rapid development of the National Endowment for the Arts (NEA), a government agency with a mission to help indigenous and folk-art forms. Those choosing dancers for the NEA, the US State Department Bureau of Educational and Cultural Affairs (CU) the Smithsonian Institution, and the Olympics Games were most often associated with the American National Theatre Academy (ANTA) Dance Panel. The handwritten November 1967 agreement mentioned above, on Smithsonian letterhead, was between Dehn and some of her dancers, granting her "the exclusive right to represent this organization [the Black American Jazz Dance Theatre], to obtain engagements for concerts, concert tours, and the Olympic Festival in Mexico City."[8] The following April, with additional support from the Rebekah Harkness Foundation, they performed at the CCNY with Blitz as manager, then took a similar program to the Smithsonian Mall in August and to the *Folk Festival* associated with the Olympic Games in October. The Lou Parks Dancers were now formally included in the company as the most contemporary act of the concerts.

A Western Union Telegram in Dehn's clippings file confirmed the "agreement to engage your *Afro-American Folk Dance Company* for a performance on the mall in Washington DC at 8:30 pm August 24, 1968," signed by James R. Morris, Director of the Division of the Smithsonian's Performing Arts.[9] Members of the

CU attended this performance, and the *Washington Post* review described how: "They strutted. They swaggered. They rolled their hips. They cut their eyes. They stepped high. They bowed low. It was Harlem and Basin Street and all those saints marching in and way down on the Swanee River."[10] The Smithsonian was also involved in getting the company to the 1968 Olympic Games in Mexico that October, which were the first ever to be fully televised worldwide. Consequently most countries took great care that selected images were presented of themselves. The athletes in the opening ceremonies largely wore traditional dress, and many musicians and dancers were sent to give performances representing their native cultures. Following a heralded concert at its *Folk Festival*, Dehn was asked to head the newly formed International Organization of Traditional Dance, Music, and Song (IOTDMS), and her company was invited to its conference in Kingston, Jamaica. The IOTDMS may have been short-lived, as the only mention of it in Dehn's Collection was when she was elected president with the aim to deepen and extend understanding between people through the folkloric arts. Chief Counselor for the Cultural Olympics, Dr. Rubin de la Borbolla, later served as a sponsor of her TJDC.[11]

Charles Reinhart lived in New York City at that time (before directing the *American Dance Festival* for many decades), managing several dance companies, and was approached by the NEA to develop a dance touring program.[12] Dehn's company auditioned for that program on December 10, 1968, which was observed by two members of ANTA, Reinhart and William Bales (Dean of Dance at the State University of New York), and Beverly Gerstein of the CU's Cultural Presentations Programs (CP).[13] The CU by this time had been sending dance abroad to further the image of America as creative, promoting freedom and individual expression.[14] The audition was noted as extremely successful, and by December 20 Mura was in Washington, DC to discuss an Afro-American Folk Dance Theatre tour to Africa[15] the company was later booked as the Jazz Dance Theatre: Rag to Rock.[16] A Department of State memorandum dated December 27, 1968 indicated that Mura was intending to visit her brother in Lausanne for a few months. She made a slight error in a press release for the upcoming tour, to which Blitz, as company manager, responded "unfortunately within the last month, Miss Dehn had to mourn the passing of her brother Boris and her very close friend James Berry. The toll she has endured within so short a period has been tragic and even though Miss Dehn has displayed an enormous amount of strength she nevertheless has not been quite herself."[17] Her trip to Switzerland was canceled, yet despite the personal losses she continued to work on performances and the upcoming tour.

Jazz Comes Home

The CU develops and manages US international educational and cultural exchange activities; its Historical Collection is housed at the University of Arkansas (UArk) Libraries in Fayetteville, AR. Part of the State Department, it was associated with, and later merged with, the United States Information Agency (USIA) and United States Information Service. The exchange of culture as a significant tool of US international relations began in the early years of the Cold War between the United States and Russia. Cultural diplomacy mixed an imperialist desire to "impress American values on others" with a "gentler, high-minded vision of mutuality and respect," and was evidenced by the fact that both the USIA (information) and CU (cultural) programs were enacted and supervised by the same people.[18] The State Department used ANTA's Dance Panel to choose candidates for its touring programs, which were then reviewed by the CU, USIA, Department of Defense, Central Intelligence Agency, Library of Congress, Smithsonian Institution, National Gallery of Art, Commission on Fine Arts, and a separate Advisory Committee on the Arts. The CU and the USIA were required to report all aspects of the tours, including budgets, to Congress, and evaluate each program's efficacy.[19] At UArk, the CU's Collection, MC468, Group II, Box 67, Folders 13–16, holds 614 pages of the bureau's reports on every aspect of the JDT African tour, including travel, performances, and report narratives from every American embassy that hosted the company. The tour at times raised money for different State Department causes, such as the Nigerian Red Cross, but was primarily intended for the exchange of goodwill between countries. A thorough read reveals additional objectives to use the arts as positive propaganda, to positively influence the psychological climate toward the United States, and to provide an image of it as a land of creative freedom and individual liberty. A remarkable film documentary of the two-month tour, titled *Jazz Comes Home*, is housed in the National Archives in College Park, Maryland. The program accompanying the film states:

> AMERICA'S cultural presentation of the Jazz Dance Theatre tour in Africa has been filmed in color so that it could be permanently preserved for those Africans who were unable to see the original performances—and also for those who would like to recapture the excitement of the live programs. The film's director, Harry Keith of Washington, D.C., and Bill Simon of Tunis, Tunisia, travelled more than 10,000 miles with the troupe through eight countries, recording not only their performances but their many colorful side trips to historic sites,

universities, marketplaces, craft workshops, and homes. Prints of this film may be obtained from the nearest American Embassy or U.S. Information Service (USIS) Library.[20]

The program presented on the tour was very similar to those in 1968 at the CCNY, the Smithsonian, and the Olympics, with a few cast and number changes. Dehn's scrapbooks are filled with numerous outstanding newspaper reviews, as are the reports from the embassies. The company was received in regal fashion, and the concerts were attended by heads of state. The tour offered both the American dancers and the African hosts a chance see their connections through the body and movement. Retrospectively, Pepsi Bethel called it "as much a pilgrimage as it was a cultural tour." He recounted it as a "trip of a lifetime," during which the reception of the company by the African hosts was nothing less than extraordinary.[21] Dehn was so impressed with Allen Blitz after the CCNY performance that she asked him to be the company manager for the tour. Chenault Spence was hired as the lighting designer and production manager.

Chenault Spence (1939–) was born in Concord, NC and majored in theater and lighting for dance and opera at the University of North Carolina, then moved to SoHo in New York to be in the capital of theater. His first lighting job in the city was at the original Duplex on Grove Street, where he used five rotary household dimmers to provide lighting, which may have prepared him for touring Africa.[22] Chenault worked with modern dance legends José Limon and Erick Hawkins before accepting the lighting designer/production manager position on the tour. The *JDT* traveled with no lighting equipment, and Spence worked in venues ranging from theaters with facilities that were well-equipped to having no lights at all. Soon after the JDT tour he was hired by the Alvin Ailey American Dance Theatre and returned to Africa on a similar State Department-sponsored event. When Chenault joined the Ailey company there had been a period of some turbulence and "The great thing about the State Department was being paid wasn't a question."[23] Spence designed lights for Alvin Ailey for the next twenty years. He also designed the lights for *The Damnation of Faust* (1986), *An Evening with Mikhail Baryshnikov* (1999), and *Artemisia: Light And Shadow* (2018).

After retiring from the Ailey company he spent twenty years as a supervisor, then President of the English Language Programs of the Cetana Educational Foundation in Myanmar. Later he became a public member on the Landmarks Committee of the Community Board in the Village, New York.[24] Chenault was called back to work with the Ailey company for the 2023 season at City Center in New York as the new designers needed someone to explain the particular ambience expected for Alvin's creations. Allen Blitz introduced this writer to Mr. Spence in 2023, and both were happy to share their experiences of this remarkable tour.

The State Department "Recapitulation" of the JDT tour indicated: *8 Weeks, 22 Persons, 8 Countries, 18 Cities, 31,970 Spectators, 30 Off-stage Activities*;[25] a summary of the two-month program read: "Special Factors and Problems JDT June 7–Aug 3, 1969":

> This Afro-American company stirred some 32,000 target spectators in its victorious and wide-ranging tour of the huge African continent. Key audiences and intense local enthusiasm for the troupe marked the presentation. Minor tremors of disapproval were heard from some posts (Rabat, Tunis, Lagos) who felt that Uncle-Tom-ism was somewhat implied in the first half of the program performed by the old time Negro dancers. This interpretation was heavily outweighed by the generous critical acclamation awarded the JDT throughout its overall tour. The department in its evaluation of JDT had found that the scenes of developing Negro music and dance, rather than reflecting Uncle Tom-ism, portrayed authentically a rich Afro-American tradition that appears to be disappearing. This position was strongly supported by some of the more knowledgeable critics in Africa. Jazz Dance Theater merits the confidence extended it by the Department and deserves prime consideration for future presentations.[26]

The press release sent to the embassies for distribution to local newspapers and radio stations contained the following information and was also printed in the JDT post-tour program. Context is so important here, as these actors were playing themselves and sharing their personal journeys, with no intention of self-deprecation. However, when the context was not considered, concerns naturally arose as the movement toward racial equality often viewed the minstrel images with disdain and perpetuating negative stereotypes:

> The Negro [sic] has brought to the dance in America a unique heritage which not only reflects his ethnic origins but also his exuberance and vitality. Negro [sic] folk dancers first appeared on the American scene in the late 1840's, bringing with them the early "jazz dance"—the tap dance, the "Buck and Wing," and a host of others often created spontaneously by the performers on stage. These early dance forms, along with the music and routines which accompanied them, formed the core of America's popular entertainment of the nineteenth century— the minstrel show.

Later, during the era of ragtime, jazz and swing, came other dances such as the Charleston and Lindy Hop whose stage was the ballroom rather than the vaudeville theatre. It is the history and spirit of these dances, routines, and rhythms which The Jazz Dance Theatre captures in the first part of its vibrant revue called From Rag to Rock. Featured here are the gentlemen of the jazz dance: the multi-talented Avon Long, the comedy dance team of Cook and Brown, dancer comedian Albert Gibson, James "Stump" Cross, Buster Brown, and Pepsi Bethel—all top figures in the American entertainment world who are also solo performers when they are not with the company.

The second part of the Theatre program includes dances of more recent history the age of rock 'n roll. This presentation under the direction of Miss Lou Parks, is an exploration of the history of rock 'n roll forms and an exciting demonstration of the dances of the contemporary rock scene.

The names of the dances on the program depict exactly what was presented. Albert Gibson helped with group arrangements and choreography for Part I. Dehn was responsible for all pre-tour interactions with the State Department, the program coordination, costume assembling, publicity, and rehearsals, and during the tour overall direction and interaction with dignitaries and heads of state. Blitz managed the coordination of company details, Spence managed lighting and production.

The Program

The Jazz Dance Theatre in
From *Rag to Rock* A Program Of Afro/American Dance Creations
Organizer-Director: Mura Dehn

Part I: Dancers Of The Theater

Overture	Dick Vance and his Orchestra, Eddie Barefield, Joe Marshall, Milt Sealey, Bernard Upson
1. *New Orleans Parade*	Dancers of the Company.
2. *Work Song,*	
a. *Woman's Song,*	
b. *Freedom Song*	Avon Long
3. *Tramp Act and Name Game*	
4. *Evolution of the Tap Dance*	Cook & Brown, Albert Gibson, James Cross

    a. *Swanee River*
    b. *Time Step Variations*
    c. *Tap Chorus*
    d. *Taps & Chairs*
    e. *Bojangles*
5. *Old Time Steps*
6. *Musical Interlude* — Dick Vance and His Orchestra
7. *Cake Walk* — Pepsi Bethel
8. *Strut* — Avon Long with Cook & Brown, Albert Gibson, Buster Brown, James Cross, and Pepsi Bethel
9. *Courtship, Old & New* — Buster Brown
10. *Old Man Time* — Cook & Brown
11. *It Ain't Necessarily So* — Avon Long
12. *Sporting Life* — Avon Long with Cook & Brown, Albert Gibson, Buster Brown, James Cross, and Pepsi Bethel
13. *Jazz Step Vocabulary* — Avon Long with Cook & Brown, Albert Gibson, Buster Brown, James Cross, and Pepsi Bethel

Part II: Dancers Of The Ballroom

1. *Lindy Hop Swingout* — Lou Parks and her dancers with Pepsi Bethel
2. *Big Apple*
3. *Jazz Song* — Avon Long
4. *Aerial Lindy* — Lou Parks with Gloria Thompson, Gigi Brown, Micky Wall, Gregory Arnold, David Butts, and Dickie Harris
5. *Musical Interlude* — Dick Vance and his Orchestra

Part III: Evolution Of Rock 'N' Roll

6. *Rock 'N' Roll Step Vocabulary* — Lou Parks and her Dancers
7. *Current Trends in Rock 'N' Roll*

Company Manager – Allen Blitz   Lighting Designer – Stage Manager Chenault Spence[27]

All of the dancers and musicians were African American; the biographies below were compiled from those created for the USIA by Blitz, Dehn and the performers themselves, supplemented by relevant post-tour sources. This is meant as a tribute to these dance sensations, most of whom performed with Dehn intermittently from 1960 to 1974.

The Orchestra

Every performance began with an overture, and the band continued playing as the dancers paraded in to "When the Saints Go Marching In." Most of the band had performed in famous big bands and orchestras of the 1930s, 1940s, and 1950s, and all continued stellar musical careers throughout their lives. The orchestra leader and trumpet player **Dick Vance** (1914–85) was born in Kentucky and first studied violin before moving to Ohio and blowing his trumpet at high school dances. He trained at Juilliard, taught brass at Father Rice High School in Manhattan, and his career extended into every facet of the industry, including playing with Fletcher Henderson's orchestra from 1936 through 1938, where he was the lead trumpeter and an occasional vocalist.[28] Vance played with the great names of the big band era, namely Chick Webb, Charley Barnett, and Eddie Haywood, and arranged music for Duke Ellington, Cab Calloway, Ella Fitzgerald, and Lena Horne. He toured with Don Redman and was a regular at the Savoy through the 1950s. Among the many Broadway shows he blew trumpet for were *Pal Joey*, *A Streetcar Named Desire*, *House of Flowers*, and *Hallelujah Baby*, and he was a featured soloist at Radio City Music Hall. He released three albums in the 1960s featuring Dixie Land styles and rhythms, copies of which he gave as gifts to some of his African hosts during the tour. He accompanied Dehn to the Olympic Games festival in Mexico City, and then toured Europe with Eddie Barefield in 1969. Dick Vance played with Dehn's TJDC from its inception and continued through 1973.[29] In 1979 he was cited as the composer for the documentary film *No Maps on My Taps*, starring Lionel Hampton and Howard Sims.[30]

Raised in Des Moines, Iowa by his coalmining, guitar-playing father and piano-playing mother, **Edward Emanuel "Eddie" Barefield** (1909–91) had a productive sixty-year career. He began playing in the Midwest with Benne Moten, and at age twenty-four joined Cab Calloway's orchestra, for which he wrote and arranged music for forty years. He also composed and arranged for Benny Goodman, Glenn Miller, Paul Whiteman, and Jimmy Dorsey, and worked as an arranger of the ABC Orchestra and for the *Endorsed by Dorsey* program.[31] A star saxophonist, he fronted the Ella Fitzgerald band for several months as the only Black saxophonist at the NBC studios in 1942.[32] Barefield played on multiple recordings with the Kansas City Orchestra, Don Redman, Benny Carter, and Eddie Haywood.[33] On Broadway, he was the musical director for the original Broadway production of *Streetcar Named Desire* in 1947. Occasionally returning to Cab Calloway, he also played with Wilbur DeParis before joining the circus band of the Ringling Brothers (1971–82). During that time he continued to play intermittently with Dehn's Traditional Jazz Dance Company and recorded the albums *Eddie Barefield* (1974), *The Indestructible Eddie Barefield* (1977), and *Jazz* (1982). Barefield freelanced for many orchestras, musicians, and events in the 1970s and 1980s, and recorded a 1977 album as a leader for Famous Door. His wife, Connie Harris, was a successful dancer who performed in over thirty films.[34]

Drummer **Joe Marshall** (1913–92), whose mother also played piano, was born in the "redneck Riviera" of Florida and brought up in Chicago. His first professional gigs were in the early 1930s in the Chicago jazz scene, then he spent nearly three years on the road with the Burns Campbell Band.[35] In the early 1940s Marshall played with Milt Larkin's band, from 1942 through 1947 he had a seat in the orchestra of Jimmie Lunceford, and he later played with the Duke Ellington Orchestra.[36] Marshall played drums for over six decades, adapting to changing public tastes and the actual types of jobs available. At times he was mistaken for the older Joseph "Kaiser" Marshall, another drummer who was active with Fletcher Henderson in the 1920s and died in the late 1940s; each appeared on over 100 recordings, though the younger Marshall was also associated with rhythm and blues and the doo-wop music of the 1950s, In 1952 Marshall played with a New York-based quintet led by Ben Webster, with Harold Baker, Cyril Hines, and Bill Pemberton. (Hines would also work with Dick Vance and Mura Dehn on several events.) In 1958 he worked on television in *Arthur Godfrey's Talent Scouts*, and in 1960 appeared on Al Sears' *Swing's the Thing* album. He combined television work, with Broadway shows, playing in the pit bands in stage productions involving classic jazz, such as *Bubblin' Brown Sugar* and *Ain't Misbehavin'*, and touring internationally with Benny Goodman and Coleman Hawkins. Marshall played in the rhythm section for Tyree Glenn during the 1970s, continued to work with Dehn and Dick Vance through 1973,[37] and continued to record until at least 1989.

On piano and accordion was **Milton "Milt" Randolph Sealey** (1928–2000), one of eleven children born in Montreal, Canada. Milt worked with his brothers Hugh and George in the Sealey Brothers Band in the late 1940s after studying at Montreal Conservatory and often gigged in New York. In 1953 he moved to France, where he studied at the Paris Conservatory, and later toured Europe and North Africa. He went back to Montreal for the latter part of the 1950s, moved to the United States in the early 1960s, and recorded the singles "Kansas Fields" and "Billy Billy" in 1955 and "Jelly Bean" in 1967 while serving as the musical director and pianist for The Platters. His "Black Diamond" was recorded by Rahsaan Roland Kirk in 1965. He recorded the album *Milton Sealey* in 1979 and *It's Christmas Magic* in 1981. The Milton Sealey Trio had a steady gig at Windows on the World, atop the World Trade Center in New York City, in the early 1990s and recorded the *Windows on the World* CD.[38] Sealey recorded the album *Image in the Mirror: The Triptych* with singer and composer Jeri Brown in 2000, and shortly after passed away. Brown went on to receive international praise for the album, garnering the Canadian Juno nomination and the coveted Martin Luther King Jr. Achievement Award for her one-woman play of the same title. She wrote on her web page that Sealey was "comfortable playing and composing in many styles, but he especially loved playing and composing in the jazz genre. It is my hope and aim that all of Canada and the world will remember him. He was brilliant and so special."[39]

Bass player **Andrew Bernard "Bernie" Upson** (1937–2014), was born in New York City and spent his early years in Harlem until his family moved to Queens when he was a teenager. He began playing double bass, then electric bass and bass guitar, was passionate about jazz, and was touring the East Coast by the age of twenty.[40] According to his Facebook page Upson was involved in the music business for more than fifty years.[41] He served in the US Army before music took him around the world. Beginning in the late 1950s he performed with Roy Haynes, Buddy Tate, Quincy Jones, Marvin Gaye, and George Benson, and toured Europe and the Caribbean. A tribute to him on Facebook is accompanied by his soothing, delicious jazz vibes with pictures of Lou Parks with her Soul-Jazz Revue, which included his first wife Gigi Brown. After returning from Africa Upson was in the Louis Panassié film *L'Aventure du Jazz*, which was filmed during 1970–2 in New York and France.[42] Upson graced the stages of Carnegie Hall, the Lincoln Center, and the Kennedy Center in addition to the Apollo. He spent the last twenty-five years of his life in Ithaca playing regularly with the Bernie Upson Trio, some of the region's finest musicians. In 2003 he married Deborah Clover. Amelia Sauter, co-owner of Felicia's Atomic Lounge where he often played, said: "In the beginning, we booked him because of his music and then fell in love with him."[43]

Dancers of the Theater

Part I of the JDT program was meant to be a revue of the acts performed by Black entertainers from the late 1800s through the 1930s. Dehn's company were the greatest Black dancers and artists of their time and created their own skits.

Notably Cross, Gibson, Brown, Cook, and Brown were five of the seven tap dancers featured in the classic documentary *Great Feats of Feet: A Portrait of the Jazz and Tap Dancer*, where each dancer speaks of his life and his art, "revealing the creative spirit and individuality that have personified each artist through their long careers."[44] Brief biographies of the "old-timers" follow. Pepsi Bethel's biography is in Chapter 4.

Avon Long (1910–84) was born in Baltimore, MD, attended Frederick Douglass High School, and created his own style of jazz dance. A *New York Times* review noted, "Avon Long was known internationally as 'Sporting Life' in *Porgy and Bess* (1942–1944) and dances as though his legs were steel springs."[45] He danced and sang in the Cotton Club with the bands of Cab Calloway and Duke Ellington, and performed on New York stages in 1936 in *Black Rhythm* (1939), *Very Warm for May*, *Carib Song*, and *Memphis Bound* (all 1945), was in the 1945 *Ziegfeld Follies*, the 1946 Broadway production of *Beggar's Holiday*, 1951's *The Green Pastures*, the 1952 revival of *Shuffle Along*, and in 1954's *Mrs. Patterson*.[46] Long was also in the television mini-series *Roots: The Next Generation* and appeared in the films *Finian's Rainbow*, *The Sting*, and *Harry and Tonto*. He was nominated for a Tony Award for his role of Brother Dave in *Don't Play Us Cheap*; the all-Black play opened on May 16, 1972 and ran for 164 performances, then he re-created his roles later in the 1973 film adaptation of the musical. Long originated the role of John in *Bubbling Brown Sugar* in 766 performances at the August Wilson Theatre (1976–7).[47] One of the great American dancers in the JDT company, about the tour he said: "Each individual movement when I am dancing is an expression of myself, a development of my life—or the non-development of it. . . . Coming to Africa it is a great moment, a new dimension.[48]

Born in Chicago, **Charles "Cookie" Cook** (1917–91) grew up in Detroit and was raised by a mother who ran a boarding house for Black performers. (Though other sources list his birthday as 1914, the passport he submitted to the State Department for the tour lists February 2, 1917, so is used here.) He began by playing garbage cans and touring Black vaudeville circuits with Mama and her Picanini's, a famous Negro vaudeville act which included novelties such as juggling, trampoline, and a Russian dance with taps.[49] At age twelve he met thirteen-year-old Ernest "Brownie" Brown, who would later become his dance partner. Cook was the "straight," tall, grouchy foil to Brownie's "funny guy."[50] Though they tried to avoid the practice as much as possible, at times they had to continue the tradition of "blacking up" by wearing burnt cork.[51] Cook and Brown were a very successful comedy act, extensively mentioned in Marshall Stearns' *Jazz Dance*. They appeared at the Cotton Club, Apollo Theatre, Miami's

Fountainbleu, such famous European nightspots as the Latin Casino in Paris and London's Palladium, and in 1939 at New York's Radio City Music Hall. They were featured in the 1943 film *Chatter*, in the Broadway musical *Kiss Me Kate*, where their routines to "Too Darn Hot" and "Brush Up Your Shakespeare" stopped the show, and were seen on TV with Sammy Davis Jr.[52] In 1949 they joined and performed regularly with other famous tap dancers in The Copasetics dance troupe to keep the art of tap dance alive. Notably they appeared with Cholly Atkins, Honi Coles, Chuck Green, and Pete Nugent in 1963 at the *Newport Jazz Festival* which was organized by Marshall Stearns.[53] Cook and Brown performed with Dehn at the Olympic Games festival. They also performed in *An Evening with Charles Cook and Friends* (1984) and in *Cookie and Friends* (1989). Noted as a tap master and teacher, he was passionate about passing on tap routines that he wanted to preserve to students. He was inducted into the International Tap Dance Hall of Fame in 2008.[54]

Cook met his longtime dancing partner **Ernest Brown** (1916–2009) in Chicago at age thirteen, and they created their own act called Legomania in the early 1930s. They combined tumbling and acrobatics with superb tap dancing when two-man comedy teams were at their peak.[55] Brown, being 4 feet 10 inches tall, was the "funny" half to Cook's straight," tall, grouchy foil.[56] "Blacking up" with burnt cork, as mentioned above, was an inevitable part of their early career. In addition to the above, at the height of the tap dance renaissance Brown appeared in the film *The Cotton Club* (1984), performed at the 1984 Summer Olympic Games, and at the 92nd Street Y in *Fifty Years of Tap Dancing*. He also performed in *An Evening with Charles Cook and Friends* (1984), in Jane Goldberg's *Shoot Me While I'm Happy* (1985), and *Cookie and Friends* (1989). At the age of eighty, Brown formed a partnership with Reggio McLaughlin, who was almost half his age. They performed at the 2008 *Tap City Festival* in New York City and the documentary *JUBA: Masters of Tap and Percussive Dance*. Brown received the American Tap Dance Foundation's Hoofer Award in 2004 and was inducted into the International Tap Dance Hall of Fame in 2008.[57]

The choreographer for many of the "old-timers'" routines was **Albert "Gip" Gibson** (1913–1990), who was born into the theater in Atlanta, GA as a member of the famous Gibson family.[58] Bethel Gibson Sr. ran Gibson's Minstrels and Gibson's Chocolate Revue, which played the Elmont Theater in Pittsburgh in 1925.[59] A review stated that the big star was Albert: "Al is something of an artist despite his tender age [of fifteen]." It went on to describe how the youngster combined tap with eccentric and Russian dancing "with a freedom and naturalness that forces the customers to cheer him lustily."[60] In his childhood

Gibson toured with carnivals, minstrel shows, vaudeville, and later on in burlesque, night clubs, and musical comedies. He was the creator of the world-traveled musical comedy trio The Three Chocolateers with Bethel "Duke" Gibson Jr and Guss Moore, with whom he originated his outstanding number "Peckin'" (which Benny Goodman recorded in 1937). They were regarded as three of the best comedy dancers of their time, appearing with Duke Ellington the same year in Chicago and with the Cab Calloway in the *Cotton Club Parade* fall revue.[61] His career also extended to Hollywood, where he appeared in *New Faces of 1937*, *A Day at the Races* with the Marx Brothers, and 1942's *Moonlight Masquerade*. As mentioned in Chapter 4, Albert "Gip" Gibson met Sandra (Mildred Pollack) at a party thrown by Mura Dehn; they married, and later Sandra and Gip had a show together called *The Mad Gibsons*. In 1982 Gibson and Paul Black were part of a musical called *Tappin' Uptown* that gave three performances at the Brooklyn Academy of Music. Others in the cast included Harold Nicholas, Peg Leg Bates, Honi Coles, and James "Buster" Brown.[62] The Changing Times Tap Dancing Company paid tribute to Gip Gibson as part of *By Word of Foot II*, a festival presented on December 3 and 4, 1982.[63]

The sixth of eight children and the only male, **James Richard "Buster" Brown** (1916–2002) was born in Baltimore.[64] He started his career as a child performing at family gatherings where he learned the steps and styles of previous generations.[65] Brown attended Frederick Douglas High School in Baltimore, where he and two friends formed The Three Aces, started touring the United States in the 1930s and changed their name to The Speed Kings due to their speed and precision.[66] Speed Kings 2 arrived in New York in 1939, played the Apollo and Smalls Paradise, and Brown danced for a brief time as one of the Chocolateers with Albert Gibson.[67] He appeared in the 1943 musical *Something to Shout About*.[68] As a soloist, Brown toured the United States with Rudy Vallee, South America with Cab Calloway, and performed in George Wien's festival in Europe. In 1966 he appeared with Duke Ellington and was the featured dancer with The Sacred Concert Tours.[69] That year he also performed in jazz festivals in European cities with The Harlem Uptown All-Star Dancers, who later turned into "Hoofers"; Buster had the distinction of being a member of both The Hoofers and The Copasetics. A flash jazz and tap dancer, he was invited by Dehn to join her company for his personal style of elegance and intermittently performed in her concerts beginning in 1962 at Cooper Union, at the 1968 Olympic festival, and others through 1973.

Brown danced in the film documentaries *Great Feats of Feet*, *Fancy Feet*, and *Tap Dancin'* in the 1970s, the films *Tap* and *The Cotton Club* in the 1980s, in two

PBS specials, *Tap Dance in America* and *The Gershwin Gala*, and on Broadway in *Bubbling Brown Sugar* and *Black and Blue*. He served as a master of ceremonies from 1997 to 2002 at Swing 46 in New York City, where he was loved for his wry, insouciant charm. Stars such as Savion Glover acknowledged the speed of his dancing and up-tempo close polyrhythms as a major influence, and he toured with Glover in *Footnotes* in 2000. In February 2002 Brown received an honorary doctorate from Oklahoma City University.[70]

James "Stump" Cross (1919–81) was born in Ocean City, New Jersey.[71] He was nine when he and his friend Eddie Hartman appeared on *The Horn and Hardart Radio Hour* in Philadelphia, and by their teens they were the comedy act Stump and Stumpy.[72] Regulars in the 1930s and 1940s at the Apollo Theatre, they capitalized on their contrasting heights and personalities, "combining comic banter, scat singing, and a swinging style of tap."[73] Master of ceremonies Willie Bryant would announce: "Here's a very fine team, a little different, because one's about down here and one's about up here, but you put them together and you really got something."[74] They toured the country with Duke Ellington and Count Basie, toured Europe with Chick Webb, and appeared in the films *This Is the Army* (1943), and *Ship Ahoy* (1942).[75] Their act opened with a song, followed by a series of "solo specialties in which one out-did the other," and ended with the taller Stump throwing Stumpy through Lindy hop aerial moves. They appeared on television in 1950 on *The Bands of Bands* with Lionel Hampton and His Orchestra. After the death of Hartman in 1951 Cross, with a new partner, Harold Cromer, toured with singers Nat "King" Cole, Ella Fitzgerald, Sarah Vaughn, and The Ink Spots to the Cotton Club, the Copacabana, and the Paramount in New York City and the Desert Inn in Las Vegas. They also appeared on the *Milton Berle* and *Kate Smith* television shows and *Your Show of Shows* with Sid Caesar. The act lasted until 1963, when Cross joined The Copasetics.[76] James Cross was one of the many artists who visited James Berry often, where he met Dehn. He performed with her company at the Olympic Games, at Chicago's Goodman Theater (1972) and in New York at the Town Hall in 1973. His unique style of comedy tap dancing was captured in *Great Feats of Feet*.[77] In 2008 Stump and Stumpy were both inducted into the International Tap Dance Hall of Fame.

Dancers of the Ballroom

Fortunately, due to the current generation of Lindy hop/swing dance enthusiasts, teachers, scholars, and the internet, there is well-deserved, salient information available on Mama Lou Parks and several of her dancers that were on the tour (though much harder to find in print). Her company was referred to by various names over three generations, but on the African tour they were listed as The Lou Parks Dancers (LPD). Unfortunately, space limitations for this monograph will only allow a few hundred words about each of them, so the reader is urged to visit the resources listed in the endnotes for fuller descriptions of their careers. Two of the dancers, Gloria Thompson Caldwell and David Butts Cairns (as well as Debra Youngblood, profiled in Chapter 6) were still alive at this writing and still participating in Lindy events around the world.

Mama Lou is remembered by the swing dance community with a hero's status, and dance was her ministry.[78] She was a kind but demanding pillar of Harlem who led her dancers from the streets to stages all over the world. **Louise "Mama Lou" Olive Parks Duncanson** (1925–90) was born in Raleigh, North Carolina, then moved to Boston where she attended Emerson College. Though her family wanted her to be a minister, she had worked her way through college jazz dancing in chorus lines, so ventured toward performing arts and appeared in various productions, including *Cotton Comes to Harlem, Come Back Charleston Blue,* and *The Spirit Moves.* Parks spent summers working as a hat check girl at the Savoy with her godfather Charles Buchanan, watching the masters of Black social dances.[79] In 1955 she was living in Harlem when the state began a cultural program that was part of an attempt to introduce the residents of Harlem to some of the "finer" things in life.[80] They wanted her to teach square dancing to young people, but knowing Harlem, she thought jazz dancing to be more suitable. She was assigned to PS 68, which during non-school hours served as a community center and later a rehearsal hall for the Harvest Moon Ball preliminaries.[81] Many of Parks' dancers came to her as children—for example, Maurice and Gregory Hines and their dad Maurice.[82] Her three-month summer classes became an annual event that trained the next generations to be in her companies and in the HMB, an event she was instrumental in for three decades.[83] By 1958 she was an instructor at the Savoy and her Parkettes were mentioned in the newspapers.[84] She was surrounded by HMB rock 'n' roll winners in a picture in *The Daily News* in 1960, captioned "SENSATIONAL—and Community Center 68 has done it again! The [PS 68] center's dance group took 1st, 2nd and 3rd prize at the Harvest Moon Ball in the Rock and Roll Divisions."[85]

Several of Lou Parks' dancers' performed at the Carnegie Recital Hall in which James Berry made his return to the stage. The 1969 cast notes Blitz and Dehn sent to the CP for the African tour included:

> The Lou Parks Dancers are considered to be [a] foremost group in America. A few months ago, the group had a special invitation to perform at President Nixon's inaugural ball. They appear regularly at the Apollo Theatre in Harlem, frequently on television, in leading night spots throughout the country and have toured Europe and South America. They appeared (with JDT) recently at the Olympic Games Festival and the Smithsonian. Lou Parks is an incredibly hard worker who trains champion aerial lindy teams every year. She appeared as a featured performer in the Broadway production of "Hallelujah" with Leslie Uggams last year in the part of the Little Mama.[86]

As chroniclers of Black dancing as an expression of creativity, Parks and Dehn were determined to not let anyone forget its importance as an art; her company performed with Dehn through 1973 and later toured with Bethel's company.[87] In the UK in 1981 she taught dance workshops and influenced Terry Monaghan and Warren Heyes to set up a British Lindy hop dance troupe, which became the Jiving Lindy Hoppers. That year a British TV company paid her to re-create one of the dance competitions in Harlem, which documented the "goings on at Smalls Paradise in Harlem and the story of the Lindy Hop."[88] The footage, aired on *The South Bank Show*, generated so much interest that Parks and her dance company toured the UK again in 1983 and 1984.[89] Her group also performed in Brooklyn Academy of Music's 1983 production *Dance Black America*, then began a three-year regular gig, *Jitterbug Jazz*, at the Village Gate with The Harlem Blues and Jazz Band.[90] In December 1988 the Bronx Arts Council honored Parks at Lincoln Center and former protégé Gregory Hines appeared with some of tap dancers of The Copasetics who had toured Africa with her and Dehn. In June 1989 her company performed with the Basie Band at Carnegie Hall for Joe Williams' seventieth birthday party. Legally blind and suffering from diabetes, Parks fell ill and died in 1990. That year her Harvest Moon Ball was cancelled and never re-staged. Some of the surviving Lou Parks Dancers honored her at the *Count Basie Centennial Ball* in 2004.[91]

The Lou Parks Dancers' three decades of industrious work and performances helped to revitalize Black social dances everywhere they were seen. They were "her" dancers, however, and largely unnamed on programs as individuals; rather they were listed as her "Parkets," "Parkettes," "Dancers," or "Company," making it difficult to research them and know exactly which, for instance, were at Carnegie Hall, the Smithsonian, or the Olympic festival. The six she brought on tour to Africa are in the State Department reports. All of them were HMB contest winners, and all of them were in *The Spirit Moves*.

Richard "Dickie" Harris (1948–2003) was born in New York, but little could be found on him save a few items by Monaghan, and his work with LPD and

Dehn. He was just twenty-one when they went to Africa, and was part of the "new generation of great Lindy Hoppers who arose from Mama Lou and her champion coaches."[92] Dickie was the "backbone of the company," wrote Monaghan, and the success of the company lay in the talents of the dancers, "aptly demonstrated by Harris' victory at the 1966 HMB with Thelma Grant." He was also in the first group of Lindy Hoppers to perform at Radio City Music Hall since Whitey's Hoppers in the 1930s.[93] Excerpts of him dancing at an event honoring Mama Lou lay bare his unbelievably fast and exciting dancing and footwork, exuding the type of joy referred to by Dehn and White.[94] Most likely the performances and workshops the LPD did each summer in Stockholm throughout the 1970s were largely responsible for the Lindy craze throughout Italy, France, Germany, and Switzerland, the founding of the Swedish Swing Society in 1977, and the development of the Herrang Dance Camp.[95] Harris would have been leading that charge as he and Joya Jaimes won a "decisive victory" in the 1985 TV entertainment competition *Star Search*.[96]

Harris was known to be very engaging and went on to lead Parks' company after her death. Primarily a touring group with full-time jobs on the side, the LPD rehearsed weekly in New York City and taught regularly in Florida through the 1990s with Harris as artistic director. In a bulletin for The Mama Lu Experience Traditional Jazz Dancers, Harris wrote, "On behalf of Mama Lu we must provide a service to the community through teaching and performing." The newsletter also lists himself as Artistic Director, Debra Youngblood as Contracts and Promotion Director, and David Butts as a Managing Associate.[97] With his big smile and ferocious footwork, Harris performed for the last time in July of 2003 with Ernest Brown at the New York City Tap City Festival.

Named after his father, **David Butts Cairns** (1944–) was born in Harlem and largely raised by his grandmother after his parents died. At the time of this writing he was still dancing and teaching. He told this author almost everything listed below which is corrboated in YouTube interviews. Cairns met Lou Parks at PS 68; he had been in a bit of trouble as a youngster and was told by a judge he had "better find something to do" or he would be "sent away." He called himself a "street kid" mandated to go to the afternoon program.[98] Parks recognized his talent immediately, and when he was just fifteen invited him into The Parkettes. Singer James Brown visited the Apollo Theater where the LPD were billed as the "World's Greatest Twisters" and invited them to go on tour; they left on Christmas Eve and were on the road for six months. When asked how his grandmother responded to him going away at such a young age, he replied: "She never tried to stop me, anything was better than hanging out on the streets." He said: "It was a good program, Mama Lou made us do it right; she took us to places most people only dream of." He told Peter Strom in 2020, "We rehearsed every night from 6–9:30pm, Mama was wonderful but a task master also. I called her LOP (Louise Olive Parks), we butted heads a lot, I had my opinions and was not afraid to speak up but she respected me."[99] He felt performing with Parks made him "a better person, it kept my anger down . . . I was a sort of rough and ready you know let's beat up somebody . . . but I was too tired to make trouble—it made me calm. Dance saved my life." Butts and Betty Silva won the HMB Jitterbug Jive division in 1962.

Cairns traveled with the LPD across the United States in the 1960s teaching Lindy hop and jitterbug and performing with various artists such as Chubby Checker, The Harlem Blues and Jazz Band, Lionel Hampton, B.B. King, and Cab Calloway. He went to the Olympic festival before going to Africa with Dehn in 1969 and later danced in *The Spirit Moves*. When asked about his most important memories of the African tour with TJDC and what he would want history to remember about his career, he replied: "All of it. That I did it. Coming from Harlem as a street kid and doing the things that I did, other kids seeing me on TV, it was a wonderful time."[100] He worked with Dehn through 1973, then went back to Africa in 1974 with James Brown for a three-night music festival in Zaire featuring musical legends B.B. King, Bill Withers, Celia Cruz among others. He and Lola Love can be seen dancing with Brown in *Soul Power*, a 2008 documentary film about the event directed by Jeff Levy-Hinte. Talking about Brown, he said: "He was a good guy; he had his moments but he treated me well. He called me on stage; he gave me money; dancers didn't get paid much. We went all over the world with James Brown, he was crazy about us. You had to dance and watch him and smile at your audience at the same time because his signals told [us] what he was going to do." He was still dancing in 2024, and when asked what he loves most about Lindy hop, he responded with "I love it because I'm free to be me."[101]

It was very difficult to find information about **Eunice "Micky" Wall Richardson** (1943–), a.k.a. Micky Wall. Her passport listed in the State Department records indicates her birth name was Eunice and she was born in New York.[102] The records also show that by the African tour she was married to Private First-Class Charles B. Richardson, who was stationed at the US Army Fort Drum base. *The Daily News* wrote that she won the HMB in 1961,[103] so was most likely one of Parks' original dancers, and toured with Gloria and David Butts with James Brown. The JDT post-tour program included this statement: "The slim, alert female artists of this unusual dance ensemble, Gloria Thompson,

Gigi Brown, and Micky Wall said they had enjoyed every aspect of their visit here. Our participation in this cultural event gained us a lot of experiences and long-lasting memories."[104] Wall also said: "It was wonderful meeting Emperor Haile Selassie, I wanted to bow, not because I had to, because l wanted to." The CU records also indicate that Wall was first sick in Guinea, then had to leave the tour a few days early due to colitis, arriving in Kennedy Airport in New York and being transported to a military hospital.[105]

Wall is listed as "Micky Richardson" in Dehn's *American Jazz Dance Theatre Rag to Rock* program in New York City with Vance, Barefield, Blitz, and student performers courtesy of Brandeis High School and Walter J. Damrosch Junior High School. She appeared in the TJDC's Town Hall concert, in the university tour funded by the NEA, at the Walnut Street Theatre in Philadelphia and the University of North Carolina in 1974.[106]

Born in South Carolina, **Mary Jessie "Gigi" Brown** (1935–?), according to her passport filed with the State Department, was born Mary Brown,[107] but she signed the tour agreement with Dehn as Jessie Brown and was listed in all JDT and TJDC programs as Gigi.[108] A thorough search turned up little else except what we know from Dehn's papers, which matches Micky Wall's almost to the point. Gigi danced in *The Spirit Moves*, the Town Hall concert in March 1973, and *Rag to Rock* in 1974. Butts said, "I danced with Gigi for years until she had a brain aneurysm then I went back to Debra."[109] At the time of this writing there was a beautiful video of Gigi Brown dancing with Ed Johnson while Johnny Lee Hooker sings the blues in 1969 on the Harlem Swing Dance Society Facebook page.[110] Allen Blitz said: "Everyday there was a picture of Gigi Brown in the press, she became the star, very popular in Nigeria, so beautiful and fit, and so talented."[111] Most of the press photos of solo performers in Mura's collection are of Brown.

Raised in Harlem, **Gregory "Waco" Arnold** (1937–2016) was one of Mama Lu's original dancers and was at the Apollo when they were billed as the "World's Greatest Twisters."[112] He participated with the JDT and LPD on the 1969 Africa tour, and there is an amazing 1971 promotional clip of him dancing with the other tour dancers that can sometimes be seen on *Swungover*, though it is unnamed and unsourced.[113] As one of the Lou Parks Dancers, he participated in Dehn's *Rag to Rock* program with Thompson, Brown, Wall, Butts, and Harris, appeared in her 1973 Town Hall concert, the 1974 University Concert tours funded by the NEA, and in 1974 at the Walnut Street Theatre and the University of North Carolina.[114] Arnold was a supporter of The Harlem Swing Dance Society (THSDS) from its inception, frequently giving lectures and sharing his memorabilia. In October 2013 he spoke an event at the Lt. Joseph P. Kennedy Community Center in Harlem in which the Savoy "Old Guard" and newcomers met each other. THSDS described him "As a keeper of the flame and one of our cherished Lindy Hop legends." He also appeared with them in 2016, where he "set the record straight as far as the Lindy Hop and jazz dance facts are concerned."[115]

Arnold's main partner was **Gloria Thompson Caldwell** (1938–), who was born in Missouri, raised in Indiana, and later the family moved to New York City. Her father wanted her to hear the best live music in New York, so he took her to the Savoy. He watched her closely, allowing her to dance but making sure she and the men she danced with were on their best behavior.[116] She learned quickly and was sought after by those who wanted to train for the HMB. She told Strom: "You were happy, you danced, you sweat; it was how you felt. . . . That's why they called it Home of Happy Feet, we loved it, we loved the challenge."[117] She met Parks, who was working in the hat check room, "I started to talk to her and you know we had a very friendly relationship. . . . Parks was a good person, she didn't disrespect the children at all, she would take the time to teach. She knew where the Lindy Hop came from, and it represented the Black people and she wanted the children to know that."[118] She said Parks "ruled with an iron hand; if you made a commitment, she wanted you to stand by it. We called her Miss Parks; we gave her respect with no half stepping or nothing, we gave it our whole each time we hit that floor."[119]

Thompson was one of the originals Parks rehearsed for the HMB, and she and Lee Moates placed second in 1958. Their first major gig was with James Brown at the Apollo, where they did new routines every week. "We did everything after that, Twist, the Monkey, the Jerk, Boogaloo, and always had to Lindy Hop fast at the end."[120] Brown was often called the hardest-working man in showbusiness, and Gloria said Mama Lu was the hardest-working woman. "She never stopped, the Savoy closed, she rented the Savoy Manor, and we stayed in the HMB. She knew how to Lindy and she rehearsed and practiced like we did." After the Apollo they played Radio City, then "oh my goodness I think the first time out of the country was Africa"; it was a cultural affair, the group performed then often would teach classes.[121] "They would show us what they did and there were similarities to things that we did." She, like the other five dancers Parks hired for Africa, danced with Dehn through 1974. She and her father were delighted she was able to travel the world through dance.

Gloria said: "your partner becomes like a part of you, you can read signals you don't have time to say well okay we going to do this routine or this step . . . make sure that you have the right hand contact and a good grip, and don't pull no surprises on them."[122] "We didn't know what it was to go slow, we never warmed up, we loved to dance." She and Butts said the same thing: "at BAM everyone was warming up, but we danced to warm up; we danced to bring the people into what we were doing—the audience got more excited than we did."[123] She told Strom when she was seventy-one that she never stopped dancing, she had moved to New Orleans after her daughter was killed, but she would come back anytime anyone wanted her to teach or perform.[124] Gloria emphasized that each decade Lindy gets a little bit more popular, but it is important to remember, "the heart of Lindy Hop is Black . . . way back in the '20s and '30s if you heard about somebody doing it they were Black, so, make sure to give credit where credit is due."[125]

Plate 1 Mura Dehn and Adolf Dehn, Paris, *c.* 1926

Plate 2 Mura Dehn, Art Deco, *c.* 1930

Plate 3 Mura Dehn in Kaminsky costume, *c.* 1937

Plate 4 Asadata Dafora, Mura Dehn, and Coker in *Bird of Prey*, c. 1940s

Plate 5 Sandra Gibson, Pepsi Bethel, Al Minns, Esther Washington, and Leon James, *c.* 1945

Plate 6 James Berry, *c.* 1950

Plate 7 Gigi Brown, Gloria Thompson, Micky Wall, and Dickie Harris

Plate 8 Debra Youngblood with David Butts Cairns

Plate 9 David Butts Cairns, Lou Parks, Bernard Upson, Gloria Thompson, Milton Sealey, Gigi Brown, and Micky Wall

Plate 10 Gloria Thompson, Gigi Brown, Chenault Spence, Ed Barefield, Gregory Arnold, Charles Cook, Dickie Harris, Mura Dehn, Allen Blitz, Ernest Brown, David Butts Cairns, Tasca, Lou Parks, Milton Sealey, and Pepsi Bethel

Plate 11 Allen Blitz, Pepsi Bethel, Milt Sealey, Eddie Barefield, Ernest Brown, Mura Dehn, Dick Vance, Avon Long, Joe Marshall, Buster Brown, James Stump Cross, and Charles Cook

7

Rag to Rock, Section II

The African Tour

The artists of the *Jazz Dance Theatre* not only proved themselves to be accomplished performers but should be heralded for their integrity as representatives of the United States: in every way they were professional, generous, and patient, inimitable ambassadors and guests. Naima Prevots and Tsung-Hsin Lee in separate texts reason that after the Second World War President Eisenhower, the general who had "led the Allied troops to victory," began using the arts instead of military power "to win friends and influence policy." A new social and aesthetic order, a progressive ideology which connected artistic freedom and expression to the "difference between a free society and totalitarianism," was becoming a part of US foreign policy.[1] In the 1960s, as the Civil Rights movement grew, Black artists were sent abroad as the importance of their heritage to American dance was increasingly acknowledged. Artists on CU/USIA tours were not trained as diplomats, but onstage and off were American citizens and observed, whether in performance, master classes, or impromptu events and parties, making them highly valuable resources through human connections and artistic impressions. This type of cultural diplomacy required the cooperation of the embassy posts, the local press, and the citizens in each host country.

The following summary of the tour is compiled from the State Department reports with assistance from Allen Blitz and Chenault Spence. In the reports USIS and USIA are seemingly used interchangeably, CU refers to the Bureau of Cultural Affairs, and CP to the Presentations. Although the information exists, due to space restrictions the airflight and bus travel details are not included. If the success of this cultural diplomacy is measured by media coverage, audience attendance, and reports from US embassy posts, then Dehn's African tour exceeded every expectation. (See Table 7.1.)

Allen Blitz was twenty-one years old when he signed on as company manager. Henrietta Yurchenco and Mura Dehn both had immense confidence in him, and

Table 7.1 Jazz Dance Theatre Africa Tour Summary

Jazz Dance Theatre Africa June 7 - August 3, 1969					
22 Persons + one escort officer $129,985.81- Total Obligation; $75,581.00 Contracts; Transportation $44,748.81 Other 9,719.00					
Country (8)	City (18) 17	Date	Performances (28)	Attendance 31,970	Off Stage Activities (30)
Morocco	Tangier	6/9	1	820	1. Recorded radio broadcast; estimated audience 700,000.
	Marrakesh	6/11	1	500	
	Casablanca	6/12	1	1,000	2. Recorded TV program; estimated audience 400,000.
	Rabat	6/13	1	2,100	
				4,420	
Tunisia	Hammamet	6/16	1	500	1. Recorded TV program est. aud. 250,000
	Tunis	6/18	1	450	2. Recorded Hammamet radio interview in French with Director Mura Dehn. est. audience 100,000.
				950	
Ethiopia	Addis Ababa	6/23-24	3	2,600	1. Recorded 25-minute video tape for TV. 2. Workshops and clinics with Orchestra Ethiopia and dancers of Haile Selassie I Theater.
Somalia Republic	Mogadishu	6/26-27-29-30	4	5,000	1. Three receptions and two-night club people-to-people visits. 2. Impromptu attendance at national independence celebrations.
Nigeria	Lagos	7/6-7-8	3	4,575	1. Dinner-dance; 200 guests.
	Ibadan	7/9-10	2	1,500	2. NBC-TV shot several hundred feet news film.
	Kaduna	7/14	1	1,000	3. Taped TV show for Nigerian broadcasting firm.
	Kano	7/15	1	425	
				7,500	
Guinea	Conakry	7/19, 23	2	3,000	1. Reception by Guinea youth organization.
	Kindia	7/20	1	2,000	2. Luncheons, dinners, receptions in Conakry, Kindia and Mamou.
	Mamou	7/22	1	2,000)	
				7,000	
Senegal	Dakar	7/26-27-30	3	3,750	1. USIS shot film of troupe.
	Thies	7/28	1	250	2. Buffets, receptions; an evening as guests of Senegalese folk artists.
The Gambia	Bathurst	7/31	1	500	

subsequently for eight weeks he was in charge of the costumes and props and carried around $10,000 worth of traveler's cheques, the daily per diems of the dancers and musicians. Pepsi Bethel's book relates that the dancers "had no way of knowing the political ramifications involved." Blitz wrote: "The members of the Jazz Dance Theatre (JDT), through their personal integrity and discretion, made the trip enjoyable without incident or scandal."[2] Perhaps one of the most significant results of the JDT's tour was the opportunity it afforded both the performers and their hosts to meet and exchange thoughts and ideas.[3] It began in Morocco.

Morocco: Supporting the Mission's "Americana" Program Objectives

The first stop was Tangier, where they landed safely on June 8, 1969, though none of their air freight was on board. It arrived the next day, delaying the performance for twenty minutes. The American Embassy post, the person in charge of the tour in that country and communication with the CU/

USIA/USIS, wrote that the "JDT gave four dazzling performances of song and dance and drew highest praise from spectators and press alike." A single unfavorable reaction to the performance was from an American teacher at the American School of Tangier who felt the show presented a derogatory image of the American Negro. The teacher wrote to the embassy that "at a time when American ghettos are boiling, [the JDT] perpetuates the myth of the happy, toothsome Negro, the bumbling head-scratching Negro."[4] Other Americans and Moroccans, however, did not react to the performance as negative social commentary, but rather "top-quality" entertainment which elicited laughter, cheers, and applause. US Ambassador Henry Tasca filed a Joint Embassy report from Tangier, Marrakesh, Casablanca, and Rabat, writing: "Performances of the JDT troupe in Morocco resulted in one of the most successful cultural presentations the mission has ever sponsored." The extensive coverage by the press indicated that the JDT was "a very effective presentation supporting the Mission's 'Americana' program objective." He thought it was an example of how "talented artists reflecting a valid and important US art form can relate to African audiences—goodwill in the short term and appreciation of American culture in the long term." He continued that only one comment in the Arabic-language daily *Al Alam*, "which never misses an occasion to criticize the United States," was an almost amusing if non-sequitur observation that "the police at the doors of the Rabat Theatre turned away Moroccans who did not wear ties when President Johnson was noted for receiving visitors at his Texas ranch in casual dress."[5] More than 4,000 Moroccans saw live performances, and another 400,000 had the opportunity to see an hour-long television re-broadcast of the Rabat performance (see Table 7.1).

The concerts in every country were attended by many government officials; in Morocco alone the Minister of Primary Education from Rabat, the Governor of Marrakesh Province, the Secretary General, the Pasha, the Vice President of the Municipal Council, the President of the Regional Tribunal, and Princes Moulay Mehdi Alaoui and Sidi Mohammed enjoyed the performances.[6] "The princes wanted to sit on stage and dancers had to adjust, trying not to knock them into the pit," recalled Chenault Spence. Receptions with dignitaries, the company, and invited guests followed almost every performance. "Here," he said, "Mura had an advantage, in that she was tall, dressed beautifully, had an international air and spoke many languages so could talk to each head of state."[7] In Morocco the biggest impact, however, was on the youth in the lycées and universities, who, even though they couldn't understand the lyrics, preferred the music to that sung in French or Arabic. An embassy post named Woolf from Casablanca wrote: "The universal beat of the music and dance produced a response from even the most conservative members of the audience and the JDT provided us with a rare and profitable opportunity to establish or renew valuable contacts with Moroccan young people."[8] Growing up with rock as an integral part of their own culture, *Rag to Rock* "gave them the chance to see—in an elegant and sophisticated form—the origins of the music and dance," wrote Tasca. He concluded by strongly urging "that brilliant troupes of this kind" be programmed far more frequently. "The message of a free, dynamic America striving for self-expression at the individual level is a powerful antidote to rigid dogma and ideologies of all varieties which violate the desire of people to realize certain of their deepest aspirations."[9]

Harry Hirsch, the CP escort officer assigned to the JDT, intermittently submitted reports to Thomas Huff and Frank Walters at the CU in Washington, DC. Dehn and Blitz both recalled his effectiveness as a guide and itinerary mediator, though his reports were hardly diplomatic (more like diaries), favored the salacious details (such as one of the older performers forgetting his false teeth in New York and the drinking of two others), and he often meddled in affairs outside of his official business (Dehn's control over the older men performers).[10] This led Walters to actually write to Huff a handwritten note over one report: "I would like to tell HH that we will ask for his opinion when we want it,"[11] and on another wrote, "None of his goddamn business." It was obvious Hirsch and his allies preferred the Eurocentric-leaning and classically tailored presentations of Alvin Ailey's company, which had toured Africa the year before, rather than the Black social and folk forms of the JDT.[12] Hirsch's reports wavered depending on who he was talking to during the tour, ranging from at first writing that it was "a good, strong presentation and will go over everywhere" to "the USIS photographer thinks we could never get away with presenting such a show in the US in this day and age."[13] Admittedly there were several isolated remarks throughout the eight weeks concerning the depiction of the Black American culture; it is also true that after returning to the United States, the Traditional Jazz Dance Company continued to perform the same show, with rave reviews, through 1974.

Ambassador Tasca included in his report that the requests for tickets could have filled the 2,100 seats of the Mohammed V Theater several times, and remarked that the "overwhelmingly enthusiastic audience reaction was best told by press reviews" such as "Jazz + Dance = Triumph" and "American Jazz Dance Theatre has Conquered the Town."[14] A local journalist told the American Consulate in Casablanca that he "had never before witnessed a full house in the Municipal Theatre for a cultural presentation nor such an enthusiastic, responsive audience."[15] The "frequently lethargic Casablanca audience being carried away with enthusiasm" resulted in "one of the most successful cultural presentations the mission has ever sponsored."[16]

Tunisia: Where the Fresh Air Is Mixed with the Smell of Jasmine

The format, depth, breadth, and the documents included, such as newspaper reviews of the performances, in the reports varied from embassy to embassy, though the sentiments from Morocco were repeated in the next seven countries, with the exception of Tunisia, whose embassy post, E.W. Mulcahy, was not impressed. Mulcahy's report began by saying, The JDT was a popular success. Audiences at both Hammamet and Tunis obviously enjoyed this fast paced, professional show. The orchestra was of extremely high quality."[17] He went on to say that the members were "engaging, likeable people" who were so cooperative that "providing logistical support was easier than anticipated." The JDT enjoyed all aspects of their time on tour, which included watching the Tunisian folklore dancers in a rehearsal, a cocktail party hosted by the ambassador, and informal dancing with the locals. However, he felt that while performances may have been successful, they did not support the "American objectives." Mulcahy believed the JDT's male dancers put on a vaudeville act that reminded him of the minstrel shows of the 1920s and 1930s: "The act was pure slapstick." In actuality, it was *exactly* that, and the performers were recreating acts they had successfully performed on vaudeville stages. Allen Blitz said "the origins of the routines were the street dances of their childhood; this Black dance culture is evolving constantly, [Mura] said that all the time."[18] The announcements for the program in both the June 13 *Le Petit Moroccan* and the June 19 *La Presse* quoted Dehn: "I want to present in this program as a synthesis of what the Afro-Americans have created in this century. Their style, humor, feeling of life and rhythms. The remarkable point is a continuously high level of creativity which always finds the expression of what is most actual at that particular moment."[19] Mulcahy continued that the "image of the [Negro] as a gay, carefree figure with an almost childlike innocence" was always false, even "grotesque in 1969." He explained that the racial prejudice among the "otherwise tolerant and very civilized" Tunisians was due to most uninformed foreigners believing everyone in the country was Black, and "Tunisians are especially eager to advertise their whiteness and to disassociate themselves culturally from the Black peoples of the continent." He said: "we need shows that permit [Black Americans] to display talents that Tunisians look up to and realize they cannot yet emulate. The Alvin Ailey Dancers is such a show."

An unsigned report/review took a different stance. Titled "An Excellent Jazz Dance Concert at Hammamet Cultural Center," it was picturesque writing (which included the ellipses):

> The road is empty except of few cars rushing to the Center . . . lights were out to be replaced by resonant music . . . dance started and the audience started applauding and cheering and bowing heads with excitement . . . reacting to the strong and moving jazz rhythms . . . and the beats of the feet of the band members . . . In this romantic atmosphere where the fresh air is mixed with the smell of jasmine, harmony between the dancers and the audience reached its peak and a wave of real hysteria prevailed over the audience which was standing, applauding, and cheering and saluting . . . The last dances were beautiful jazz dances which most of the audience dream of and which [Negroes] knew and developed with their spirit . . . it is natural dance, primitive and inspiring . . . The performance was sponsored by the American Embassy in cooperation with Cultural Center . . . our thanks to both for this present . . .[20]

Escort Hirsch had written: "in sub-Sahara countries there is a considerable amount of knowledge about American [negroes], their lives, their heritage and their recent (daily) struggles to erase the depiction of the [negro] as he was presented on the vaudeville stage." He pointed out "the raggedy hats, the washboard and drumming on buckets" in the first half.[21] These opposing points of view are understandable and the issue potent as the Civil Rights movement of the time was trying to erase a particular Black narrative. The 2022 movie *Uprooted* includes statements from jazz historians Bob Boross and Moncell Durden, who speak about jazz dance as a history of America's truths which is always creatively aligned with political possibility.[22] Also in 1968, Black artist/activist Larry Neal wrote: "The motive behind the Black aesthetic is the destruction of the white thing, the destruction of white ideas and white ways of looking at the world." His basic questions were: "Whose vision of the world is finally more meaningful, ours or the white Oppressors? What is truth? Or more precisely whose truth shall we express, that of the oppressed or the oppressor?"[23] While Ailey chose Black themes and American Black music, he was using white constructions and aesthetics; his programs were modeled on white concerts and white ideals of design and beauty. Lou Parks said: "Our training is handed down generation to generation. Some folks ask why I don't teach ballet or some of the more formal dances? Tap dancing, Buck dancing, the Cakewalk this is our heritage and we should not be ashamed of it."[24]

Neal argued that Black art speaks "directly to the needs and aspirations of Black America. . . . A main theory of Black power is the necessity for Black people to define the world in their own terms." He was emphatically opposed to "any concept of the artist that separates him from his community."[25] Dehn spoke and wrote about the meaning in Black social and folk dances as connected to life, *always*. Had they read the advance press (included above), Hirsch or Mulcahy would have known that Dehn's point of view likened the dances of her vaudeville stars to the satire used as social comment by the actors of commedia Dell'arte, which agreed with Katrina Hazzard-Gordon's argument that the buffoonery was a safer tool for criticizing white masters who could not be openly ridiculed in the practice of slavery.[26] The same adaptive techniques were used in minstrelsy and early vaudeville, especially the Lindy hop, and the arts of African Americans through the present day. Again, it is complicated, contextualization is key, and there is no absolutism in this instance. Blitz's final report suggested there were different criticisms in the French-speaking countries (Tunisia, Guinea, and Senegal): "the audience could not understand the English the dancers used on stage." The performers utilized conversation between dance numbers to give them time to catch "their breath and keep the rhythm of the show going." However, the responses of the audience and the applause attested to the quality of the show.[27]

Ethiopia: Attended by His Imperial Majesty Emperor Haile Selassie

Following the shows in Tunisia, the company had to board a plane to Rome (where Blitz was able to pick up the errant dentures), as Italy had tried to colonize Ethiopia between 1936 and 1947, and though they were ultimately unsuccessful, Air Italia was still Ethiopia's national airline. They flew back two days later to Addis Ababa. Contrary to Tunisia, the post from Addis Ababa observed that the JDT's concerts "met all objectives of the State Department," were an "Outstanding Success," were attended by His Imperial Majesty Emperor Haile Selassie, and the "Prime Minister even joined in the Hallelujah Chorus."

The company gave a mini-performance for 400 underprivileged children and there was excellent press, radio, and TV coverage, with eighteen newspapers posting announcements and reviews.[28] They did three performances in two days. Military and community leaders, members of the diplomatic corps, and invited guests comprised capacity audiences at the Haile Selassie I Theater and the National Patriots Association Hall. "Receptions and luncheons by mission members allowed considerable personal contact with Ethiopian cultural leaders" during the visit.

Co-sponsoring organizations the Young Men's Christian Association and Young Women's Christian Association netted US $1,444 each from funds generated by two performances, and the *Ethiopian Herald* on Wednesday July 2, wrote that the "Proceeds from Recent Jazz Show is $8,498" (proceeds from the performances in all countries were split between local organizations and the embassies).[29] The *Herald* also published an article on June 29, 1969 proclaiming that the JDT had "conquered the hearts of many Ethiopians."[30] Solomon Deressa of the *Addis Reporter Weekly Magazine* loved the first half, "the unselfconscious bawdy slapstick humor," but not so much the youngsters in the second half.[31] The company attended receptions, luncheons, workshops, and clinics with Orchestra Ethiopia and traditional dancers. Allen Blitz wrote: "At invitational performances the audiences were as enthusiastic in their own way as the shows before the general public." Pepsi recalled:

"A deep red carpet was spread from the sidewalk in front of the theater, up a flight of steps, through the theater doors, and up onto the stage where a gilded chair awaited the Emperor. When the Monarch set his foot upon the carpet, such a hush came over the spectators, that one could have heard a pin drop. In this royal setting, our company out did itself with a brilliant performance." Emperor Haile Selassie I of Ethiopia seemed very pleased with the JDT and, according to Allen: "showed his pleasure as he invited the company to his box and presented souvenir coins to each of us after the curtain."[32] Blitz thought the company was well cared for by the Ethiopians. Costumes, despite the exorbitant cost, were dry-cleaned as needed. "They had tables, chairs, mirrors, clothes racks, beverages, lights for the dressing rooms, people to iron costumes, and the case of Addis Ababa oxygen for the high attitude."[33] The embassy report also stated that despite the cheering crowds and praise for the performances the post did not "wish this to be the only side of the [Negro] American's culture presented in Africa ... however the appearance of the JDT made an excellent contribution to a better understanding of one aspect of US cultural life." Mura Dehn thought the Africans found themselves in the various movement representations of jazz, but were most moved by the performance of "Soul Dance," the dance on the program which represented the late 1950s–1960s and was accompanied by soul music. Blitz agreed and said what happened in the clubs after the performances was even better, as the dancers and the Africans saw themselves in each other and *both* groups responded, "That's what *we do*."[34] When questioned about the relation of soul to African religious dance, the director of the Addis Ababa National Museum answered, "This is beauty."[35]

Somalia: Unselfconscious, Bawdy, Slapstick Humor

Fifty members of the Somali Radio Artists met the JDT at the airport,[36] and 4,500 Somalis later witnessed "uniformly excellent" performances with enthusiastic responses and comments.[37] In Mogadiscio, the post wrote that four performances, on June 26, 27, 29, and 30, raised $1,690. The first performance was before an enthusiastic audience which included the prime minister, Mohamed Haji Ibrahim Egal, members of his cabinet, and members of the diplomatic community, including recent arrival US Ambassador Fred L. Hadsel.[38] The report goes on to say that the JDT "played to a standing-room-only audience of over 1,500 in the Somali national theater, the audience participated avidly with Lou Parks and her group in singing the rousing spiritual Amen." It also noted "great interest in the first half of program which traced the history of American dancing from New Orleans beginnings through work songs, women's songs, freedom songs, and name games to the evolution of tap dancing." Viewers had a "special affinity" with the second half, which received an "even more vociferous" response. Dehn wrote: "Africans of various nationalities recognize themselves in the Afro-American dance. They seem surprised and flattered to be recreated by their descendants. They find their folk traits in some of the jazz periods and their village fool in the antics of the comedians, but Soul moves them."[39] Notably the Mogadiscio embassy post also saw the "the similarity of some of the group's dances to traditional native dances" and wrote that a highlight of the group's stay was the celebration of Somali Independence Day on July 1, during which the company were honored guests at a reception given by President Abdirashid Ali Shermarke at the Presidential Palace. "The presence of the JDT at impromptu gatherings in the city's squares added zest to the occasion."[40]

The same report asserted that the JDT "proved themselves to be outstanding representatives of their country in the way they conducted themselves both on and off stage" and they should be commended for their "outstanding manner."

They were described as cooperative and "understanding concerning the difficulties of travel in Africa," and went on stage only two hours after arriving in Mogadiscio. Pepsi Bethel also wrote: "I'm sure that no one in the cast, and that includes myself, will ever forget those memorable days abroad. And I never before had been on the road with such a harmonious group of performers."[41] Further, the embassy post wrote that the accommodations were "5th rate, rooms were dirty, no hot water, insects abound, without one complaint." Ambassador Hadsel signed off with "It is hard to conceive of a cultural presentation that would have been better received in Somalia, I am confident that relations between our two countries will be even more friendly in the years to come."[42]

Nigeria: Requests for Additional TV and Radio Exposure Too Numerous to Meet

The USIS film crew shot footage in every country, and the company recorded radio or TV shows in Morocco, Tunisia, Ethiopia, and Nigeria, where NBC-TV took several hundred feet of news film. The embassy post in Nigeria reported: "Requests for additional TV and Radio exposure too numerous to meet."[43] The Nigerian stops were Lagos, Ibadan, Kaduna, and Kano, to combined audiences totaling 7,500, and countless more watched on TV. The eleven-day tour included "six overwhelmingly successful performances," which benefited the Nigerian National Red Cross Society. They appeared on three television shows, performed once before a high-level invited audience, and were guests of honor at two well-attended representational functions. In short, wrote the post, "the performance was both a worthy cultural presentation of Jazz Dance forms and a triumph in cultural diplomacy."[44]

Airline operations to the next stop disrupted the company's travel plans, and the company arrived in Lagos on July 6, three days and three performances behind schedule, due to the "plane not being available" in Somalia, causing them to miss a command performance with General Yokuba Gowan (though he made it to a later performance and personally congratulated them afterward). Blitz said: "We flew to Ghana, for the trip to Lagos. I looked out the window and most of stuff was on the tarmac, instruments, costumes, clothes, but when we landed in Lagos we had an official reception."[45] They were met by Ben Enwonwu, Chief Cultural Advisor to the Federal Military Government, who had been designated officially to welcome them. At the first performance the dancers were hampered somewhat by lack of a raised platform, and the band was out of uniform. "I had to borrow the only thing available, sheer pants, from the bass player and was asked by a Nigerian if it was the latest style."[46] The standing-room-only audience of over 800, including guests of honor Ambassador Elbert G. Mathews and twenty senior officials of the Red Cross, did not notice or did not care. They "laughed, applauded, sang, shouted, and tapped their feet," a response that set the pace for the remainder of the visit, and was followed by a buffet-dinner-dance for over 200 people at the post's home. "The performers . . . are highly sociable and the guests had a thoroughly enjoyable time talking and dancing with them." The next day the USIS was deluged with requests for tickets for the next two shows, "even Federal Executive Council, Chief Obatemi Awolowo, telephoned the ACAO to reserve tickets for his family." Those were also standing room only, and many people had to be turned away and many others peered in from outside the glass doors.[47] The JDT won acclaim for its public performance. The *Ibadan Sunday Sketch* critic Biodun Famojuro said, "never in the history of theatrical entertainment by foreigners in Nigeria has any show carried away or enticed the adults, the ardent critics of soul and twist dances, like the jazz show."[48]

The JDT's appearances in Ibadan on July 9 and 10 were also effective. The post wrote: ". . . from the Military Governor to the 'man on the street'—everyone had heard about the dancers . . . and everyone wanted to see them." He thought the audience "understood the message: the American dance finds its genesis in the Afro-American heritage."[49] Blitz's report stated: "the frequency of performances proved not be too taxing . . . although in Ibadan we had a day consisting of television taping in the afternoon, a performance in the evening, a cocktail party afterwards, and a bus ride the next morning." When they reached Kaduna they were quite tired. "The most demanding aspect of the schedule were these cocktail parties. We did enjoy them for they gave us the opportunity to meet many interesting people."[50] There 500 officials, and leaders were led in laughter and applause by General R.A. Adebayo, Military Governor of the Western State who later executed steps from the "boogaloo" when being introduced to the performers. Spectators were captivated by Avon Long and the veteran performers. *The Post* wrote: "Audience reaction: Old and young, Black and White ECSTATIC. "The performers no doubt succeeded in fostering Afro-American solidarity via the realm of modern theatre."[51] Avon Long commented: "Our dances originated here . . . very similar . . . and I saw dance steps I wish I could take back home . . . but their steps often are more complicated than ours. Africans have this sense of 'I'm black and I'm proud' and I knew was at home."[52]

Although obviously tired, when they arrived in Kaduna the JDT observed a group of Fulani dancers, rested, then reported to the BCNN radio/TV station for rehearsal and performance on live TV. The master of ceremonies of the show interviewed Mura Dehn and Lou Parks to provide listeners with background of the group.[53] That same evening the post and his wife hosted an outdoor buffet dinner party for over 150 invited guests, including the military governor and members of his executive council, Cultural Society officials, Red Cross officials, radio and television producers and directors, and certain journalists. At the next performance 1,000 spectators joined Lou Park's rendition of "Amen" and the audience rose to its feet with rhythmic clapping.[54] "After the finale, North Central State Governor Col. Abba Kyari went on stage. Carried away by the spirit of the moment, the usually reticent Governor rendered his dance version of 'When the Saints Go Marching In' and the 'Twist.'" Dehn wrote: "In Nigeria, at war with the Ibos, the chief commander of armed forces jumps onto the stage and joins the dancers in a finale of soul. He is like an immense white bird, dancing in his white flowing robes."[55] Lou Parks' thoughts were: "In Nigeria I said, 'this is my mother's home because all the ladies have happy faces which I identified with my family in America and it made me proud to be Black.'"[56]

On July 9 Dehn air-messaged Walters: "Please confirm my position with company. Hirsch criticizes my decisions. Orders company before notifying me. It harms work."[57] On July 11 Walters wrote to Huff: "We have received information Hirsch and Dehn maybe at cross purposes.[58] As obnoxious as Harry is he seems to keep the company moving; I do not intend to make an issue of this."[59] Also in that folder, a letter to Walters from Hirsch on July 13 gossips:

> Miss Dehn is very tired and had a mild nervous breakdown. She wanted to go home but I didn't pay too much attention to her request as these things have a habit of straightening themselves out after a good night's sleep. She is still with us after a couple of doctors in Ibadan gave her some medicine. She is not in control of her group. None of the guys like her. She is really neither a director nor a choreographer, just a dreamer.

Hirsch was not a doctor, producer, or a choreographer either, and knew not of Dehn's (or the company's) history or her four decades of artistic productions. Blitz had commented in our conversation, "The guys had their routine, it was not really a company, rather a group of soloists with Lou's dancers." Chenault agreed, "She knew it all but didn't do a run through, or warm-up, that type of directorial thing. Allen and I glued it together."[60] Hirsch went on to describe financial "problems" which were none of his concern and was ignorant of the full picture of the pre-tour costs of costumes, promotion, and coordination that were Dehn's sole responsibilities. He referred to Mura and Lou as "the dames."[61] Huff responded on July 14 to Hirsch that it was "Essential you continue to work in close harmony with Dehn. She is artistic director, contractor and company manager and your principle [sic] point of contact with the company."[62] Kaduna post Hutchinson messaged the CU on July 14: "Organizer-Director Of Jazz Dance Theatre Mura Dehn Unable Proceed To Guinea Due To Illness. Will remain In Kaduna Until Recovered. Hopes to Rejoin Group In Dakar."[63]

"There was tension there between Mura and the hoofers, I remember her being frustrated by their obstinance," Blitz recounted during one of our meetings. The young dancers were a unit and Lou Parks their strong, disciplined leader, but the dynamics among the older group were dissimilar. "There was probably stuff that happened but understandably because here's this white European woman who was like a doyenne; she didn't walk she floated; she didn't touch the ground." He could not remember any specific incident, but noted: "the guys were drinkers, wonderful, but the race difference, sexual difference, she was the boss, it was only a natural cultural divide."[64] Dehn sent a letter to Huff from Kaduna on July 13 summarizing the experience of the JDT and her gratitude to the USIS for the care and effort they had provided in making the tour so comfortable. In five weeks they had visited five countries, staged nineteen performances, recorded seven radio and TV shows, participated in numerous workshops and clinics, and attended over a dozen receptions. She felt the company was welcomed by the ambassadors, their wives, and members of the foreign service community and were frequently honored at lavish affairs and royal receptions. Every post had seen that that their professional needs were met, and even commended Hirsch pertaining to transportation and accommodations. "Unfortunately," she continued, "Mr. Hirsch has the repeating tendency to take on those affairs of the company which belong in the realm of the director." She continued, saying that he incessantly neglected to consult her and bypassed her to take certain propositions directly to the members of the company, which led to the demise of the lines of communication and caused her much humiliation. He not only "contradicted and undermined my plans for meaningful exchange with the artists and students" but also impeded the workings of the USIS.[65] Dehn later left the tour and returned to New York, though it is unclear exactly when or why. In the same conversation Allen Blitz told me, "tours were such hell anyway," and by that point Mura was only involved in the promotional and reception parts of the tour; he, the company, Parks, Spence, and Hirsch were able to continue without her.

"The Jazz Dance Theatre was without question the most important and the most successful program of the USIS in Kano during the past three years," reported the post Ted E.G. Tanen, "JDT had attracted the largest audience in a single room they had ever seen." He indicated he was "highly pleased" in terms of the mission's cultural objectives; though he added: "On the negative side, there were a few young, militant Black Americans who commented on the Uncle-[Tomism] of the first part of the performance." He stated the comments were few in number, and to his knowledge no Nigerian expressed such a negative view. Virtually all the residents who attended the show in his opinion "viewed it as a marvelous expression of a dying art." Most, including Governor Kyari, saw it as an "historical piece of jazz dance."[66] "Moreover," he wrote: "we are fully satisfied that our audiences were in all cases composed of the most influential and important strata of Nigerian society," and "numerous new contacts with important Nigerians were realized" as a result. The JDT took part in a number of social activities, "to the advantage of the mission." He praised them for not once complaining about the "Staging facilities [that] were never the best and often extremely poor" or "traveling within Nigeria [which] is at best a trying pastime and is always exhausting." Tanen firmly believed that the overall positive effect of the visit was "equal to many months of normal Post cultural activity." However, his summary of the month was: "basic problems of US-Nigerian relations remain. . . . During July, the JDT and Apollo Il landing on the moon spread a soothing balm over the anti-American rash that has been endemic to Nigeria since the start of the civil war. Both events provided Nigerians a chance to blow off steam."[67] "Jazz Dance Theater merits the confidence extended it by the Department and deserves prime consideration for future presentations."[68]

Guinea: A Marvelous Expression of a Dying Art

Allen Blitz related that Guinea was the only country aligned with more socialist countries and had joined the French community. Stokey Carmichael, the Black American political activist, was "big into folk arts" and was living in Guinea at the time, so came to a performance. When they pulled in to Conakry, because it was so poor Blitz went up to look at the accommodations, which were "disgusting." When they found a better hotel, there were two other groups staying there, Romanian folk dancers, and Irish Otis Elevator installers working at the Russian embassy. The latter were on a free tab for whatever they wanted to eat and drink, and the three companies partied together with "really good east European beer."[69]

Chenault Spence recounted that the conditions of the theaters they performed in varied greatly from one country to the next. Mura hired the lighting designer, saying she wanted the dancers to shimmer, "to look like they were in a cube of ice." The reality was "there was every deviation of lighting, we were doing the best we could with whatever equipment we found."[70] Allen agreed that in some places such as Rabat, Casablanca, Tunis, Addis Ababa, and Conakry they had to also makeshift a suitable backstage area.[71] He doubted any other dance company would have adapted so well to the "sub-standard conditions. It was miraculous that no major injuries occurred on stage." "In Conakry, Spence said: "we played in the Magnificent Chinese-built Palace of the People equipped with every modern theatrical convenience. Later in Kindia we performed on a stage lit by a single 100-watt light bulb. The Post rushed home and collected several 100-watt bulbs, a drop cord, and aluminum foil to fashion a reflector and brought them back to the hall." Allen and Chenault remembered that Cookie at one point fell off the stage and scrambled back up; the audience didn't realize it was the lighting and thought it part of the show.[72] The director of the Voice of the Revolution (Guinea's national radio station) was most helpful, providing a sound system and technicians. The post also carried twelve sheets of plywood to Kindia and made the stage floor on which the group performed later that evening. Promises by local officials to clean the toilet facilities were not kept. Blitz disclosed that everyone got sick at one point: "in Rabat I was so sick the bus driver had to carry me upstairs." One dancer who had diarrhea in Kindia had to be carried by the governor's chief of protocol to the governor's home to use his facilities.[73] Allen later confirmed the dancer was Micky Wall, and recollected:

> I believe it was in Kindia, perhaps Mamou. We were staying in what I believe to have been a French plantation before independence. The troupe was divided to spend the night in various bungalows set in a tall canopy jungle. During the day you could see monkeys flinging themselves high through the trees. I was preparing to go to bed when I received notice that a troupe member needed medication I had in my first aid box. I didn't have a flashlight so I had to walk down narrow paths through this jungle in the dark. It may have been only 100 yards to my destination but we were warned that there were creatures that you wouldn't want to meet on a jaunt through the brush. I clearly remember feeling like I was a seven-year-old walking alone in the forest.[74]

The JDT was a success in Guinea with 7,000 spectators, the governor of Mamou calling the show "Truly sensational. Despite cleanliness problems, luggage problems, toilets not working there were still no complaints from the company, and they made every effort to mix with Guineans despite the language barrier."[75] Some of the American artists socialized post-performance with the locals. Blitz reminisced that he and several of The Copasetics were invited by a "fellow who worked at the local TV station" to walk through "dark and forbidding narrow winding streets" where they climbed "a stairway with delicately carved balusters and tiled risers. It led to the second story which opened to a large space under the night sky," which he described as a setting "straight out of 1001 Arabian Nights." He recalled sitting on a "red leather pouf as we smoked kif [hashish]. Would you believe," he asked, "I don't remember anything else about the evening?"[76]

The post wrote of the social events:

> Outstanding among this group was Gregory Arnold who drew such a crowd on the dance floor in Mamou, the police had to protect him from admiring Guineans who wanted to get a better look as he demonstrated some new steps. At one point four girls tried to dance with him simultaneously, prompting a Mamou official who was enjoying the spectacle to comment: 'That fellow is getting more attention than a Chief of State.' Arnold did not speak French, but he certainly communicated.[77]

Gloria Thompson shared: "We see a lot of us in the dances done here. The steps are the same but the rhythm is a bit different. We're going to take back some of [your] dances and put them into our routines and name them for African cities where we've visited."[78] Mura said: "It was an exchange, a real exchange, and my dancers now understand that they do have a real African heritage. . . . They gained strength from being in Africa . . . and the Africans said they recognized their own movements in our dances."[79]

The report included that on Sunday morning, July 20, 1969, the day of the famous American Apollo II flight, the group embarked by road to Kindia. On the road someone told Chenault the Americans had landed safely on the moon. The CU had anticipated the event and on the bus for the company had metal badges showing the landing. The governor provided a "lavish lunch as well a visit to the Biological Institute that many of the Americans remarked was a highlight of their African tour." The theater that evening was packed with 2,000 audience members and the ovation given to the American artists was "overwhelming."[80] The report also stated that Guineans were able to "put politics aside and relax while being entertained" by the JDT and would be "talking about the performance for a long time. It was an effective instrument in promoting goodwill... and each Guinean spectator who had been continuously bombarded with anti-American criticisms was actually applauding the pleasure of having Americans among them." It was hoped this would bring some balance to anti-American propaganda being peddled by the Sino-Soviet bloc.[81]

Senegal and The Gambia: "We Had the Stars and The Moons In Our Eyes"

The company was in Dakar, Senegal ON July 26, 27, and 30; the embassy Post Andrews reported: "To say that the JDT had a considerable impact on the audiences for which they performed would be an understatement.[82] Despite the language barrier and their typical reserve, Senegalese audiences were highly enthusiastic; the Gambian audience response was simply overwhelming." This report covered both of the final two countries Senegal and The Gambia. There were five performances, three in Dakar, one in Thies, and one in Bathurst which was the final performance of the tour. The first was held at a University in Dakar with an audience of 250 Senegalese leaders and members of the diplomatic corps, and the second in the basketball court of Stade Demba Diop, where several thousand cheered and some even joined in the finale. The situation got slightly out of hand when "many youths got a bit carried away with the audience participation thing."[83] The following night torrential rains kept part of the audience at home, but those who made it to Thies "enjoyed themselves thoroughly."[84] The next performance, after a day off, was given at the Senegalese military headquarters, Camp Dial Diop, for 500 invited military officers. Here the USIA film crew spent time shooting exteriors and establishing shots, offstage activities included a buffet supper at the Ambassador's residence, a cocktail reception, and the group were guests at a *Soirée Folklorique* given at N'Gor, the most enjoyable African dancing some dancers said they had seen on the whole trip.

Andrews commented that though the show had the "desired impact" and was entertaining, certain Americans felt the first half of the show was superior to the second and recommended that the next time a group like this one was sent out that they bring along their own sound system and an electronic piano. It was noted that due to former contract obligations Avon Long returned to the United States on July 26. Allen reported that members of the company "frequently suffered from diarrhea and constipation, but we were always well supplied with Kaopectate and laxatives. . . . Luckily, no serious illness or injuries occurred and the embassy doctors were always at our disposal." Due to colitis, however, Micky Wall left the tour, returned to the Unites States on July 30, and missed the final performance.[85] The long overland bus rides were the most tiring, especially the grueling trip from Dakar to Bathurst in The Gambia, wrote Blitz.[86] After a five-hour bus ride they took a ferry over the River Gambia on the shores of the Atlantic ocean. This final performance took place in the Grab Island High School, where an audience of 500-plus, headed by the prime minister, gave a standing ovation. Several members of the group said that this last performance was perhaps the best of the tour; certainly, the audience must have been one of the best they had had in Africa.[87] M.K. Manneh of *The Gambia News Bulletin* wrote on August 2: "We had the stars and the moons in our eyes." Hundreds of people, including dignitaries such as Sir Dawda Jawara and Lady Chiel, went wild with excitement and responded with cheers echoing through the halls. "What a Night! First the jazz dancers brought the audience to its feet and then we were treated in the interval (intermission) to the 15-minute film of Apollo II—with Armstrong and Aldrin landing on the moon! We loved you and thank the American State Department for sending you!"[88]

Blitz's report ended: "In conclusion, I'd like to point out that all the personnel at the diplomatic posts were always very helpful and considerate. Our African tour was successful in every respect and provided for everyone who performed, worked backstage, and for those who were our audience a memorable and meaningful experience. Very truly yours." Albert Gibson said: "My brothers in America and my brothers in Africa are one . . . it's beautiful."[89]

On August 7, 1969 Assistant Secretary for Educational and Cultural Affairs John Richardson Jr. wrote:

Dear Miss Dehn:

On behalf of the State Department, I want to express my appreciation to you and your company for the superb performance that distinguished the Jazz Dance Theater tour in Africa. May I mention in particular Miss Lou Parks, Mr. Avon Long and Mr. Dick Vance who lent excellence to the presentations. The reports received from our embassies in the countries in which you performed attest to the unqualified success which you achieved. For this we are very grateful. We hope that, as you recall your tour in the days ahead, you will take great pride and satisfaction in the knowledge that you and the company made significant personal and artistic contributions to the accomplishment of the objectives of our cultural exchange program.[90]

Mura believed the African Americans felt that they had a heritage of 400 years in the United States, but that they came back to Africa with something to give. "l am an African by heritage and by descent—but l am a Black American," said pianist Milt Sealey, "My roots are here in Africa and perhaps someday I'll have a chance to trace them back here."[91]

8

The Traditional Jazz Dance Company, 1969–74

In rock 'n' roll the dancers had found a live wire to the spirit of their ancestors and appreciated the act for the drama it embraced. This reincarnation of the imaginary past is wonderful theater. Theater acted out in life, and life acted as theater.[1]

Boris

Lyena Dodge's family also emigrated to Vienna and had known the Tsiperovitsches in Odessa. She remembered Boris' illness, saying that Mura tried to "fix" her brother, taking him everywhere—to Europe, Switzerland, and Israel.[2] It appears he spent the early part of the 1920s in London with his father, the latter part in Paris with Mura, Chaprik, and Adolf, and by the 1930s was in a sanitorium in Switzerland. The few pictures of Mura and Boris in her collection reveal they were close in age, though he was of slightly larger build, with almost identical facial features. Mura was very close to Boris and tried but was unable to assume financial responsibility for him and bring him to the United States in 1952, but they wrote to each other often.[3] Each of his letters began with the salutation, "My dearest only love darling sister Mura," then often went on to respond to her last letter, report on how he was feeling, and his visitors in Prilly, where he was institutionalized. Letters indicate that when she went to Europe she stayed long enough to rent a nearby apartment, and she traveled by sea to Europe; he was happy her last visit was going to be by ship, as usual, instead of flying. He knew many details about the Smithsonian and the Olympics; in February 1968 he wrote, "I am proud my support and love are your treasures." The September before he passed, a letter states, "I am happy that your work goes well and is so rewarding, I hope with all my forces the African engagement will come through."[4]

Friends from several countries sent letters to Mura about her loss. Many of the sympathy notes are not signed, nor envelopes always included, but in her collection are items from Lausanne, Spain, Mexico, and France. Several refer to Mlle. Antoinette Büher, who must have been an intermediary for presents between Mura and Boris, as she delivered gifts to him, and he wrote of giving her the money Mura sent to buy items he needed. A friend named Jacques wrote, "Life goes on, we are left with the memory of something very valuable and the consolation that Boris had a quiet, happy, and painless hour of death. But for you, who grew so close with him, I pray to God for strength and courage and consolation." He informed Mura that Mlle. Büher as well as another ten members of the community paid their last respects, and to him: "it was an honor to help carry the coffin." One letter read: "Knowing how great your attachment was for this sick brother, I can easily imagine your sorrow, I am sure that Boris will be missed by Jacques who became very attached to him, as one becomes attached to a big, suffering child," and another, "the greatest sorrow was that he passed just days before you were leaving to join him and so close to your dancer's death." [5]

Sympathy letters concerning James Berry also poured in, notably from Prince Omar Ky Khan and dance ethnologist Joann Kealiinhomoku, expressing the "loss to the dance world" and the loss of a longtime friend. "There must be consolation," the latter wrote, "to know that some of his work was filmed, and that he felt appreciated—thanks to you.[6]

Within a year Mura had endured illness, a gall bladder operation, the deaths of her first husband Adolf whom she had remained close to, her brother, and dear friend James Berry, and an exciting but exhausting tour to Africa. Her tenacity again reigned, and within months of her return to the United States she was steeped in the development of a new phase of the Traditional Jazz Dance Company, now with a full a board of sponsors and directors, which would continue for the next five years with some support from the National Endowment for the Arts. The NEA was founded as a separate federal agency in 1965, and certainly several of her concerts before going abroad were under its auspices. These included the February 21, 1969 event at New York State University College in Purchase and the March 11, 1969 *Afro American Folk Dance Theater performance* at Sarah Lawrence College presented by the Black Student Association.[7] US government agencies such as the NEA stipulated nonprofit managing boards, and after returning from Africa she characteristically put together a stellar representation of the New York jazz/art scene which included as its sponsors Mrs. Count (Catherine) Basie, Milton Hinton, Edgar Battles, Maria Piscator, Prof. H. Yurchenko, Dr. Rachel D. Yocom, John A. Fairchild,

Roy Moyer, Dr. D.R. De La Barbolla, Prof. Raoul Helmar, Noble Sissle, John (Dizzy) Gillespie, and Charles Delaunay. The board of directors were tap dance legend Honi Coles, choreographer Donald Saddler, painter Sari Dienes, and the well-known artists' accountant Rubin L. Gorewitz. The nonprofit status also allowed her to apply for New York State Council on the Arts (NYSCA) grants. The TJDC received a $10,000 grant from the latter for administration, operating expenses, rehearsal fees, and the filming of an African American folk dance documentation project conducted by Mura Dehn in the 1970–1. Her company was now also included on the list of touring companies sponsored by the NEA.[8]

Allen Blitz graduated from the City College of New York in August 1970 and continued to manage the company for the next few years. On September 2 they were part of the *New York Dance Festival* made possible by the NYSCA with the title *Mura Dehn's Traditional Jazz Dance Company From Rag to Rock—A Panorama of Authentic Black American Dance Creations from 1900 Till 1970*. Notes from the program read that the TJDC was "a new name for the *Afro-American Folk Dance Theater*, . . . reorganized [and] larger in scope, including a wider range of great tap dancers, comedians and church artists, all authentic artists of the era they represent." The group choreography was again by Albert Gibson, and a slightly different Dick Vance Orchestra accompanied.[9] Don McDonough of the *New York Times* remarked that among the eye-boggling routines were the acrobatic team of Cook and Brown and Chuck Green, and the latter "manages to produce a patter of subtle sounds that makes one strain forward so as not to miss the delicacy of his special artistry." Dance critic Anna Kisselgoff of the *New York Times* wrote: "For the tap-dance buff the TJDC is a must."[10]

Folder 242

The company papers in the Mura Dehn Papers, Folder 242 imply that the next phase was at times a bumpy road. The first meeting of the board of directors was held at the offices of Gorewitz and Mancewitz on August 10, 1971. Present were Mura Dehn, Rubin Gorewitz, Robert Mancewitz, and Donald D. Saddler; not present were Sari Dienes and Honi Coles. At the meeting she reported on the first NYSCA grant, plans for the future, and plans for the establishment of a permanent center for Black ethnic dance. She informed the directors that to date she had taken no salary for herself, or the dancers for rehearsals, they were only paid for actual performances. The company reports are a bit confusing, numbered oddly, there are multiple drafts, and dates sometimes do not align with newspaper announcements and concert reviews. What is obvious is an attempt to organize, plan, and enlist the help of others in the process, though the difficulties of doing so are apparent. On a partially typed legal-size piece of paper are notes that indicate from the concerts, and if the engagements were fulfilled, the net income for the artists of the company would be $17,000 plus the $3,000 paid out in 1970 at the *Delacorte* (New York) *Dance Festival*; in the years 1970–1 and by the beginning of 1972 the company would have earned $20,000; for the two weeks of the college tour they would receive a salary of about $75 for five rehearsals. It also says that over 400 pages of a chronicle of jazz dance had been typed, probably referring to her unpublished manuscript. She had submitted a new proposal to the Council of the Arts to enlarge the company, create new programs with rehearsal salaries for artists, and to complete the making of a documentary, *Oldtimers and New Trends*. Included also are plans for research in New Orleans and Jamaica, to continue to edit *TSM* with Herbert Matter, and the establishment of a permanent center for Black ethnic dance. Another paper documents the expenses of filming.

There is also the statement, "They [the older dancers] do not understand that M.D. paid out thousands of dollars for rehearsals." The report says she received money from the grants but would have less than $8,000 to make the film, to pay for the material, cameraman and equipment, and "consequently we will see that they get a percentage of residuals." Evidence of that compensation was not found in company reports.[11] Additional pages in the folder are related but not sequential. On another is written, "Miss Dehn said there was difficulty in the group. A meeting is to be called requesting them to air their views and state what they have against her. They have been rude, and very offensive. Miss Dehn's only interest is in the dancing and if someone else can manage them any better, Miss Dehn said she would 'bow-out.'" It is difficult to identify the author, as Dehn is referred to in the third person, but the report goes on to state, "She suggests that she receive at least respect and a chance to be heard. She wants to get it out in the open . . . and has spent her lifetime in the 'black and white' dance situation and will probably get another group of Black dancers???" (The multiple question marks are in the original.) Mr. Saddler suggested a cocktail party in the dancers' honor to get them to come to a meeting, to tell them what things were being done for them, and how she was spending the grant money, and also to hang pictures of the dancers around the walls at engagements and perhaps show them some films. When asked about the situation, Allen Blitz wrote to me: "Regarding her frustrations it was rather mutual and fairly evident at times.

Grousing and bickering understandably took place during the long sessions in the dive rehearsal studios on 8th Avenue near the old Madison Square Garden." Blitz and I had previously discussed her "imperious bent" that he said, "raised the hackles of the hoofers, and they perceived Mura as an outsider, a woman, and white." He continued:

> A lifetime of confronting exploitative conditions made them sensitive to perceived disrespect. I can remember one evening on tour in Georgia hanging out in a motel room with Charles Cook, Ernest Brown, Honi Coles, and Buster Brown. They regaled each other with stories of being mistreated by nightclub owners, agents, and promoters throughout the world. Looking back on these experiences, although presented as funny at the time of their occurrence, was anything but humorous. I think they were particularly sensitive to her ideas.[12]

He explained that that "there was considerable outside pressure of the Black consciousness movements extant at the time," so her attempt to present the acts as history conflicted with their not wanting to portray tap dancing as retro or "steppin' fetchit."[13] There was no mention in the folder of how the situation was resolved.

The Annual Report of the TJDC the following October reveals that Dehn and Herbert Matter edited material and added music to *Dancing in the Savoy Ballroom and Jazz Dances—1900 to 1950*. She was invited by Henrietta Yurchenco to participate in the *International Folk Music & Dance Conference* from August 25 to September 4 in Kingston, Jamaica, where her above-mentioned film was presented and received with exceptional interest and applause. The Company now had about twenty minutes of recorded material of Jamaican folklore. Additionally, Dehn had visited New Orleans and researched current moods in Black dancing, talked to various artists, and filmed a parade with an 8 mm. camera. A film of the Harvest Moon Ball and contemporary dances was made with Louise Parks and Dancers on September 23, 26, and 28, and the agent of the TJDC, Miss Farinon, secured a two-week engagement in 1972 with New York State University, sponsored by the NEA.[14]

The February 1972 tours saw the company at the State University of New York at Cobleskill, Brockport, and Binghamton. From September 20 to September 22 they performed, presented lecture-demonstrations, jam sessions, and seminars at Louisburg College in North Carolina, sponsored by both an NEA Grant and the North Carolina Arts Council, and on October 16 at the Goodman Theater in Chicago.[15] The *Democrat and Chronicle* in Rochester, New York State reported on February 24: "What the Brockport audience expected to see from the Dehn

Jazz Dance Theater, I don't know. What they got was a lesson in American dance history and a whopping good time." The seven older pros who presented the first progression of dance steps were "winning and ageless."[16] Nancy Moore of Chicago opined, in an undated, unsourced clipping, "In keeping with the steps and music of the period they reconstruct, the dancers crack the same jokes that were made then. If I had not spoken to the artistic director of the company, Miss Mura Dehn, I might have thought that some bit of 19th century Uncle Tom-ism had slipped through time into the twentieth century, unnoticed." She went on to wonder how a Chicago audience might respond to the group, "some of whom make jokes that white folks won't understand and jokes which black folks may not appreciate." She seemed surprised that no one seemed outwardly disturbed; rather, at the end of the concert, the audience came onstage and she saw "such phenomena as vaudevillian Albert Gibson strutting about with a little, bespeckled middle-aged lady, and children attempting the high kicks of the Cakewalk." Glenna Syse of the *Chicago Sun Times* loved the first half but not so much the second, as did another reviewer in an article titled "Creative Black Artist a Delight": "The audience had a great time, more so with the tap dance veterans of Harlem's Cotton Club and the world's music halls than with exuberant prizewinners of Harvest Moon Balls, Savoy Ballroom style." Linda Winer of the *Chicago Tribune* wrote under the heading "The Jitterbug Is Back in Town," "It was all there. . . . The tapping that predates Sammy Davis Jr., the truckin' that came before R. Crumb's comix, and the old minstrel humor we've been taught not to enjoy because it comes from a time we'd like to forget." She said, "Based on the premise that the genre created should not be dumped with its racist bathwater, the NY company tries to show us why. The case is undeniable."[17]

Made possible by the NYSCA grant, with many cameras on hand to record what might be lost, "Lou Parks' dancers swept the audience up into their own exuberance," wrote Anna Kisselgoff in the *New York Times*; the show at the Town Hall on March 15, 1973 and the TJDC served as a "reminder that many Black vaudeville comedians were good dancers." The stars of Black vaudeville "were still remarkably impressive in their tap or acrobatic technique, masters of their art."[18] They were Cook & Brown, Albert Gibson, Buster Brown, James Cross, Ralph Brown, and Pigmeat Markham with Baby Seals. Highlights of the program included *Mardi Gras Parade, Here Comes the Judge, Rent Party, Strut and Tap Dance,* and *Harvest Moon Ball.*[19] Pigmeat Markham and Baby Seals had appeared as a team with Mura Dehn several times in the 1970s: at the Town Hall mentioned above, in *The Spirit Moves,* Part V, and at the Walnut Street Theatre in Philadelphia in 1974.[20]

He was in his eighties in 1973 when **Ernest "Baby" Seals** (c. 1890s–?) according to a Jacob's Pillow advertisement in the *Village Voice*, was to teach "the [Negro] minstrels he learned at the turn of the century," and Mura Dehn "will teach a special course in social dances of the twenties."[21] Ernest was a comedian, producer, choreographer, dancer, and writer, and a nephew of Franklin "Baby" Seals, (c. 1880–1915), the vaudevillian who wrote the successful "Baby Seals' Blues."[22] Ernest was prominent in the Theater Owners' Booking Association (TOBA), the vaudeville circuit for African American performers in the 1920s, primarily in the Southern, Southwest and several Northern cities. Emma Mitchell, his wife and a blues singer, was Seals' leading lady in a show he created and produced on the circuit, which had a seven-year run from 1924 to 1931 with up to twenty-four performers.[23] He generated material on the road, continuously finding new talent and incorporating it into seventy-five minutes which included singers, comedy skits, chorus routines, and dancing to the swinging rhythms of a small jazz band. His "flexible approach encouraged improvisation" and drove "the evolution of vernacular dance."[24] On February 14, 1925 *The Afro American*, under the title "Stage Music," stated, "Seals' and Mitchell's Melody Lane Girls are pleasing [audiences] in Petersburg and Virginia, with Norfolk to follow."[25] Two weeks later the same newspaper published Seals' poem "C.A.U. Blues," which appears to cajole readers to join a union. He had a byline of entertainment notices which appeared in the *Afro-American* and *Indianapolis Recorder*.[26] For the latter he wrote, "After a very successful two-day run in Philadelphia" the *Brownskin Models* opened on February 13 in Hartford, Connecticut for a five-day run at the State Theatre. "When the curtain went up there sat 4,500 patrons and when the curtain came down on the last show 42,000 theatregoers had seen Irvin C. Miller's 1938 edition."[27]

Ernest performed for five years (1932–7) in *Brownskin Models*, a popular touring revue from 1925–54 which mimicked successful white revues such as *The Ziegfeld Follies* but glorified gorgeously gowned brown-skinned dancing girls. The production, with comedy routines, lively songs, and other specialty acts, played large Black *and* white theatre chains.[28] Seals stayed exceptionally busy through the 1940s in take-offs of the production such as *Brown Skin Manikans* in Baltimore, at the Ritz Theatre in Daytona Beach, and in Miami, Palm Beach, and Tampa.[29] He was also the "master-fun maker" at the Apollo in the *Stopping the Traffic Revue*,[30] he "quit the Palace Theater" in New Orleans following a rift with the manager,[31] but was "tossing fun" there with Sweetie Walker in September.[32] The *Baltimore Afro-American* had a picture of him in blackface which accompanied "the internationally known comic who is tops in the field, kept the SRO sign hanging out" during a summer tour of Charles A. Taylor's *Club Harlem Revue* in 1943.[33] The veteran comedian toured army camps with the United Service Organizations in 1945,[34] was the "laugh getter" in the show *Moulin Rouge* at the Midway in Phoenix, and that year he did comedy again in *Harlem in Havana*.[35] As the "funnyman" he often played Chick's Show Bar in Baltimore.[36] In an advertisement on page 17 for Rockhead's nightclub in 1962, *The Montreal Gazette* called Baby Seals an "Hilarious Comedy Star."[37]

Seals also enjoyed celebrity in the 1960s as Pigmeat Markham's "second banana" with whom he made several recordings, and he danced with Mura intermittently in the 1970s. In New Orleans he met **Dewey "Pigmeat" Markham** (1904–81), who was born in Hayti, North Carolina on what was later named Markham Street.[38] Like Seals, Pigmeat's story is fascinating and a microcosm of Black comedians in the twentieth century. He ran away from home at age fourteen as, though Black Americans were "free," it was still very difficult for many to find work and becoming an entertainer with a traveling minstrel show was an alluring option. At his very first gig his boss presented a can of burnt cork and showed the performers how to apply it. Markham started in carnival and medicine shows touring Georgia, North Carolina, Alabama, and Tennessee, working constantly and learning a wide variety of dances and songs; as minstrel shows dwindled, he entered the vaudeville circuit. He adopted the moniker "Pigmeat," performed non-stop, and amassed a repertoire of dance steps, jokes, sketches, and stunts. He toured with *Bessie Smith's Traveling Revue*, appeared in A.D. Price's *Sugar Cane Revue* from 1925 through 1928, and had logged thousands of performances by the time he was twenty-four years old.[39]

By the early 1930s Markham started appearing in Harlem as a regular at the Alhambra Ballroom. His experience allowed him to upstage the more established comedians and he soon appeared at the Apollo Theater. White comics such as Milton Berle and Henny Youngman were known to copy his jokes. Roger Dodge wrote about Markham: "He appeared in several Broadway musicals such as *Hot Rhythm* (1930), *Blackberries of 1932*, *Blackbirds of 1939*, and *Ecstatic Ebony* (1939) which kept him in top dancing form. He was the originator of the dance steps Susie-Q, The Boogie-Woogie, and Truckin,' which swept the country."[40] Markham wrote and worked in two comedy shorts in Hollywood, *Mr. Smith Goes Ghost* and *One Big Mistake*, and performed at the Lincoln Theater in Los Angeles in a program starring The Andrews Sisters. The Los Angeles Black community at that time, however, was not thrilled to see Markham on stage acting out depictions they felt were holding back the advancement of their race. Markham said he acknowledged that his act might reinforce stereotypes, but they offered him money because he was funny, "not historical—funny. I was born and raised black. I learned my comedy from black comedians. The earliest skits and bits I did ... were invented by black men. The audiences I learned to please ... they were mostly black, too."[41] One of America's most popular African American comedians at the time, Markham was unapologetic about blackface, a "mask," Gottschild wrote, that "was both a deception and protection."[42] Nesteroff quotes Markham:

> You may wonder why a [Negro] had to do that, and all I can tell you is that's the way it was. Just about every Black entertainer in those days worked in burnt cork and lip make-up. I never went before an audience without my burnt cork until 1943. I'd been working in blackface for so many years that I was scared to go on without it.[43]

The unfathomable practice of blackface, white men applying burnt cork to their faces to make mockery of the Black performers while at the same time copying their acts, was both offensive and common at the turn of the century. Stranger were Black minstrels, such as Pigmeat's hero Bert Williams, who engaged in the same practice. Williams explained it was a result of supply-and-demand economics. White minstrels in blackface took work away from actual Black performers; African Americans performed in blackface to win back some of the work. He and his comedy partner Walker decided that if white men were billing themselves as "coons," they would bill themselves as "The Two Real Coons."[44] Eventually the cork was polarizing and Markham became a marked man by the NAACP, the Urban League and Negro advancement societies wishing an end to 'Uncle Tom.' In 1943 confronted backstage by some young Black men who said blackface caused a lot of pain, he agreed to stop. His stand-up career faded a bit, but he was able film *Fight that Ghost* (1946) and *House Rent Party* (1946). Markham went back to the Apollo, though his act was waning in popularity at a time when *Ebony* magazine declared: "No Negro in his right mind would dare venture upon an American stage and do a minstrel act unless he wanted to become the guest of honor at the first all-colored lynching in history."[45] Ed Sullivan saw him several times at the Apollo and asked Pigmeat to bring his *Here Come da Judge* routine (which he wrote and first performed in 1928) to his show in 1947 at Maxim's Theater.[46] Sitting at an elevated bench in a black graduation cap and gown, he delivered his "judgments," as well as frustrations with the accused. In 1949 Sullivan booked Markham on his TV show *Toast of the Town*. Sullivan, against the wishes of racist producers, made it a practice to present outstanding African American acts such as the Harvest Moon Ball champions and The Harlem Globetrotters, and probably "did more to advance race relations in America than any of his contemporaries in the television industry." His progressive booking policies helped African American comedians make inroads into mainstream entertainment.[47]

Comedians started making records on jazz labels in the late 1950s, and every stand-up comic working made an album. Pigmeat Markham churned out a series on Chess Records, resurrecting his career.[48] As "Here Come da Judge" became a hit, Sammy Davis Jr. said the phrase during a guest shot on Rowan and Martin's television show *Laugh-In*. The producers then hired Pigmeat for about eight different episodes. With Dick Alen he turned the skit into a song and brought it to back to Chess Records, where it became very successful, earning royalties through the 1980s. The catch phrase uttered by a Black comic in 1928 echoed across the nation forty years later. At a time when "Black Power" resonated from "Watts to Vietnam," Markham's style of vaudeville had an unexpected resurgence.[49] Revamping the sketches he had used for years, most of which had been performed originally in blackface, Markham helped bridge the tension between races with his unlikely blend of old-fashioned comedy. Though he performed with Dehn's TJDC in several concerts, he insisted:

> My act is not history, it's comedy. It's not white-man's comedy, it's Negro-born and Negro-popular. It's not aimed at ridiculing anyone; the characters I've created are no more a slur on the Negro than Jackie Gleason's hot-headed bus driver or Art Carney's sewer cleaner or Dean Martin's drunk are a slur on white men. I am an American Negro Comedian and I'm proud to be all three.[50]

"Here Come da Judge" was accompanied by music with a funky beat and topped the charts in 1968, causing Pigmeat Markham to be regarded as a forerunner of rappers and one of the precursors of rap music.[51]

The year 1973 was heralded as when breakdancing/hip-hop started, though in February 2024 Rennie Harris said the phrase "hip" meant aware and "hop" meant consciousness, so "hip hop" was essentially a peace gathering manifested in social dances and went all the way back to the Lindy. The three laws of hip-hop—individuality, creativity, and innovation—that were evident in the Lindy carried forward into breakdancing; Black expression and creative resistance remained indigenous to the dancer's place and purpose.[52] While the Black Power movement of the previous decade may have struggled to find new directions combining "political issues and economic issues,"[53] by 1973 the DJs, music, breakdancers, and graffiti artists were recognized as core elements of hip-hop responding to the current social and economic inequalities. There were glimmering hopes that the goals of brotherhood had advanced, and signs of progress in the workforce, education, and politics, but anti-white feelings remained as the average Black family still had an income that was 59 percent that of a white family in America. The move toward racial equality had proved arduous and painful; the results of which were complex and filled with contradiction.[54]

Against that backdrop was the TJDC's concert at the Town Hall and the surprising responses found in the reviews. In addition to Kisselgoff's quoted above, on March 15 Joseph Gale of the *Daily News* reported that he saw in the audience a "greater heterogeneity than he was accustomed to ... from 6 to 70 from tuxedos to levis responded with a serious and knowledgeable appreciation and left with glistening eyes, shaking heads and wondering smiles."[55] What Dehn presented, "for one time only, which is a shame, was a pastiche of vaudeville burlesque comedy and dazzling tap dancing." The critic Robe wrote in *Variety* that the traditional portion was highlighted by a "brilliant turn by Cook and Brown, followed closely by Pigmeat and Seals," and the comedy ranged from "superb to passable" and the dancing by Lou Parks; Dancers, Gigi Brown, Micky (Wall) Richardson, Gloria Thompson, Gregory Arnold, David Butts (Cairns), Dickie Harris, with the addition Edward Johnson, was "generally excellent." The "Vaudeville fans, and they grow every day, would have loved seeing some wonderful old routines getting faultless and hilarious treatment from these veterans."[56] That year Dehn also filmed *Old Timers* with Pigmeat Markham and Baby Seals.

Folder 242 also includes a document indicating Dehn had submitted a proposal to the NYSCA to establish a creative workshop and a school to teach the fundamentals of jazz by members of the company. It included a request for rehearsal and teachers' fees. Another indicated she hoped to finally realize her aims with an expanded company embracing the entire field of Black folklore with a permanent organization, a professional performing company, a school of authentic jazz dance, and an archive of movies, documentaries, and books on the history and people. By the mid-1970s several scholars working on jazz dance studies took note of her films. In the 1973 Kandilakis interview she said:

> The social dance of today is dominated by the Americas, all over the world. Maybe China is excluded, but Russia is not. Neither is India, Africa, Europe, or Japan. It is truly amazing—it is the dance of today. That's why I feel it should have its focus, And it's great creators should have a place for themselves. There are all kinds of ethnic groups, but there is no center for Black American social dance.[57]

The TJDC's March 19, 1974 performance in the University of North Carolina's Aycock Theater had a slightly smaller cast and band but a very similar program;

three days later the full company was back (though Gloria Thompson was replaced by Joya Jaimeson and Edward Johnson danced for David Butts Cairns) and they were accompanied by Dick Vance's Trio. The performances on March 22–24 at Philadelphia's Walnut Theater sponsored by the NEA and Pennsylvania Council for the Arts netted several reviews. Bob Nelson of KYW News radio loved the "Kaleidoscope Of Vaudeville," writing: "Make no mistake about this show. It is not a slickly choreographed panorama of dance. This is folk dancing in the true nature of that term. Tap dancing, now an almost lost art, is brought back in all its multifaceted forms . . . one of the most amazing folk-jazz presentations I've ever seen." He mentioned Pigmeat, Albert Gibson and the Lou Parks Dancers, stating, "They'll dance your hearts away."[58] Ellen Shaw's review noted "there was a hot time in the old town last night as TJDC turned the Walnut into a swinging, swaying, revival meeting. . . . Those that remember will vibrate with nostalgia those that don't will love the history lesson. . . . No matter what the chronology, everyone winds up on their feet belting out the spiritual 'Amen.'[59]

Rock 'n' Roll

The TJDC concerts reflected Dehn's intrigue with the evolution of contemporary social dance. Though not as extensive as her writings on the "Golden Era," which was her foremost commitment, her rock 'n' roll chronicles include ethnographic accounts of the popular dances she observed, such as the twist and watusi; many she believed were created by public school young teenagers in Harlem and Brooklyn. Pages 64–5 of her manuscript describe the "Eyewitness Accounts Schools 1960–64," which are flavored with a perceptive insight that communicates nuance, feeling, and the atmosphere of the event:

> I watch the very beginning of rock 'n roll steps in a P.S. school in Harlem. Two boys and a girl are doing the slop and didi-bop walk. They seem to be wading in a stream on slippery pebbles. Floating backwards on the slide of the slop, they turn about with a flip of the fishtail; advance, trembling in the air, one foot lifted, the other undermining stability with multiple beats . . . . the little girl gives out squeaks of delight. They are not gripping the floor—they float above it.[60]

Dehn described the intricate, roundabout motions of the boys and girls at PS 28 in Brooklyn, the "turning wrists, rolling pelvises, trembling feet. Their bodies, undefined like jellyfish, blur the outlines, elude precision. I joke, 'What African dance is this?' The kids laugh. It is Popeye the Sailor, Marilyn Monroe, and the swim." She continued: "But the mainstay of rock is the African undulation of the torso. Steps like jerk, dog, monkey, do away with motion in space. The dance becomes almost stationary. A wide stance and flexed knees bring the necessary stability." Her research into this aspect was fed by her collaborations and interviews over two decades with Mama Lou Parks.[61]

In 1975 Dehn wrote that rock 'n' roll had again "changed social dance in a radical way," and listed the changes she felt were brought about for the first time in this century:

1. The role of the woman is as creative in invention and display as that of the man.
2. The dance is without a leader.
3. The group dance has no formation.
4. Arm movements are an integral part of the social dance.
5. African body movements became a western social dance.
6. All age groups adapted dances created by children.
7. The couple dance is banned. And there is still another first: the quality of relations between whites and [Blacks] in rock 'n roll depends on the initiative of the blacks.[62]

Unfortunately the list is not elaborated on, yet it does illustrate that Dehn considered not only the technical aspects of dance (points 3, 4, and 5 above) but also the social and political implications of social dance (points 1, 2, 6, and 7). Looking at dance as a complex, layered phenomenon, Dehn was able to recognize multiple meanings. Not only did the roles of women and men reflect the political ethos of the time, but race relations, reflective of the Civil Rights movements, ushered in a renewed interest and display of African dance movements by both European and African Americans. Black Americans were then able to assert a role of authority in dance. Dehn credited dancers as able to embody this ethos, and when imbued with a political or social overtone, she termed it "Black Awareness." Her accounts of the dancers and the dance illuminated the ways in which bodies unconsciously, but very knowingly, can operate with an almost independent agency.

9

Rhythm: A Driving Force

They use the support of rhythm—much kinder and more powerful ally.[1]

Sculpted Verse

Le Jazz Hot, no. 355 (1975) was the seventh volume Mura contributed to, this time using James Berry's words taken from interviews which were then translated by Laurent Goddet into French. Berry thought Harlem during his time had "good vibrations: no racism. White people danced with Black people; Black people danced with white people; everyone was happy dancing to the jazz rhythm. We did whatever came to mind to a Charleston beat. There was 'Cherry Picking,' the 'Flying Charleston,' the 'Little White Charleston, tap dances, and the aero plane in Charleston rhythm."[2] In her earlier writing Dehn was struck by this "obedience to the rhythmic force," where the jazz dancer is "an instrument of invisible rhythm, which enters the body and demands its release through movement."[3] She also marveled at a "surprising technical dexterity which is naturally subtle and sophisticated." There is also "withheld rhythmic energy which produces anticipation, a kinetic excitement." She described Leon James as a master "in withholding, producing a teasing, and humorous suspense."[4]

Lillian Morrison explained that rhythm, as in the "ebb and flow of a tide, or the way originality, gesture, spirit, meaning and emotion are expressed in movement, was a driving force" behind Dehn's life.[5] It was a source of inspiration and energy; its power carried through her work, evidenced in her dances, her productions, and her films. Her style was infused with color; she sculpted verse from a rich history of language coupled with passion and a sense of humor. She was not afraid to make mistakes, telling Morrison: "I don't mind, I go from error to insight." Her friends commented on her "original and surprising opinions about almost everything" for instance on describing a mutual friend's weaving as "immaculate non-conceptions," and about a Godunov opera: "all pauses and darkness."[6] The sheer number of written materials she generated then bequeathed to her friends suggests she wrote constantly, using language as a way to decipher jazz and life.

In 1976, at the beginning of what became a very successful performing career, Eiko & Koma (Eiko Yamada Otake and Takashi Koma Otake) came to New York City from Japan. Eiko was twenty-three years old. One of the first people she met and established a relationship with was Mura Dehn. Having been given tickets to the Roseland Ballroom, Eiko & Koma were simply sitting and eating as they were unfamiliar with the social dances of the country. Next to them was a man fifty years their senior, doing the same. A conversation began which lasted throughout the evening. He introduced himself as "Dutch" Thomas and said his wife, Mura, was out on the dance floor as Dutch did not dance. Eiko said Mura "was lovely" at age seventy-four; she still danced beautifully. That evening the four walked together to the subway; a few days later, in the office of *Dance Magazine*, Eiko and Mura met while both were submitting information. Dehn invited her to tea at her apartment, and Eiko felt they quickly became friends, more like family. She was "one of Mura's three girls: the Japanese one."[7] The other two, Ruthie, the first wife of Charlie Dorkins, and Lynn Carlo, also had similar grandmother/granddaughter-style relationships with the elder artist. Carlo lived in the same building and had also been close to Dutch. Eiko and Carlo thought of Dehn fondly. Both believed the elder supported their artistic endeavors: Eiko's dance and Carlo's painting. Both visited Dehn often: Dehn taught Eiko some jazz during her almost weekly visits, even a dance to a Bruce Springsteen song, and during the final years of Dehn's life Carlo and Dehn dined together nightly. Eiko said that Dehn "did not know how to cook—nothing."[8] Still, she entertained friends often, and Eiko, Allen Blitz, and Mark Scherzer were among those who frequented her apartment through her last decade, much of which was spent writing poetry and distributing her films.

Letters in Folder 186 from 1977 confirm the interest of UNESCO to bring the Traditional Jazz Dance Company and *The Spirit Moves* to Paris. Mura wrote three others on October 8, to Jean Rouch about bringing the company to the Musée de l'Homme, to Sue Weill at the NEA about a grant to edit another part of *TSM*, and to Mary Myerson to bring both the TJDC and *TSM* to the Cinémathèque Française. There is no evidence of concerts after 1974, but Dehn received a grant in 1978 for more editing, and according to a letter from Dutch was in Europe that year.[9] On February 5, 1979, *TSM* was introduced by Walter Terry at the *Lincoln Center Dance Collection Film Series*, and that March her drawings (she started drawing in her late seventies) were on view at the Baecker and Harpsichord Studios in New York City. As there are examples of Mura's artwork in her papers, it is surprising, but not shocking, that they would be alongside the prize-winning children's books of Remy Charlip, the giant paper constructions of Sylvia Palacios Whitman, the found art of James Waring, and the drawings of Sophia Delza, Simone Forti, Midi Garth, David Gordon, Ana Halprin, and Steve Paxton.[10] The next year Dehn was afforded some recognition as the TJDC received support from the NEA to edit and refine the post war-era part of *TSM*, and by her inclusion in the International Dance Council, Inc. (the American Division of UNESCO) in Paris, France. The conference focused on the preservation and dissemination of American dance. Dehn was on a panel focused on African American dance which included anthropologists Judith Lynne Hanna, Alan Lomax, and dancer Lavinia Williams. Irmgard Bartenieff discussed Laban Movement Analysis, and Genevieve Oswald, then curator of the New York Public Library Dance Collection, also participated.[11]

What is both surprising and shocking are the letters concerning the estate of Benjamin Benno.[12] Benno Greenstein Benjamin was born in London in 1901 of Russian-Jewish heritage. On the death of his mother in 1905 he was sent to Russia and raised by his maternal grandparents until his father brought him to New York, where he immediately began to study painting in 1912. Benno went to France at the age of twenty-six, and during his stay became acquainted with various masters who recognized his talent and originality. His paintings appear in museums in the United States and in private collections, including that of his friend Pablo Picasso.[13] The rest of his paintings, drawings, and watercolors, were willed to Mura.[14] Also in the folder are several pages of an appraisal document listing 255 items for a total of $104,730. While they may have known each other in Russia, it is much more likely Mura and Benno were friends in Paris along with the other ex-pat, anarchist, avant-garde artists they knew there. They may have had contact over the years, were not close, but "he trusted her," Mark Scherzer told me. Benno had drafted his will in 1947, and "it surprised everyone he left his entire estate to her upon his death in 1980."[15]

Scherzer, Mura's lawyer from roughly 1980 through her demise, had just started his practice when his partner Peter, a dealer in Middle Eastern nomadic art and textiles, introduced him to Dehn and her coterie of 80-year-old lady friends. They included photographer Stella Snead, painter Sari Dienes, and poet Lillian Morrison. Scherzer remembered a fashion show in Peter's loft where they modeled some his merchandise: "Mura, with her erect bearing carried herself as a dancer and made for a great runway model even at such an advanced age."[16]

Mura was tall, he said, "with an air. . . . She always wore these capes and berets so she looked like an artist, it was fun to go out with her." Peter found a gallery that bought the bulk of the Benno collection; he had not made any kind of deal with Dehn for compensation, so she gave him a few little paintings, at which he bristled. "She could be direct and demanding and Peter thought I jumped through too many hoops for her," Mark told me, adding, "Most important is what she did to document the dance, it took vision and incredible determination in spades and it wasn't appreciated but she was so sure of the importance of it at time most people weren't. . . . it was really a tremendous service to humanity and for cultural history."[17] There is mention in the same folder of Dehn giving other paintings to dancers and friends, and later paying for Benno's funeral expenses and tombstone.

Film Screenings and Festivals

A Celebration of Women in Dance, the March 1981 Thelma Hill Performing Arts Center's gala, honored the Black dancers of Katherine Dunham's first New York company, and Mura Dehn. Lavinia Williams introduced her at the awards ceremony, saying she was "One of our greatest pioneers," noting her organization, promotion, and presentations over four decades. She added that Dehn was "one of the first to recognize the [Negro] in the development of jazz and folk dancing."[18] That June her films were screened at the *International Dance Film and Videotape Festival and Conference* at the New York Public Library, and *TSM*, Part II was shown at the *Dance Critics Association Conference*. Sally Sommer, conference chair, expressed her deep appreciation to Dehn in two different thank you notes, writing, "Seeing this film was one of the highlights of our conference this year, many of us were thrilled and surprised at viewing this extraordinary dance, at realizing the vibrant and rich heritage of joyous movement which has so profoundly shaped us." She went on to say that this jazz dance was relatively unknown and unseen, so it was a "rare treat" to see the dance and the many TJDC dancers—'the flesh behind the images'—who attended. Sommer continued: *TSM* was a "magnificent document of a piece of dance history that has been neglected and left largely unrecorded," and that the conference members "were very moved. Your knowledge, zeal and pioneering spirit have made you one of our most prized dance historians."[19]

Film festivals are not usually monetizing events, though the Hamburger Kinotage paid for one print as a result of its showing, and Dehn had offers to buy a print from the *London Festival* and Columbia University in New York City. A letter from Alan Lomax indicates that an early version of the *Harvest Moon Ball* film was in New York Public Library by 1972; Scherzer revealed the other segments of *TSM* were in the archives of the Lincoln Center and the State Film Centre in East Melbourne, Australia by 1984, and were sought by the Cinémathèque Française and Musée de l'Homme in Paris. In a letter to Peter Foster he wrote: "The film has been shown to great acclaim at international film festivals in London, where it was recognized as the outstanding film of 1982, Nantes, where in 1981 it won a best film award at the *Festival des 3 Continents*, and it received a medal from the city of Berlin, where it was recognized as the most interesting entry in 1982, and *La Biennale de Venice*.[20] Celia Epiotis of ARC Videodance's *Eye on Dance* television series interviewed Mura about her films in June 1982 for a segment called: "Glances of the Past: Documentation of Jazz Dance."[21]

The next year *TSM* was a featured film at *Filmex*, the *Los Angeles International Film Exposition* of 1983. The films were also shown at Houston Museum of Fine Arts in May 1983, and Mura attended the New York State University when they were shown at Columbia, and at the now storied *Dance Black America* festival at Brooklyn Academy of Music.[22] Also, the debut of *The Sparkle Image Show* on cable Channel J was "proud to announce" there would be a mixture of award-winning material including *TSM*, a documentary on the 100-year history of jazz dance in America.[23]

Herman Dutch Thomas

According to a letter from neighbor Rose Meyer on Fort Washington Street, Mura was staying with Mary Myerson in Paris in December 1981, and wrote: "Should I not write you again, please let me extend to you greetings for Chanukah and Christmas, and again don't worry, we will look after Dutch."[24] Scherzer and Blitz talked about Dutch fondly, both had "sat around" the Dehns' apartment in Fort Washington and both thought they were an unlikely couple, she the tall, classy artiste with a Russian accent, and he a short "salty old seaman" with a Dutch accent. "She wasn't a snob, Scherzer said, she met him in a bar on 11th Street"; they were married for almost forty years. They were very independent, but when together at home were mutually "tender, caring, and devoted to each other." Allen said: "I loved Dutch, he was straight out of central casting, a tough guy with a rough voice, looked like Popeye; so different than her, no connection with art or dance; he was a Merchant Marine, came here in the 30's and was an organizer of a national maritime union (a red-hot union); both were real die-hard leftists."[25]

Dutch was not thrilled with some of Mura's dancers because he knew that she was being disrespected; Blitz also said he was a "fighter and a doer with old time integrity." Lillian Morrison believed he was supportive and accepting of James Berry in spite of his drinking and emotional problems and all of the dancing that went on in their apartment. Dutch had savings, a good pension, supported her financially and emotionally, and did all the cooking and cleaning while she devoted herself to dance. Charlie Dorkins felt that the beginning of Dutch's ultimate demise was when he was hit by a car in 1982.[26] He died of an aneurysm, on the operating table, six months later at the age of eighty-two. His death inspired Dehn to compose several poems, an activity she had increasingly done in her seventies and eighties. Lillian, a poet herself, said Mura who had a unique gift for apt and original metaphor added to her love of rhythm in movement of the spoken word.

On The Death of My husband (IV)
Body divorced from movement,
heart from kindness,
the soul is wilting, an unwatered plant.
I do not give an ounce of love.
There are no people in my life.
The salt is gone.[27]

Though he had passed three years prior, there are a series of handwritten letters to Dutch dated February 22, 1985 in Mura's papers. They begin with "My love Darling" and reveal she read his letters almost every night, and they gave her "so much of what [she] needed." Some talk of her friends, another of looking for a home for herself. Dutch's letters were comforting even when he was firm and "planted in life." Another said she re-read his letters often as he "always came alive, reassuring, interesting, meaningful and full of love." She regretted not seeing him before his fateful operation but still loved him dearly, even the "times it was not there as you hid it does not take it away; you wanted the two of us together exclusively, exclusively—just what I want now." She wrote she had read *Cosmos* by Carl Sagan without criticizing and got a lot out of it. Another letter says she knew she stayed with Boris too long so he went to Ireland without her; in another she admits her preoccupation with her films. Overall, the letters illustrate a marriage with both love and regrets, she was happy even when they fought, and she needed him always and understood it. Another states she is alright but "semi-alive physically" and remembers "the constant words of love you gave me all of your life" and she has to accept living by herself.[28] In the same folder is a handwritten, line-by-line budget of household expenses, adding up to $1,611, leaving her $389.00 in her bank account. Sally Sommer and Lillian Morrison both told me Mura died almost penniless; Eiko mentioned she'd often give important items such as pictures, pieces of film, drawings, and paintings away indiscriminately. Even so, after gifting some of Benno's collection and covering the expenses of his estate, selling the rest of his paintings could have provided some support in her last years.[29]

Rhythm of Words

The extension of her writing into poetry was a natural development of her love of language and rhythm, though it would be impossible to determine when she began as so much of her prose crosses the boundaries into the poetic sphere. *Lion Tamer* is a collection of forty Dehn originals that were published posthumously by Morrison. Lillian wrote in the preface that Mura Dehn came to poetry late in life, when she was compelled to register new and strange changes which were happening to her in old age.[30] In Dehn's Collection are three folders containing versions of hundreds of poems, and a list of nearly fifty poems she sent out to literary journals including *The Poetry Review*. She had published two poems in the anthology *Timeless Voices*, and another in the anthology *When I Am an Old Woman I Shall Wear Purple*.[31] Very often the subjects of her poems were people: Roger Dodge, Dutch, Chaprik, and James Berry. Recurring themes of movement, rhythm, and the body figured in many cases as she recorded the transformation occurring with her advancing age. Most aging dancers know the frustration and the struggle of growing old, a fading instrument, and changing abilities; Dehn put these feelings into verse:

Old Age I
My skin is comfortably loose
a size too large
I like it slow

no need to tighten up
the muscle corset is now a blouse
The seventy's rolled over[32]

The charming 28-minute film *In a Jazz Way: A Portrait of Mura Dehn*,[33] a snapshot of her life, shows Mura dancing with lifelong friend Al Leagins, describing her work, and includes excerpts of *TSM*. Shot in 1980 and released in 1986, it won a Blue Ribbon in the 1987 *American Film Festival* and was available from Alexander Street Press at the time of this writing. *The Spirit Moves* was shown in New York at the Public Theatre in 1986 (as part of Joseph Papp's *Film at the Public* series), which Allen Blitz attended with Henrietta Yurchenco and called a monumental event. Jack Anderson's piece in the *New York Times* described how one part of the film in a "deliberately undecorated studio" created a "strange kind of timelessness," and another when the camera is standing still in a ballroom "immortalized anyone who came within its frame." "A film would be the first real book we had about these dances," said Dehn, these films are "a portrait of our century because all of the important events of our time were reflected in dance in one way or another."[34]

Dehn's poetry themes turned toward death. Lillian Morrison told those gathered at Dehn's funeral service that "as might have been expected, she wrote about getting old in a way that no-one else has done before, not only with complete candor and exactitude, but with great wit."[35] Dehn recalls the death of her friends, the encroachment of death's right of way. The previous "To Old Age" refers to age and youth as "envelopes, bringing the message, but once delivered of no account." In another she wrote:

Lion Tamer
My pride, my years
turned on me.
I goad them with a chair,
whip them with hoops,
command them to sit on haunches
and wave their paws.
They growl. They leap.
They form a pyramid.
I'm in the act.
I must perform my part
and lay my head
into their open mouths.[36]

Eiko remembered: "Mura called me one day and told me 'I almost died yesterday, but came back, having told myself I cannot die until I finish editing *The Spirit Moves*. She did that."[37] Mura finished editing her films in late 1986, and died on February 11, 1987, Her obituary in the *New York Times* read:

> Mura Dehn . . . a specialist in American [B]lack dance, died Wednesday at her home in Manhattan. . . . [She] was considered a pioneer in documenting the various styles of black social dance. . . . the highly praised *The Spirit Moves* . . . [is] considered among the most valuable archive footage in a field that covers both social and theatrical history.[38]

Alan Lomax spoke at Dehn's service, predicting she would be discovered for the pioneer she was, saying: "Her films show black creativity in one of its shining moments, and will serve as a witness and resource in the achievements of Afro-American culture for future generations."[39] Yet Dehn felt her voice was never fully heard and that dance academics were still unconvinced about the value of jazz in the late 1980s. She would be happy to know her films and materials are now some of the "most visited" at the Dance Division in New York Public Library.[40] Through the last moments of her life she continued to work on her manuscript and on the documentation and preservation of Black social dance and jazz dance. Dehn felt Eiko had the necessary skills and affinities to sort through her belongings and divide her possessions among the benefactors of her estate. As Mura and Dutch had no children, she left her possessions to her friends: Ruthie Dorkins received some of Benno's paintings, Lynn Carlo her photographs and other paintings, and Lillian Morrison the rights to her poetry and books.[41] Eiko became the custodian of the bulk of Dehn's materials after her death; she received copies and the rights to *The Spirit Moves*, as Dehn believed her films to be very valuable and that they could assist in putting the Otake children through college.[42] Eiko sold a copy of the first three *TSM* volumes to Dancetime Publications in 2010, where it was available for a few years, and there were used copies on sale at Amazon at the time of this writing, and many clips have made it to the internet, on personal YouTube channels. She had negatives and copies of the films made and donated them to institutions where she felt they could be the most useful, such as the library of New York University.

Informants interviewed for this study agreed that Dehn was one of the strongest women they knew, and one they missed the most. Her strength was evident in the ways she moved throughout the world, in her early eighties, even riding the A-Train (subway) alone in New York, which she considered "home";[43] it was evident in her physicality, holding herself "beautifully, 'til the end,"[44] and dancing, as *In a Jazz Way* illustrates, with style and grace even at age eighty. Her strength was also evident in the determination she enlisted in following her life's mission. Friends and colleagues also concur that Mura Dehn was a brilliant, often difficult woman, with astounding ideas and an art for colorful, metaphoric, even profound language. Her scholarly inquiries delved into the heart of the jazz idiom, and her exceptional use of metaphor and imagery in her writing on jazz lends itself to a particular understanding of the form. While she did not use the lexicon of a seasoned academician, her unique style was able to translate a nuance in the elusive jazz form that others did not. Though she was nearly fifty when she began filming at the Savoy, Dehn considered this to be her primary occupation. *The Spirit Moves* will remain one of her enduring contributions. When she could not dance anymore she became an impresario and documenter; when she could not move she turned to the rhythm of words, her poetry suggesting a complex individual with an indomitable spirit. With chutzpah and humor, she dedicated herself to her vision, and rhythm was the most consistent force in her life and work.

10

Lessons from the Academy

> *I am sure my perceptions and understanding may seem to completely miss the point to the Black creators. They draw from roots unfelt and unknown to me, it has a different meaning to them which I could never express.*
>
> *I can only say that I lived and loved this dance and felt free to create it, not like an outsider but as part of it at all times. I was, and am aware, that the deep source which inspires us all comes always from the Black people.*
>
> Mura Dehn[1]

Jazz Scholars, Fellows, and Aficionados

Mura Dehn, with typical effervesce, wrote that to the Savoy originators jazz was a "belief in a miraculous future."[2] Learning a cakewalk in 1912, visiting the underground jazz cafés in Paris, frequenting the Home of Happy Feet in Harlem, hers was a lifetime of dancing, observing, writing, documenting, and promoting, without pause and often without appreciation. Her colorful language and passion sometimes eluded articulation, and she was apt to romanticize, writing in stream of consciousness with little self-editing. Some scholars were disconcerted by and misunderstood her statement: "I believed this to be more important than the advent of the Diaghileff's Ballet Russe. Here were not only the virtuosos but the very originators of the global dance craze! Not only the Black Nijinsky, but Black Vestris and Black Noverre."[3] The insinuation was not that she was Diaghilev, but that in addition to the reconsideration of form and performers as that impresario sought, she felt the originators and creators should also be supported and venerated. She deemed herself a producer, she was exceedingly confident, and complicated, but never condescending; her mission was to cultivate, recover, and preserve, and her zeal sometimes superseded delivery. The list of scholars, fellows, and afficionados able to embrace that gestalt attest to the significance of, and the lessons to be learned from Dehn's work.

Mura Dehn and Asadata Dafora established the Academy of Swing to define and teach its form, subtext, and history. Peppered throughout her collection are notes about intended lectures concerning the dance's human impact, and the discovery of its primeval movements. The academy would address the "Orgiastic Quality of Social Dancing, its comparison to the Antiquity of Africa, and of the [Negro] Church as a Dance Repository." Under these headings were the role of Negroes and whites in the creation and practice of social dance, the unprecedented dance renaissance due to jazz, European avant-garde artists and jazz, and the postwar period—the great breakup.[4] The next section of the course was titled "Historical Survey." It began with the Congo square dances in New Orleans, then examined the structure of movement in African American dance as compared to European folk dance and ballet. Plantations, saloons, dance halls, minstrels, carnivals, medicine men shows, vaudeville, burlesque, and musicals were given consideration; "Post-Civil War and the Ragtime Era" comprised another unit, and that segment's ending was devoted to the merging of two dance cultures. A third section began with "The Jazz Explosion and Its Triumphal Conquest of Europe," which led into "The Golden Era of Jazz, 1920–1940, then "Bebop, Mambo, the Cools, and Rock 'n' Roll" were covered before the social aspects of the dance were explored. The outline also included Dehn's analyses of the folk creation as it happened before one's eyes, its function, and a simultaneous survey of what she termed "the entire dance achievement." She wrote: "Folk art is the only mirror in which man sees not himself, but the world as it is." Finally, she planned to discuss "the meaning of rhythm in our century." The course's entirety would result in a deep understanding of the history, ingredients, and essentials of the jazz dance form.[5]

Form, Function, and Characteristics: Resisting a Hierarchal Ladder

John Dewey began the twentieth century with a plea on behalf of the education of the "whole" child;[6] dance educators in response argued for the inclusion of movement in the classroom, and an argument can also be made for the inclusion of the classroom in the studio. I entered a career of dance teaching in higher education which placed ballet and modern dance on the top rungs of a hierarchal ladder. Studying Dehn's work led me to turn the ladder horizontal and view all dance forms side by side, examining each with the same questions: "What is the genre, what is its purpose and meaning to those who created it, and what are the particular attributes that make it unique?"—a process I called *Form, Function, and Characteristics*. History and context layers movement experience with enriching multiple meanings which can be lost in a traditional, purely kinetic experience. "Could we have gotten to the moon without Newtonian physics?" asked Wynton Marsalis, suggesting that the greatest jazzmen are finely practiced and knowledgeable in their art form, so that improvisation and invention emanate from a highly skilled and articulate foundation.[7] Likewise, we can't fully understand the potency of a dance form without knowing its social, psychic, and aesthetic meanings. In order to keep the ladder on its side and examine all genres evenly aesthetic objects must be considered in relation to the environment where they exist as practices; art and artifacts are deeply significant and firmly anchored in their designers' ways of living. Dance teaching that includes analysis of essences and ingredients honors each form's complexity, originality, and passion; establishing context is key. At its inception jazz dance was a social, folk form, constantly developed and shaped by the participants, so must be investigated from that perspective. *Form, Function, and Characteristics* does so, and aligns with both Susan Koff's and Karen Hubbard's writings on dance teaching. The latter proposes learning the history and style of authentic jazz dance from the perspective of African American culture[8] and the former suggests a shift from past dance education practices to a pedagogy with a holistic framework, hence a socio-cultural and philosophical perspective.[9]

Comprehension of the rhythmic imperative is enhanced when contemporary jazz is deliberated in relation to the "Golden Era." This imperative, which moved a generation, was in part responsible for its virtuosity, vitality, and brilliant styles. Reflection on the past helps us to understand our present and move forward into a future which is enriched by erudition. As Marsalis asks: "How can something new and eccentric be developed . . . when the meaning of what's old is not known?"[10] Dehn believed jazz music and jazz dance had great influence in the forming of the American character and were significant barometers of culture; important as art and folk art, but also important as human and social documents. Jazz offered dancers a structure that was socially uplifting, through which they could creatively interact with their environment, affirm their selves, and mediate relationships and meanings through movement. Partners embodied rhythm and music with swung eighth-notes and released it through known and invented signifying movement responses. The whole person, mind and body, acted together, and philosophies were mapped onto the figure of the dancer. The body through dance became a site of creative resistance, and the political was personal. Just as the blue note illustrates a new morphosis of different tonal scales superimposed over each other, the body attitudes in jazz dance were new creations of diverse parentage. When examining each, then, culturally relevant frameworks have to be applied that examine the aesthetic object in relation to the environment where it exists. Joann Kealiinohomoku pointed out that a speaker's own aesthetic judgment does not refer to the values of the performer, rather, "To say that 'sports are not dance' really means that the sport does not live up to the aesthetic standards of the speaker. In short, to label something as a dance art or not a dance art, tells us more about the speaker than it does about the phenomenon and performers in question."[11] In order, then, to grasp the ways in which diverse cultures convey images, it is necessary "to understand how *they see themselves* in relation to the world, since [their] images are a result of concepts of perception."[12] A reading of African American social dance would necessarily include its role as a social mediator, an interpretation Mura Dehn referred as early as 1936.

A Knowing Body: American Is Part African

That jazz dance has been marginalized in academia is due in part to the Western distancing which has produced an abyss of misunderstanding between the dances of diverse cultures and the mind and its body. Yet all knowledge is socially constructed and defined through particular contexts, experiences, and histories, so the abyss must somehow be bridged, especially in regard to the primacy of the body. Dehn observed changes in attitude and disposition that were reflected in the body, movement, and dance. She explained the art of social dancing as "knowing how to hold your body and how to let it go," implying that it is actually the body itself that knows.[13] Movement is behavior, and it is feeling. Responsiveness creates and reveals our sense of identity.[14] The attitudes represented in the dancing body are indicative of a philosophy; recognition of which acknowledges the whole person. Dehn felt the films she made of jazz dance chronicled a time of prewar optimism for African Americans to the pessimism and disaffiliation of the postwar bebop and the frustration evidenced in breakdancing. This gives credence to the body as having a particular way of knowing; the body absorbs and has access to a strand of knowledge that the conscious mind does not necessarily have to understand. The body's faculties and capacities cannot be unconnected from the experience of knowing; it is through bodily engagement and interaction with our environments that we become aware of and sensitive to people and comprehend our past and present experiences. All human cognition comes through our senses, so is bodily in nature and acquired through a kind of absorption, as it were, "known in a way that largely escapes articulation by the knower him- or herself. An example is we can say we know how to ride a bicycle if, and only if, we can actually ride a bicycle."[15] We only know how to Lindy if we can do the Lindy.

Dehn's work revealed that the body did not only act, it was a receptacle of consciousness and knowledge, and through dance, ideals of cultural unity and individuality were recognized by a shared community. The communal joy experienced when people move together in rhythm binds us. Anyone who has a attended a swing dance event or a rock 'n' roll concert will testify that those connections are real, if unexplainable, and provide an internal narrative for who we are. As Dehn wrote, "His dance is an answer and a guide to actuality."[16] Black social/jazz dance of the Golden Era merged aural, felt, improvised African aesthetics with visual, learned, codified European dances, recognizably changing the collective dancing body. Dehn's contribution to dance history, then, unveiled the ways in which Americans, through this new idea of movement and the body, are part African.

Moved by the Spirit

Mura Dehn loved to dance, and reveled in the sensation. She loved her life, her work, and the dancers with whom she worked and learned from; she acknowledged their prowess, resourcefulness, and knowing bodies. Most importantly, she loved the joy, and the "spirit" they maintained regardless of circumstance. She consistently explored, adapted, tailored, and acclimated over her 84-plus years, sparkling in her jazz way. Mura hoped to realize her goals with a permanent organization, including a professional performing company, a school of authentic Black dance, and an archive of movies and books on the history and people of jazz dance. While the permanent organization never developed, she did have the Academy of Swing for several years, a performing company for over twenty years, interviewed many dozens of dancers, wrote copious articles on jazz dance, and produced fifteen films. Hopefully, this monograph, with its short bio-scripts of many of her remarkable dancers, partially fulfills another aspect of her dream.

Notes

Introduction

1. Author unknown, in "Foreword," Mura Dehn, "Jazz: A Folk Dance," *Dance Magazine* 19, no. 8 (1945), 8.
2. Jennifer Dunning, "The Spirit Moves: A History of Black Social Dance on Film," *The New York Times*, December 16, 1987, 22.
3. Lillian Morrison (friend of Mura), in personal communication with the author, March 1995.
4. Mura Dehn, 1902–87, The Spirit Moves Manuscript, MGZMB-res.+ 87-20, Jerome Robbins Dance Division, New York Public Library for the Performing Arts, 217.
5. Celia Epiotis and Jeff Bush, directors, *Glances at the Past: Documentation of Jazz Dance* [video recording] (New York: ArC Videodance, 1982).
6. Lynne Fauley Emery, *Black Dance: From 1619 to Today* (Princeton, NJ: Princeton Book Company, 1988), 91.
7. Marshall W. Stearns and Jean Stearns, *Jazz Dance: The Story of American Vernacular Dance* (New York: Da Capo Press, 1968).
8. Mura Dehn Papers on Afro-American Social Dance, c. 1869–1987, (S) *MGZMD 72, Box 4, Folder 107, Jerome Robbins Dance Division, New York Public Library for the Performing Arts.
9. Ibid., Folder 109.
10. Kim Chandler Vaccaro, "Moved by the Spirit: Illuminating the Voice of Mura Dehn and Her Efforts to Promote and Document Jazz Dance" (Ed.D. diss., Temple University, 1997).
11. Sally Sommer, "Heaven at the Savoy," *The Village Voice*, December 2, 1986.
12. Dehn Papers on Afro-American Social Dance, Box 21, Folder 254.
13. Terry Monaghan, interview by Elliot Donnelly, *International Lindy Hop Championships Legacy Series, Part I*, October 2, 2020, https://www.youtube.com/watch?v=1bPEgM5OYl8.
14. Eiko Otake (friend of Mura, known by her first name, Eiko), Morrison (friend) and Charlie Dorkins (friend of Mura) in personal communications with the author, 1995; Stella Snead (friend of Mura), in personal communication with the author, 1995.

15 Katrina Hazzard-Gordon, "Afro-American Core Culture Social Dance: An Examination of Four Aspects of Meaning," *Dance Research Journal* 15, no. 2 (1983): 24.
16 Morrison, (friend of Mura).
17 Stella Snead (friend of Mura).
18 Eiko Otake, *I Invited Myself, Volume III: Duets* (Philadelphia, PA: Fashion Workshop and Museum), February 22, 2024.
19 Brenda Dixon Gottschild, "The Swingin Lindy: Origins of a Legacy," *Google Arts & Culture*, retrieved February 2024, https://artsandculture.google.com/story/the-swingin-lindy-origins-of-a-legacy-by-brenda-dixon-gottschild-lincoln-center/JwWxl1IJ7CwnJQ?hl=en.
20 *History of Tap Dance*, lecture by Jason Samuel Smith, DanceNJ Professional Development Day, Ocean County Technical and Vocational School, Tom's River, NJ, November 16, 2023.

Chapter 1

1 Dehn Papers on Afro-American Social Dance, Box 2, Folder 29.
2 Wendy Oliver and Lindsay Guarino, *Jazz Dance: A History of Its Roots and Branches* (Gainesville, FL: University of Florida Press, 2014), xiv, xv.
3 Pryor Dodge, ed., *Hot Jazz and Jazz Dance* (New York: Oxford University Press, 1995), 246.
4 Roger P. Dodge, "Negro Jazz as Folk Material for Our Modern Dance," *1st National Dance Congress and Festival Proceedings* (New York: National Dance Congress, 1936), 48.
5 Leonard Feather, *The Encyclopedia of Jazz* (New York: Horizons Press, 1960).
6 Ibid., 23.
7 At the beginning of the First World War the navy had troops in New Orleans and the Secretary of War did not want them distracted, so Storyville was closed.
8 Mark Gridley, *Jazz Styles: History and Analysis,* 5th ed. (Englewood Cliffs, NJ: Prentice Hall, 1994).
9 Feather, *The Encyclopedia of Jazz*.
10 Ibid., 82.
11 Roger Dodge, "The Dance-basis of Jazz," *The Record Changer* 4, no.1 (1945): 15.
12 Loraine P. Kriegel, "Engendering Jazz (or . . . Read My Hips)," unpublished manuscript, 1994.
13 Robert Crease, "The Savoy Ballroom Remembered," *New York Swing Dance Society Footnotes: A Quarterly Newsletter* 5, no 2 (Fall 1990): 1–4.
14 Gridley, *Jazz Styles,* 37–8.

15 Stearns and Stearns, *Jazz Dance*, 141.
16 Olly Wilson, "Black Music as an Art Form," *Black Music Research Journal* (1983): 3.
17 Brenda Dixon Gottschild, *Digging the Africanist Presence in American Performance: Dance and Other Contexts* (Westport, CT: Greenwood Press, 1996); Brenda Dixon Gottschild, *Waltzing in the Dark: African American Vaudeville and Race Politics in the Swing Era* (London: Palgrave Macmillan, 2000); Thomas DeFrantz, "Hip Hop Habitus v2.0," in *Black Performance Theory* (Durham, NC: Duke University Press, 2014), 236; Brenda Dixon Gottschild, "Challenges, Chances, Changes—My Object Lesson in Reclaiming My Time," September 12, 2019, TPAC Chapel, 1837 N. Broad St., Philadelphia, PA.
18 Dehn Papers on Afro-American Social Dance, Box 1, Folder 1.
19 Wilson, "Black Music."
20 Mura Dehn, "Is Jazz Choreographic?" *Dance Magazine* (January 1948): 24–5.
21 Mura Dehn, "More Respect for the Clown," *Dance Magazine* (February 1946): 34.
22 Dehn Papers on Afro-American Social Dance, Box 2, Folder 28.
23 Brenda Dixon Gottschild (Professor, Temple University) in personal communication with author, 1994.
24 Louise Ghertler and Pamela Katz, directors, *In a Jazz Way: A Portrait of Mura Dehn* [film] (New York: Filmakers Library, 1986).
25 See note 17.
26 Joanne Kealiinohomoku, "An Anthropologist Looks at Ballet as an Ethnic Form of Dance," *Impulse* (1970): 24–33.
27 Brenda Dixon Gottschild, "Stripping the Emperor," in *Looking Out: Perspectives on Dance and Criticism in a Multicultural World*, ed. David Gere (New York: Schirmer Books, 1995), 95; Susan Spalding, "Aesthetic Standards in Old Time Dancing in Southwest Virginia: African American and European-American Threads" (Ed.D. diss., Temple University, 1993).
28 Philipa Rothfield, "Philosophies of Motion," *Writings on Dance* 11, no. 12 (1994): 77–86.
29 Dehn Papers, 1902–87, 5.
30 Caedra Scott Flaherty, "Melanie George Presents Jazz at the Joyce and More," *The Observer*, January 8, 2024, retrieved from https://observer.com/2024/01/melanie-george-presents-jazz-at-the-joyce-and-more/.
31 Feather, *The Encyclopedia of Jazz*, 16.
32 S. Carter, "Civil Rights and Southern Soul," *Z Magazine* (January 1994): 63–6.
33 Michael Ventura, "Hear That Long Snake Moan," in *Shadow Dancing in the U.S.A.* (Los Angeles, CA: Jeremy Torcher, 1985), 103–62.
34 Pamela Otto, "African American Social Dance Forms of the Harlem Renaissance: Embracing a Deeper Understanding of Jazz Dance and Aesthetic Principles," *Impulse*, 3, no. 3, 1995, 160.

35 Kariamu Asante, "Commonalities in African Dance: An Aesthetic Foundation," in M. and K.W. Asante, eds., *African Culture: The Rhythms of Unity* (Trenton, NJ: Africa World Press, 1990), 71–82.
36 Mura Dehn, "A Few Words about Jazz Dancing," *Proceedings from the 1st National Dance Congress and Festival* (New York: National Dance Congress, 1936), 43–6.
37 Feather, *The Encyclopedia of Jazz*, 16.
38 Kim Chandler Vaccaro, "Moved by the Spirit: Illuminating the Voice of Mura Dehn and Her Efforts to Promote and Document Jazz Dance" (Ed.D. diss., Temple University, 1997).
39 Leroy Ostransky, *The Anatomy of Jazz* (Seattle, WA: University of Washington Press, 1960), 24.
40 Gridley, *Jazz Styles*.
41 Gunther Schuller, *The Swing Era: The Development of Jazz, 1930–1945* (Oxford, UK: Oxford University Press, 1991).
42 Gridley, *Jazz Styles*.
43 Stanley Dance, *World of Swing* (New York: Charles Scribner's Sons, 1974), 1.
44 Schuller, *The Swing Era*, 7.
45 Brenda Dixon Gottschild, "The Swingin' Lindy: Origins of a Legacy," *Google Arts & Culture*, retrieved January 17, 2024,https://artsandculture.google.com/story/the-swingin-lindy-origins-of-a-legacy-by-brenda-dixon-gottschild-lincoln-center/JwWxl1IJ7CwnJQ?hl=en, .
46 Dehn, "A Few Words about Jazz Dancing," 22.
47 Stearns and Stearns, *Jazz Dance*, 325.
48 Dehn, "Is Jazz Choreographic?"
49 Dehn, "A Few Words about Jazz Dancing," 22–3, 39.
50 Kriegel, "Engendering Jazz."
51 Dizzy Gillespie, *To Be, or Not . . . to Bop* (Garden City, NY: Doubleday, 1979), 484.
52 Ibid.
53 Duke Ellington, *Music Is My Mistress* (New York: Doubleday, 1973), 100.
54 Dehn Papers, 1902–87, 11.
55 Brenda Dixon Gottschild, *Black Dancing Body: A Geography from Coon to Cool* (New York: Palgrave Macmillan, 2003) 223; Dehn Papers, 1902–1987, 32.
56 Dehn, "The Spirit Moves," 32.
57 Joaquim Berendt, *The Jazz Book: From Ragtime to Fusion and Beyond* (Chicago, IL: Lawrence Hill Books, 1975), 4.
58 Dehn Papers, 1902–87, 32.
59 Ibid., 31.
60 Ibid.
61 Feather, *The Encyclopedia of Jazz*.
62 Roger Dodge, "Jazz Dance, Mambo Dance, Part 1," *Jazz Review* 2, no. 10, (1959): 59, 63.

63 Katrina Hazzard-Gordon, *Jookin' The Rise of Social Dance Formations in the African American Culture* (Philadelphia, PA: Temple University Press, 1990).
64 Dodge, "Jazz Dance."
65 Dehn Papers on Afro-American Social Dance, Folder 215.
66 Ibid., Folder 212.

Chapter 2

1 Karen Wickre, "Interview with Mura Dehn," *Research Center for the Federal Theatre Project Voices of the WPA: Oral Histories of the Works Progress Administration* (Fairfax, VA: George Mason University, April 20, 1978).
2 Though her birth certificate could not be located, her date of birth on her passport registered with the US State Department for her African tour is October 7, 1902. Bureau of Educational and Cultural Affairs Special Collection ARK, MC468, Group II, Box 67, Folder 15, 89.
3 Isabella Buzynski, "Café Culture in the Jewish City," retrieved December 4, 2023, https://scalar.usc.edu/works/odessa/a-brief-history-of-odessa.
4 Friends and colleagues interviewed in 1995/6 include Lillian Morrison, Eiko, Lynne Carlo, Charlie Dorkins, and Pepsi Bethel, and in 2023 Eiko, Sally Sommer, Charles Reinhart, Carol Teten, Allen Blitz, Chenault Spence, Pryor Dodge, and her lawyer, Mark Scherzer.
5 Dehn Papers on Afro-American Social Dance, Box 5, Folder 123.
6 "About Joe," *Three Pillars Arts: The Delsarte Project*, retrieved February 2023, https://www.delsarteproject.com/joe-williams-bio.
7 Ibid.
8 Richard Kraus, Sarah Hilsendager, and Brenda Dixon, *History of the Dance in Art and Education*, 3rd edn. (Englewood Cliffs, NJ: Prentice Hall, 1991).
9 Dehn Papers on Afro-American Social Dance, Box 20, Folder 217.
10 Ibid.
11 Ibid., Box 5, Folder 123.
12 Henry Adams, *The Sensuous Life of Adolf Dehn* (Columbia, MO: University of Missouri Press, 2021).
13 Dehn Papers on Afro-American Social Dance, Box 19, Folders 209–10; Joycelyn Pang Lumsdaine and Thomas O'Sullivan, "The Prints of Adolf Dehn: A Catalogue Raisonné" (St. Paul, MN: Minnesota Historical Society, 1987).
14 Dehn Papers on Afro-American Social Dance, Box 19, Folders 209–10.
15 Lumsdaine and O'Sullivan, "The Prints of Adolf Dehn."
16 Mura Dehn, Clippings, MGZR, Jerome Robbins Dance Division, New York Public Library for the Performing Arts.

17 Dehn Papers on Afro-American Social Dance, Box 23, Folder 298.
18 Isadora Duncan, "I See America Dancing," 1927, in Sheldon Cheney, ed., *The Art of The Dance* (New York: Theatre Arts, 1928), 47–50.
19 Adolf Dehn, "Everything Explained Today," https://everything.explained.today/Adolf_Dehn/
20 Ibid.
21 Adolf Dehn Papers, 1912–87, Box 1, Folder 6, Archives of American Art, Washington, DC: Smithsonian Institution.
22 Ibid.
23 Don Heinrich Tolzmann. "Adolf Dehn: Life and Work of a German American Artist on Both Sides of the Atlantic," *Loyola Notre Dame Library*, retrieved December 1, 2023, https://Loyolanotredamelib.Org/Php/report05/Articles/Pdfs/report47-10-Adolf-Dehn-Tolzmann.pdf.
24 Henry Adams, "Adolf Dehn Biography," retrieved December 1, 2023, http://www.adolfdehnart.com/biography.
25 Lumsdaine and O'Sullivan, "The Prints of Adolf Dehn."
26 Adams, "Adolf Dehn Biography.
27 Tolzmann, "Adolf Dehn."
28 Lumsdaine and O'Sullivan, "The Prints of Adolf Dehn," 6.
29 Adolf Dehn Papers on Afro-American Social Dance, Box 1, Folder 6.
30 Lumsdaine and O'Sullivan, "The Prints of Adolf Dehn"; "Sigmund Freud Papers: Interviews and Recollections, 1914–1998; Set A, 1914–1998; Interviews and; Dehn-Thomas, Mura, 1960," *Library of Congress*, retrieved December 1, 2023, https://www.loc.gov/item/mss3999001450/.
31 Lumsdaine and O'Sullivan, "The Prints of Adolf Dehn."
32 Adams, "Adolf Dehn Biography."
33 Richard Cox, "Adolf Dehn: Satirist of the Jazz Age Author," *Archives of American Art Journal* 18, no. 2 (1978): 11–18.
34 Lumsdaine and O'Sullivan, "The Prints of Adolf Dehn," 6; Henry Adams, *The Sensuous Life of Adolf Dehn: American Master of Watercolor and Printmaking* (Columbus, MO: University of Missouri Press, 2021).
35 Ibid.; Mura Dehn, Clippings, MGZR. As previously stated, her collection is full of newspaper articles and reviews whose names and dates are removed.
36 Dehn Papers on Afro-American Social Dance, Box 23, Folder 298.
37 Lumsdaine and O'Sullivan, "The Prints of Adolf Dehn," 6.
38 Ibid., 7.
39 Dehn, "Everything Explained Today."
40 Dehn Papers on Afro-American Social Dance, Box 5, Folder 26.
41 Pryor Dodge (friend of Mura), in personal communication with author, April 2023.
42 Dehn, "Everything Explained Today."

43 Lumsdaine and O'Sullivan, "The Prints of Adolf Dehn," 8.
44 Dodge (friend of Mura).
45 Dehn Papers, 1902–87, 2.
46 Marshall Stearns, *The Story of Jazz* (New York: Oxford University Press, 1956), 109, 119.
47 "Blackface Minstrelsy: The American Experience," *Corporation for Public Broadcasting*, retrieved January 25, 2024, https://www.pbs.org/wgbh/americanexperience/features/foster-blackface-minstrelsy/.
48 Wickre, "Interview with Mura Dehn."
49 Susan Hannel, "The Influence of Jazz on Fashion," Bloomsbury Fashion Central, University of North Texas, 2019, 57–78, retrieved January 25, https://libproxy.library.unt.edu:2823/products/berg-fashion-library/bo...eth-century-american-fashion/the-influence-of-american-jazz-on-fashion, 202.
50 Chris Jenkins, "Is Classical Music Racist? An Aesthetic Approach," *Aesthetics for Birds*, February 26, 2021, retrieved from https://aestheticsforbirds.com/2021/02/26/is-classical-music-racist-an-aesthetic-approach.
51 Tyler Stovall, *Paris Noir: African Americans in the City of Light* (Boston, MA: Houghton Mifflin, 1996).
52 Henry Adams, *The Sensuous Life of Adolf Dehn, 7.* (Columbia, MO: University of Missouri Press, 2021).
53 Dehn Papers, 1902–87, 27.
54 Mura Dehn, "Jazz Dance," *Sound & Fury* 2, no. 3 (1966): 14–18.
55 Ibid.
56 Hannel, "The Influence of Jazz on Fashion."
57 Ibid.
58 W. Meek, ed., *Adolf Dehn: American Artist Retrospective Series* 4, no. 2 (Naples, FL: Harmon Meek Gallery, 1984); Snead, personal communication, 1995.
59 Dehn Papers on Afro-American Social Dance, Box 20, Folder 213.
60 Ibid., Box 23, Folder 298.
61 Adams, *The Sensuous Life of Adolf Dehn*.
62 Lumsdaine and O'Sullivan, "The Prints of Adolf Dehn," 14.
63 Dehn, Clippings, MGZR, Jerome Robbins Dance Division, New York Public Library for the Performing Arts.
64 Ibid.
65 "Ergy Landau," *Wikipedia*, retrieved January 20, 2024, https://en.wikipedia.org/wiki/Ergy_Landau.
66 Dehn Papers on Afro-American Social Dance, Box 2, Folders 14–20.
67 Dehn, Clippings, MGZR.
68 Ibid.
69 Ibid.

70 Ibid.
71 Emma Cohn, "Mura Dehn, the Preservation of Black Jazz Dance on Film," *Sightlines* (Spring 1987): 8–11.
72 Dehn, Clippings, MGZR.
73 Dehn Papers on Afro-American Social Dance, Box 5, Folder 139; Lillian Morrison, Friend of Mura Dehn in personal communication 1995; Allen Blitz, friend of Mura Dehn in personal communication 2024.
74 Dehn Papers, 1912–87, Box 1, Folders 35–8.
75 Ibid.
76 Ibid., Folders 42–4.
77 Lyena Dodge (friend of Mura), personal communication with author, March 1995.
78 Mura Dehn 1902–87 Scrapbooks, MGZR 90-9612, vol. 1, Jerome Robbins Dance Division, New York Public Library for the Performing Arts.
79 Morrison and Eiko (friends of Mura).
80 Lumsdaine and O'Sullivan, "The Prints of Adolf Dehn," 13.
81 Mura Dehn, *Lion Tamer, and Other Poems* (published posthumously) (New York: Waterford Press, 1987).
82 Lyena Dodge (friend) of Mura.
83 Mura Dehn Papers on Afro-American Social Dance, Box 19, Folder 212.
84 Mura Dehn Collection, MGZMD 483, Jerome Robbins Dance Division, New York Public Library for the Performing Arts, Box 3, Folder, 6.
85 Dehn Papers on Afro-American Social Dance, Box 18, Folder 179.
86 Dehn Papers, 1912–87, Box 1, Folders 42–4.
87 Lumsdaine and O'Sullivan, "The Prints of Adolf Dehn," 13.
88 Ibid., 14.
89 Ibid., 13.
90 "Tharpes-Roberts Affair," *Afro American* (Baltimore), July 5, 1930.
91 "Red Scare Protest Issued by Liberals," *New York Times*, May 19, 1930, 18, retrieved January 2, 2024, https://timesmachine.nytimes.com/timesmachine/1930/05/19/issue.html.
92 R.G. Harris, "Adolf Dehn's Humanity," *New York Times*, April 13,, 1930, 133.
93 "Dehn's Splendid Drawings," *New York Times*, Friday, April 4, 1931, 20.
94 Meek, *Adolf Dehn*.
95 Stella Snead, (Friend of Mura), in personal communication with author, 1995.

Chapter 3

1 Dehn Papers on Afro-American Social Dance, Box 1, Folder 2.
2 Sally Sommer, "Mura Dehn 1903–1987," *Routledge Encyclopedia of Modernism* (Colchester, UK: Informa UK, 2018).

3 Hannel, "The Influence of Jazz on Fashion."
4 Ostransky, *The Anatomy of Jazz*, 63–75.
5 Liz Williamson and Mike Moore, "That Eclectic, Elusive Dance Called Jazz," *Dance Magazine*, 49, no. 2 (1978): 63–75.
6 Barbara Engelbrecht, "Swinging at the Savoy," *Dance Research Journal*, 15, no. 2, (1983): 3–10.
7 Barbara Englebrecht, "The Savoy Ballroom Harlem, New York, 1930," *Harlem World Magazine*, retrieved October 27, 2023, https://www.harlemworldmagazine.com/the-savoy-ballroom-harlem-new-york-1930/.
8 Alexandre Abdoulaev, "Savoy: Reassessing the Role of the World's Finest Ballroom," in *Music and Culture, 1926–1958* (Boston, MA: Boston University, 2023), 84.
9 Karen Hubbard and Terry Monaghan, "Negotiating Compromise on a Burnished Wood Floor: Social Dancing at the Savoy," *Ballroom, Boogie, Shimmy Sham, Shake: A Social and Popular Dance Reader* (Champaign, IL: University of Illinois, 2009), 126–46.
10 *New York Amsterdam News* (1926), in Christi Jay Wells, "Counter-Bopaganda and Torn Riffs: Bebop as Popular Dance Music," *Between Beats: The Jazz Tradition and Black Vernacular Dance* (New York: Oxford University Press USA), 109–49.
11 Carl D. Wintz, "The Harlem Renaissance: What Was It and Why Does It Matter?" *Humanities Texas*, February 2015, retrieved from https://www.humanitiestexas.org/news/articles/harlem-renaissance-what-was-it-and-why-does-it-matter.
12 Englebrecht, "The Savoy Ballroom Harlem, New York, 1930."
13 Crease, "The Savoy Ballroom Remembered."
14 Clay Moon, "The Savoy Ballroom: Rejecting Black Exoticism through Community-Driven Design," *McGill*, June 10, 2021, retrieved from https://www.mcgill.ca/race-space/article/arch-355/savoy-ballroom-rejecting-black-exoticism-through-community-driven-design.
15 Terry Monaghan, "Savoy Ballroom," *Savoyballroom.com*, July 2011–February 2012, retrieved from Internet Archive Wayback Machine, http://www.savoyballroom.com/introduction/welcome.htm.
16 Jamin Jackson, "Why Was the Savoy Ballroom Important?" *Street Smart Swing*, August 26, 2018, retrieved from https://jaminjackson.com/the-savoy-ballroom/.
17 Abdoulaev, "Savoy."
18 Stearns and Stearns, *Jazz Dance*, 321.
19 Hubbard and Monaghan, "Negotiating Compromise on a Burnished Wood Floor."
20 Wells, "Counter-Bopaganda and Torn Riffs."
21 Hubbard and Monaghan, "Negotiating Compromise on a Burnished Wood Floor."

22 Wells, "Counter-Bopaganda and Torn Riffs."
23 Dehn, Papers on Afro-American Social Dance, Box 4, Folder 85.
24 Jackson, "Why Was the Savoy Ballroom Important?" Mills, "Savoy Gives Happy Feet a Chance to Dance."
25 Wendy Perron, "Dance in the Harlem Renaissance: Sowing Seeds," in *EmBODYing Liberation: The Black Body in American Dance*, ed. Dorothea Fischer-Hornung and Alison D. Goeller (Hamburg: LIT, Transaction Publishers, 2001), 19.
26 Moon, "The Savoy Ballroom."
27 Mills, "Savoy Gives Happy Feet a Chance to Dance."
28 Wickre, "Interview with Mura Dehn."
29 Crease, "The Savoy Ballroom Remembered."
30 Moon, "The Savoy Ballroom."
31 Stearns and Stearns, *Jazz Dance*, 322.
32 In Mills, "Savoy Gives Happy Feet a Chance to Dance."
33 Hubbard and Monaghan, "Negotiating on a Burnished Wood Floor," 129.
34 Ibid.
35 Ibid.
36 Abdoulaev, "Savoy," 51.
37 Dehn, Clippings MGZR; Stearns and Stearns, *Jazz Dance*, 317–20.
38 *Savoy Style*, "Whitey's Lindy Hoppers," *Savoy Style*, January 10, 2003, retrieved from http://www.savoystyle.com/wlh.html.
39 Dehn Papers, 1902–87, MGZMB-Res.+ 87-205, The Spirit Moves Manuscript, 13, Jerome Robbins Dance Division, New York Public Library for the Performing Arts.
40 Aniya Thompson, "Harlem Renaissance Project," *Prezi*, January 13, 2021, retrieved from https://prezi.com/p/5egoaemvyhkl/harlem-renaissance-project/#:~:text=Herbert%20Whitey%20White.
41 "Herbert 'Whitey' White," *The Kennedy Center*, retrieved February 2023, https://www.kennedy-center.org/education/resources-for-educators/classroom-resources/media-and-interactives/artists/white-herbert/.
42 Thompson, "Harlem Renaissance Project."
43 Harri Heinilä, "An Endeavor by Harlem Dancers to Achieve Equality: The Recognition of the Harlem-Based African American Jazz Dance Between 1921 and 1943" (Ed.D. diss., University of Helsinki, 2016), 135–8.
44 Terry Monaghan, "Remembering Shorty," *The Dancing Times*, July 2004, 49, 51. The article was republished at http://jassdancer.blogspot.fi/2012/10/shorty-george-snowden.html.
45 Ibid.
46 Harri Heinilä, "The Creators of the Lindy Hop," *authenticjazzdance*, retrieved February 2023, https://authenticjazzdance.wordpress.com/2012/07/04/the-creators-of-the-lindy-hop-george-shorty-snowden-and-mattie-purnell/.

47 Dehn Papers, 1902–87, 28.
48 Monaghan, "Remembering Shorty."
49 Terry Monaghan, "Alfred Leagins," *The Dancing Times*, January 2000, 349.
50 Hubbard and Monaghan, "Negotiating on a Burnished Wood Floor," 129.
51 Ibid.
52 Dehn Papers, 1902–87, 71.
53 Ghertler and Katz, *In a Jazz Way*.
54 Monaghan, "Alfred Leagins."
55 Dehn Papers, 1902–87, 72.
56 Robert Crease, "Profiles of Original Lindy Hoppers: Al Leagins," *The New York Swing Dance Society Footnotes* 1, no. 4 (1986).
57 Englebrecht, "The Savoy Ballroom Harlem, New York, 1930."
58 Moon, "The Savoy Ballroom."
59 Wells, "Counter-Bopaganda and Torn Riffs."
60 Englebrecht, "The Savoy Ballroom Harlem, New York, 1930."
61 Wickre, "Interview with Mura Dehn."
62 Mura Dehn, in Roger Pryor Dodge, "Writing and Biographical Information," (S) *MGZM-Res. Dod R, 3.
63 Pryor Dodge (friend of Mura), in personal communication with the author, February 2023.
64 "Roger Pryor Dodge," *Wikipedia*, retrieved May 24, 2024, https://en.wikipedia.org/wiki/roger_Pryor_Dodge.
65 Roger Dodge, "East St Louis 'Toodle-oo,'" *YouTube*, retrieved February 2023, https://www.youtube.com/watch?v=oVSm_dX8Jqs&t=46s.
66 Richard Warren, "Empathetic Embodiment: The Dance of Roger Pryor Dodge," retrieved May 2023, https://richardawarren.wordpress.com/2020/10/31/empathetic-embodiment-the-dance-of-roger-pryor-dodge/.
67 Roger P. Dodge, "Negro Jazz," *The Dancing Times*, October 1929.
68 Dodge (friend of Mura).
69 Dehn, Clippings, MGZR.
70 Ibid.
71 Morrison (friend of Mura).
72 Anthea Kraut, *Choreographing the Folk: The Dance Stagings of Zora Neale Hurston* (Minneapolis, MN: University of Minnesota Press, 2008).
73 Dehn Papers on Afro-American Social Dance, Box 20, Folder 217.
74 Zora Neale Hurston, *The Sanctified Church* (Berkeley, CA: Turtle Island, 1981).
75 Wickre, "Interview with Mura Dehn."
76 Kraut, *Choreographing the Folk*.
77 Mary F. Watkins, "The Dance," *Arts Weekly*, n.d., in Dehn, Clippings, MGZR, Jerome Robbins Dance Division, New York Public Library for the Performing Arts.

78 John Martin, Two Dance Concerts Full of Contrasts," *New York Times*, April 11, 1932, retrieved from https://timesmachine.nytimes.com/timesmachine/1932/04/11/100824642.pdf?pdf_redirect=true&ip=0.
79 Adolf Dehn, letter to editor, *Arts Weekly*, May 1932, in Dehn, Clippings, MGZR.
80 Ibid.
81 Kraut, "Re-Framing the Vernacular: The Dance Praxis of Zora Neale Hurston" (Ed.D. diss., Northwestern University, 2002), 355.
82 Dehn Papers on Afro-American Social Dance, Box 20, Folder 213.
83 Dehn, Clippings.
84 Dehn Papers on Afro-American Social dance, Box 23, Folder 296.
85 "New Dance Group Collection," *Library of Congress*, retrieved February 13, 2023, https://lccn.loc.gov/2013572146.
86 Ellen Graff, "Federal Dance Project (1936–1938)," *The Routledge Encyclopedia of Modernism,* September 5, 2016, https://www.rem.routledge.com/articles/federal-dance-project-1936-1938-1.
87 Elizabeth McPherson, *The New Dance Group: Transforming Individuals and Community,* September 1, 2016, https://dancetimepublications.com/dance-culture-editorial/the-new-dance-group-transforming-individuals-and-community/.
88 Wickre, "Interview with Mura Dehn."
89 Ibid.
90 *1st National Dance Congress and Festival Proceedings,* 793.04 N213, Jerome Robbins Dance Division, New York Public Library for the Performing Arts, 1936.
91 Ibid.
92 Ibid., 43–5.
93 Ibid., 47–51.
94 John Martin, "The Dance: A Convention," *New York Times,* May 17, 1936, retrieved from https://timesmachine.nytimes.com/timesmachine/1936/05/17/110048926.html?pageNumber=186.
95 John Martin, "Dance: A Congress," *New York Times,* May 27, 1936, https://timesmachine.nytimes.com/timesmachine/1936/05/31/88669393.html?pageNumber=156.
96 Wickre, "Interview with Mura Dehn."
97 Dehn Papers on Afro-American Social Dance, Box 23, Folder 299.
98 Kathleen Ann Lally, "A History of the Federal Dance Theatre of the Works Progress Administration, 1935–1939," (Ed.D. diss., Texas Woman's University, 1978), 43–5.
99 Wickre, "Interview with Mura Dehn."
100 Ibid.
101 Dehn Papers on Afro-American Social Dance, Box 23, Folder 296.

102 John Perpener III, "Asadata Dafora," *Jacob's Pillow Dance Interactive*, August 2017, retrieved from https://danceinteractive.jacobspillow.org/themes-essays/african-diaspora/asadata-dafora/.
103 Marcia Ethel Heard, "Asadata Dafora Biographical Essay," *Free to Dance Biographies*, retrieved February 17, 2024, https://www.thirteen.org/freetodance/biographies/dafora.html.
104 Asadata Dafora Papers, 1933–63, Sc MG 48, Schomburg Center for Research in Black Culture, New York Public Library.
105 Robin Kelley, *Africa Speaks, America Answers: Modern Jazz In Revolutionary Times* (Cambridge, MA: Harvard University Press, 2012), 13.
106 Perpener, "Asadata Dafora."
107 John Martin, "Native Cast Gives an African Opera: Kyunkor Produced in an East Side Playhouse Appraised as Exciting Theater Art," *New York Times*, May 9, 1934.
108 John Perpener, III, "Asadata Dafora, August 2017, https://danceinteractive.jacobspillow.org/themes-essays/african-diaspora/asadata-dafora/.
109 Perpener, "Asadata Dafora."
110 Wickre, "Interview with Mura Dehn."
111 Dehn, Clippings, MGZR.
112 Dehn, Papers on Afro-American Social Dance, Box 6, Folder 215.
113 Rennie Harris, "Workshop on Hip Hop," *DanceNJ Festival*, Rutgers University, February 3, 2024.
114 Dehn, Scrapbooks.
115 Dehn, Papers on Afro-American Social Dance, Box 4, Folder 77.
116 Dehn, Clippings, MGZR.
117 Dehn, Papers on Afro-American Social Dance, Box 23, Folder 299.
118 John Martin, "Dances in Jazz Form Given by Mura Dehn," *New York Times*, March 16, 1934, retrieved from https://timesmachine.nytimes.com/timesmachine/1945/03/16/84628698.html?pageNumber=20.
119 Dehn, Scrapbooks.
120 Dehn, Clippings.
121 Dehn, Papers on Afro-American Social Dance, Box 20, Folders 213–15.
122 Dehn, "A Few Words about Jazz Dancing," 22–3, 39.
123 Mura Dehn Collection, 1905–85, Jerome Robbins Division, (S) *MGZMD 483, 3.6.

Chapter 4

1 Dehn Papers on Afro-American Social Dance, Box 20, Folder 216.
2 Mura Dehn, Programs, MGZB, Jerome Robbins Dance Division, New York Public Library for the Performing Arts.

3. Dehn Papers, 1902–87, 23.
4. Ibid.
5. Ibid., 228.
6. Ibid., 92–102.
7. Ibid., 93.
8. Ibid., 84, 96.
9. Dehn Papers on Afro-American Social Dance, Box 20, Folder 216.
10. "Willa Mae Ricker," *Frankie Manning Foundation*, retrieved March 10, 2023, https://www.frankiemanningfoundation.org/willa-mae-ricker.
11. Terry Monaghan, "The Third Generation," *authenticjazzdance*, retrieved March 10, 2023, https://authenticjazzdance.wordpress.com/2017/03/11/the-third-generation-by-terry-monaghan/.
12. Robert White, "The 1948 Harvest Moon Ball," *Swungover*, retrieved March 10, 2023, https://swungover.wordpress.com/2022/03/16/the-1948-harvest-moon-ball/.
13. Rennie McDougall, "In Harlem, They're Still Dancing the Original Swing," *The Village Voice*, September 6, 2017, retrieved from https://www.villagevoice.com/in-harlem-theyre-still-dancing-the-original-swing/.
14. "History," *Swing on in Dance School Gold Coast*, retrieved March 10, 2023, https://swingonin.com.au/history/.
15. Harri Heinilä, "An Endeavor by Harlem Dancers to Achieve Equality: the Recognition of the Harlem-based African American Jazz Dance between 1921 and 1943 (Ed.D. diss., University of Helsinki, 2016).
16. "Frankie Manning in Melbourne 1939," *Swing Patrol London*, June 6, 2006, retrieved March 10, 2023, https://www.swingpatrol.co.uk/frankie-manning-melbourne-1939/.
17. Judy Prichett, "Billy Ricker," *Savoy Style*, retrieved March 10, 2023, http://savoystyle.com/billy-ricker.html.
18. Harri Heinilä, "An Endeavor by Harlem Dancers to Achieve Equality."
19. Felipe—EstiloSwing, "Air Mail Special (1941)," *ESTILOSwing*, retrieved December 11, 2023, https://estiloswing.es/air-mail-special-1941/.
20. Mura Dehn Traditional Jazz Dance Company, Programs, MGZR, Jerome Robbins Dance Division, New York Public Library for the Performing Arts.
21. Robert Crease, "Profiles of Original Lindy Hoppers: Sandra Gibson," *The New York Swing Dance Society: Footnotes* 2, no. 2 (1987).
22. Robert White, "Mildred "Boogie" Pollard and Sandra Gibson ISDFNKA #1," *Swungover*, retrieved March 10, 2023, https://swungover.wordpress.com/2011/02/01/mildred-boogie-pollard-and-sandra-gibson-isdfnka-1/.
23. Terry Monaghan, "Al Minns: The Incorrigible Lindy Hopper, 1920–1985," *authenticjazzdance*, January 1, 2020, https://authenticjazzdance.wordpress

.com/2020/01/01/al-minns-the-incorrigible-lindy-hopper-1920-1985-by-terry-monaghan/.
24. White, "Mildred "Boogie" Pollard and Sandra Gibson ISDFNKA #1,".
25. Ibid.
26. Monaghan, "Al Minns."
27. Crease, "Profiles of Original Lindy Hoppers: Sandra Gibson."
28. Tamara Stevens and Erin Stevens, *Swing Dancing* (New York: Bloomsbury Publishing, 2011).
29. Denise Harris, "The Pivotal Role of Al Minns in Modern Day Lindy Hop," *YouTube*, retrieved March 10, 2023, https://www.youtube.com/watch?v=jbuWlXZnBTY&t=10s.
30. James Stevenson, "Laying Down Some Leather," *The New Yorker*, February 15, 1969.
31. Crease, "Al Minns."
32. Stevenson, "Laying Down Some Leather."
33. Monaghan, "Al Minns."
34. Crease, "Al Minns."
35. "'The Jazz Dancers'—Al Minns & Leon James," *Syncopated City*, retrieved March 10, 2023, https://syncopatedcity.com/the-jazz-dancers-a-brief-survey-of-the-lives-of-al-minns-leon-james/.
36. Crease, "Al Minns.
37. Monaghan, "Al Minns.
38. Stevenson, "Laying Down Some Leather."
39. "Who Is Leon James? The Star of the Whitey's Lindy Hoppers," *Millelire*, retrieved March 10, 2023, https://www.stilemillelire.com/leon-james-lindy-hop/.
40. Stearns and Stearns, *Jazz Dance*, 317–20.
41. Stevenson, "Laying Down Some Leather."
42. Stearns and Stearns, *Jazz Dance*, 325.
43. Ibid.
44. Monaghan, "Al Minns."
45. John Wilson, "Lecture on Dance Steals Jazz Fete," *New York Times*, July 6, 1958, 50.
46. Ibid.
47. *New York Times*, November 14, 1960.
48. John S. Wilson, "Jazz Dancing Gets New Support," *New York Times*, May 22, 1962, 30.
49. Heinilä, "An Endeavor by Harlem Dancers to Achieve Equality."
50. John S. Wilson, "Two Jazz Dancers Recreate the Past," *New York Times*, January 20, 1969, 30.
51. Crease, "Al Minns."
52. "Al Minns Dancing in New York," *YouTube*, retrieved March 10, 2023, https://www.youtube.com/watch?v=dvegobsHOVE.
53. Crease, "Al Minns.

54 Ibid.
55 Ibid.
56 Monaghan, "Al Minns."
57 Jennifer Dunning, "Pepsi Bethel, 83, a Champion of American Popular Dance," *New York Times*, September 6, 2002, Section A, 21.
58 Mark Deitch, "Pepsi Bethel—Master of Jazz Dance," *New York Times*, August 6, 1978, Section D, 12.
59 Terry Monaghan, "Obituary, Pepsi Bethel," *The Guardian*, September 27, 2002, retrieved March 9, 2024, https://www.theguardian.com/news/2002/sep/28/guardianobituaries.arts.
60 Deitch, "Pepsi Bethel."
61 Monaghan, "Obituary, Pepsi Bethel."
62 Stearns and Stearns, *Jazz Dance*, 326.
63 Pepsi Bethel, *Authentic Jazz Dance: A Retrospective* (New York: American Authentic Jazz Dance Theatre, 1990), 11–12.
64 Karen Hubbard, "The Authentic Jazz Dance Legacy of Pepsi Bethel," in *Jazz Dance: A History of Roots and Branches*, ed. Lindsay Guarino and Wendy Oliver (Gainesville, FL: University of Florida Press, 2014); Pepsi Bethel, *Authentic Jazz Dance*, 22, 26, 48.
65 Deitch, "Pepsi Bethel."
66 Hubbard, "The Authentic Jazz Dance Legacy of Pepsi Bethel," 79.
67 Deitch, "Pepsi Bethel."
68 Hubbard, "The Authentic Jazz Dance Legacy of Pepsi Bethel."
69 Dehn Papers, 1902–87, 217–21.
70 Monaghan, "Obituary, Pepsi Bethel."
71 Ibid.
72 Dunning, "Pepsi Bethel, 83, a Champion of American Popular Dance."
73 Monaghan, "Obituary, Pepsi Bethel."
74 Dunning, "Pepsi Bethel, 83, a Champion of American Popular Dance."
75 Lillian Morrison, "Materials Concerning Mura Dehn," MGZM-RES Dehn M, Jerome Robbins Dance Division, New York Public Library for the Performing Arts.
76 Joanne Kealiinohomoku, "Ethical Considerations for Choreographers, Ethnologists and White Knights," *Journal of the Association of Graduate Dance Ethnologists* 5 (1981): 10–23.

Chapter 5

1 Dehn Papers on Afro-American Social Dance, Box 21, Folder 255.
2 Ibid., Box 20, Folder 228.

3 Ibid.
4 Pamela Randall, "Exploring Black Social Dance from the Viewpoint of Mura Dehn: Psychological, Sociological, and Spiritual Purposes, Functions, and Meanings"(thesis, University of California, Los Angeles, 1999), 14.
5 Dehn Papers on Afro-American Social Dance, Box 2, Folder 29.
6 Ibid.
7 Henry Louis Gates, *This Is Our Story, This Is Our Song* (London: Penguin Press, 2021).
8 Dehn Papers on Afro-American Social Dance, Box 5, Folder 120.
9 Mura Dehn, Notebooks, MGZMD 72, Jerome Robbins Dance Division, New York Public Library for the Performing Arts.
10 Dehn Papers on Afro-American Social Dance, Folder 121.
11 Ibid., Folder 123.
12 Dehn Papers, 1902–87, 11.
13 Mura Dehn, "Les Noirs et la Danse Par Mura Dehn," *Le Jazz Hot* 59 (October 1959), retrieved from https://www.jazzhot.net/PBSCProduct.asp?ItmID=3659662.
14 Dehn Papers, 1902–87, 16.
15 Michael Ventura, "Hear That Long Snake Moan," in *Shadow Dancing in the U.S.A.* (Los Angeles, CA: Jeremy Torcher, 1985), 103–62; Brenda Dixon Gottschild, *Black Dancing Body: A Geography from Coon to Cool* (New York: Palgrave Macmillan, 2003); Carl Paris, "Reading the Spirit and the Dancing Body in the Choreography of Ronald K. Brown and Reggie Wilson," in Thomas DeFrantz and Anita Gonzalez, eds., *Black Performance Theory* (Durham, NC: Duke University Press, 2014).
16 Mura Dehn, "Introduction au 'Gospel Singing' par Mura Dehn," *Le Jazz Hot* 70 (October 1952); Mura Dehn, "Georgia Peach: 'Spiritual+émotion=Gospel,' interview par Mura Dehn," *Le Jazz Hot* 173 (February 1962).
17 Dehn Papers, 1902–87, 254.
18 Dehn Papers on Afro-American Social Dance, Box 5, Folder 120.
19 Brenda Dixon Gottschild, "Stripping the Emperor," in D. Gere, ed., *Looking Out: Perspectives On Dance and Criticism in a Multicultural World* (New York: Schirmer Books), 95–122.
20 Katrina Hazzard-Gordon, *Jookin' The Rise of Social Dance Formations in the African American Culture* (Philadelphia, PA: Temple University Press, 1990).
21 Dehn Papers, 1902–87, 13.
22 Hazzard-Gordon, *Jookin'*, 5.
23 Dehn Papers, 1902–87, 13.
24 Ibid., 14.
25 Dehn Papers on Afro-American Social Dance, Box 5, Folder 120.
26 Ibid.
27 Dehn Papers, 1902–87, 44.

28 Mary Jane Aldrich Moodie, "Savoy Ballroom Style: Harlem Entertainment and Creative Black Resistance," Jerome Robbins Dance Division, New York Public Library for the Performing Arts, MGW 92-2685 (Independent Study, Barnard College, New York, 1990).

29 Dehn Papers on Afro-American Social Dance, Box 5, Folder 120.

30 Ibid.

31 Ann Douglas, *Terrible Honesty: Mongrel Manhattan in the 1920"* (New York: Farrar, Straus and Giroux,) 18.

32 Dehn Papers, 1902–87, 9.

33 Ibid., 17.

34 Langston Hughes and Zora Neale, ed. Henry Louis Gates Jr. and George Houston Bass, *Mule Bone: A Comedy of Negro Life* (New York: Harper Perennial Modern Classics, 1991), 6–7.

35 Dehn Papers on Afro-American Social Dance, Box 1, Folders 7–8.

36 Dehn Papers, 1902–87, 9.

37 Ibid., 45.

38 Ibid., 23.

39 Bob Boross, "The Legacy of Jazz Dance Historian Mura Dehn, with Kim Chandler Vaccaro of Rider University," *YouTube*, retrieved July 31, 2020, https://www.youtube.com/watch?v=u4tMjnv8bao.

40 Christi J. Wells, "And I Make My Own: Class Performance, Black Urban Identity, and Depression-era Harlem's Physical Culture," in Anthony Shay and Barbara Sellers-Young, eds., *The Oxford Handbook of Dance and Ethnicity* (Oxford, UK: Oxford University Press, 2016), 17.

41 Dehn Papers on Afro-American Social Dance, Box 23, Folder 299.

42 Robert White, "The 1950 Harvest Moon Ball," *Swungover*, retrieved from https://swungover.wordpress.com/?s=Theresa+Mason.

43 Dehn Papers on Afro-American Social Dance, MGZR Clippings, Box 23, Folder 297.

44 Dehn Papers on Afro-American Social Dance, Box 20, Folder 235.

45 Herbert Matter, "Biography," *artnet*, retrieved January 20, 2024, https://www.artnet.com/artists/herbert-matter/biography.

46 Dehn Papers on Afro-American Social Dance, Box 20, Folder 214.

47 Ibid., Box 2, Folder 27.

48 Ibid.

49 Dehn Papers on Afro-American Social Dance, Clippings, Box 23, Folder 297.

50 Charles Delaunay, "Introduction" to "Les Noirs et la Danse par Mura Dehn," *Le Jazz Hot* 59 (1952).

51 Mura Dehn, "Jazz Musique/Jazz Danse par Mura Dehn," *Le Jazz Hot* 60 (1952).

52 Dehn Papers on Afro-American Social Dance, Box 2, Folder 27.

53 Ibid., Box 1, Folder 15.
54 "James Berry," *IMDb*, retrieved March 12, 2024, https://www.imdb.com/name/nm0077569/.
55 Library of Congress Performing Arts Databases, Berry Brothers biography, retrieved March 12, 2024, https://web.archive.org/web/20230218065855/https://memory.loc.gov/diglib/ihas/loc.music.tdabio.23/default.html.
56 For a list of films, see "James Berry (Entertainer)," *Wikipedia*, retrieved March 12, 2024, https://en.wikipedia.org/wiki/James_Berry_(entertainer).
57 Library of Congress Performing Arts Databases, Berry Brothers biography.
58 Ibid.
59 Dehn Papers on Afro-American Social Dance, Scrapbooks.
60 The Berry Brothers, "Savoy Hop," *YouTube*, retrieved March 12, 2024, https://www.youtube.com/watch?v=bghET2QjVxA.
61 "James Berry (Entertainer).
62 Dehn Papers, 1902–87, 91.
63 Dehn Papers on Afro-American Social Dance, Box 21, Folder 247.
64 Ibid., Box 23, Folder 297.
65 Dehn Papers, 1902–87, 123.
66 Dehn on Afro-American Social Dance, Clippings, Box 23, Folder 297.
67 Bethel, *Authentic Jazz Dance*, 48–9.
68 Dehn Papers, 1902–1987, 128.
69 Mura Dehn and Leo Hurwitz, dir., *Dancing James Berry* [Film] (1958), retrieved August 14, 2024, https://www.eastman.org/dancing-james-berry-us-1958.
70 "Why Leo?," *Leo Hurwitz*, retrieved March 14, 2024, https://leohurwitz.com/why/.
71 Dehn and Hurwitz, *Dancing James Berry*.
72 Dehn Papers on Afro-American Social Dance, Box 23, Folder 300.
73 Ibid., Box 21, Folder 251.
74 Mura Dehn, "Be for Real: Interview with James Berry," *Dance Magazine* (1961), 32; Mura Dehn, "Jazz Profound," *Dance Scope* (1977), 18–27.
75 Stella Snead (friend of Mura Dehn), in personal communication with author, March 1995.
76 Dehn Papers, 1902–1987, 111.
77 Ibid., 106–9.
78 "Academy of Swing," MGZ, Jerome Robbins Dance Division, New York Public Library for the Performing Arts.
79 Dehn Papers, 1902–87. In this case, as is many others, the pages are marked with two numbers, "9" is typed at top middle, "117" at top right.
80 Ibid., 117–24.
81 Mura Dehn, "The ABC's of Jazz Dance," *Dance Notation Record* 8, no. 2 (1957): 3–5.

Chapter 6

1. Sally Sommer, "The Spirit Moves: A History of Black Social Dance on Film," *Village Voice,* December 2, 1986.
2. Dehn, Scrapbooks.
3. Ibid.
4. Dehn, "The ABC's of Jazz Dance"; Mura Dehn, "Negro Dance and Puritanism," *Jazz Monthly* 2 (1956); Dehn, "Jazz Dance," 14–18; Mura Dehn, "Georgia Peach: 'Spiritual+émotion=Gospel' Interview par Mura Dehn," *Le Jazz Hot* 173 (1962); Mura Dehn, "New Spirit in an Ancient Dance: World's Fair Indonesian Dancers Are Eager to Learn, Eager to Share," *Dance Magazine* 35, no. 9 (1964), 16, 18–19, 68–9.
5. Dehn Traditional Jazz Dance Company, Programs, MGZB, Jerome Robbins Dance Division, New York Public Library for the Performing Arts.
6. National Notation Bureau, "Exploration of Jazz Dance Forum: What Is Jazz Dance?" *Dance Notation Bureau*, retrieved December 5, 2023, http://dancenotation.org/news/Library_News/library_v10_n3.pdf.
7. "Authentic Jazz Dance," *Down Beat Magazine* (1964), 193; "Dance Workshops," *The Village Voice*, January 14, 1965.
8. Dehn Papers on Afro-American Social Dance, Box 20, Folder 237.
9. Ibid.
10. Ibid., Box 21, folder 254.
11. The full list is available at https://www.nypl.org/research/research-catalog/search?q=Mura%20Dehn&filters[materialType][0]=resourcetypes%3Amov.
12. Sylvia Sykes (Founder, International Lindy Hop Championships) in personal communication with the author, March 2024.
13. Morrison (friend of Mura Dehn).
14. Carol Teten (founder of Dancetime Publications), in personal communication with the author, December 2023.
15. Karen Backstein, "Dancing Images: Choreography, Cinema and Culture," (Ed.D. diss., Department of Cinema Studies, New York University, 1996), 154–6; Susie Trenka, Jumping the Color Line: Vernacular Dance In American Film 1929–1945 (Eastleigh, UK: John Libbey Publishing, 2021).
16. Mura Dehn, "More Respect for the Clown," *Dance Magazine* (February 1946), 21.
17. Mark Scherzer (Mura Dehn's lawyer), in personal communication with the author, September 2023.
18. Dehn, "More Respect for the Clown".
19. Dehn Papers, 1902–87, 86–7.

20 See Dehn's discussion with Reverend Guilbert in "Journey through the South" in Chapter 5.
21 Dehn, Clippings, MGZR.
22 White, "The 1951 Harvest Moon Ball."
23 Backstein, "Dancing Images," 173–5.
24 Claudia La Rocco, "Entertainment Review," *New York Times*, March 2, 2010, 3.
25 Terry Monaghan, "The Legacy of Jazz Dance," *Annual Review of Jazz Studies* (Newark, NJ: Institute of Jazz Studies, Rutgers University, 1997/8), 301.
26 Giltrecia Head, "Unmasking the Blues: Gẹlẹdẹ and the Creation of Blues Alchemy" (thesis, Florida State University College of the Arts 2021), 19.
27 Dorkins (friend of Mura Dehn).
28 Sommer, "The Spirit Moves."
29 Dorkins (friend of Mura Dehn).
30 Dorkins and Pepsi Bethel, in personal communications with the author, 1995.
31 Robert White (*Swungover* creator), in email correspondence with author, March 2024.
32 Ibid.
33 Alexandre McCormack, "Harlem Dancers Do a Routine," *Instagram*, retrieved February 2024, https://www.instagram.com/reel/C0QtVCZo9Ze/.
34 Dehn Papers, 1902–87, 51.
35 Robert White, "Willa Mae Ricker, the Patron Saint of Respect for Lindy Hoppers ISDFNOKA #3," *Swungover*, retrieved February 2024, https://swungover.wordpress.com/?s=Willa+Mae+ricker.
36 Ibid.
37 Riki Panganiban, https://rikomatic.com/2018/07/seven-things-you-should-know-about-hellzapoppin.html. Retrieved August 28, 2025.
38 White, "Willa Mae Ricker, the Patron Saint of Respect for Lindy Hoppers ISDFNOKA #3."
39 "Willa Mae Ricker," *Frankie Manning Foundation*, retrieved March 2024, https://www.frankiemanningfoundation.org/willa-mae-ricker.
40 *Frankie Manning Foundation*, retrieved March 2024, https://www.frankiemanningfoundation.org.
41 Ibid.
42 Robert White, "The 1952 Harvest Moon Ball," *Swungover*, March 6, 2023, https://swungover.wordpress.com/2023/04/06/the-1952-harvest-moon-ball/.
43 Robert White, "The 1953 Harvest Moon Ball," *Swungover*, August 8, 2023, https://swungover.wordpress.com/2023/08/08/the-1953-harvest-moon-ball/.
44 "Sugar Sullivan," *Beantown*, retrieved May 30, 2024, https://www.beantowncamp.com/team/special-guests/sugar-sullivan.

45. Harri Heinilä, "Sugar Sullivan—the Savoy Lindy Hopper and Jazz Dancer," *authenticjazzdance*, April 22, 2020, https://authenticjazzdance.wordpress.com/2020/04/22/sugar-sullivan-the-savoy-lindy-hopper-and-jazz-dancer.
46. Marie Ndiaye, "ISDC 2023—Sugar Sullivan & Denise Minns Harris," *YouTube*, https://www.youtube.com/watch?v=ftftdc4uWA4.
47. Robert White, "The 1956–1959 Harvest Moon Balls," *Swungover*, retrieved March 20, 2024, https://swungover.wordpress.com/?s=Sugar+Sullivan.
48. "Sugar Sullivan," *Swingin' at the Savoy*, retrieved March 1, 2024, https://swinginatthesavoy.com/staff/sugar-sullivan/.
49. Ndiaye, "Sugar Sullivan & Denise Minns Harris."
50. "Sugar Sullivan," *Swing Sistah Productions*, retrieved March 2024, https://www.swingsistah.com/index.php?id=27.
51. Peter Loggins, "So You Wanna Dance Fast?" February, 2010, https://jassdancer.blogspot.com, retrieved March 2024. To access this blog use the URL in this endnote then search for Sugar in the search bar.
52. LaTasha Brown, "Barbara Billups and Sugar Sullivan Interview, HDC 2019," *YouTube*, retrieved February 2024, https://www.youtube.com/watch?v=wLraVWqEvy8.
53. John Wilson, "Scoby Stohman Drummer-Dancer," *New York Times*, April 7, 1996, 28.
54. "An Evening of Jazz and Dance," *The Carolina Times*, June 20, 1981, 3, retrieved from https://newspapers.digitalnc.org/lccn/sn83045120/1981-06-20/ed-1/seq-19/.
55. Clarence Strohman, "Social Dancing: At the Cotton Club and the Savoy," MGZIC 9-2942, Jerome Robbins Dance Division, New York Public Library for the Performing Arts.
56. "Dance and Immigration," Jerome Robbins Dance Division, New York Public Library Digital Collections, retrieved May 30, 2024, https://digitalcollections.nypl.org/items/dad0b85c-d568-47dd-9fdc-8d5fc40eefa1.
57. "Pedro Aguilar," *Wikipedia*, retrieved March 2024, https://en.wikipedia.org/wiki/Pedro_Aguilar.
58. Joe Holley, "Dancer, Known as 'Cuban Pete,' Was Considered 'Maestro of the Mambo,'" *Washington Post*, Friday, January 23, 2009.
59. Gene Roman, "Latin Music Museum Honors Cuban Pete in NYC," *Puerto Rico Herald*, June 23, 2002, retrieved May 28, 2024, https://puertoricoherald.com/issues/2002/vol6n27/LatMuseumCubanPt-en.html.
60. Cuban Pete, retrieved March 2024, https://en.wikipedia.org/wiki/Pedro_Aguilar.
61. Jimmy Delgado, "Millie Donay Passed Away," *SalsaForums*, July 17, 2005, retrieved March 2024, https://www.salsaforums.com/threads/millie-donay-passed-away.4738.

62 Alan Feuerstein, "Mambo Legends Cuban Pete and Millie: Architects of Excitement," *History of Mambo*, retrieved May 28, 2024, http://www.justsalsa.com/culture/mambo/history/articles/alanfeuerstein/mambolegendscubanpeteandmille/.

63 Robert White, "Mama Lu," *Swungover*, December 12, 2023, retrieved from https://swungover.wordpress.com/2023/12/21/mama-lu/.

64 Judy Pritchett, "The Call of the Jitterbug," *Archives of Early Lindy Hop*, 1988, retrieved August 11, 2011, http://www.savoystyle.com/call_of_jitterbug.html.

65 Harri Heinilä, "A Great Weekend in Harlem," *authenticjazzdance*, May 19, 2013, retrieved from https://authenticjazzdance.wordpress.com/2013/05/19/a-great-weekend-in-harlem/.

66 Mike McDermott, "LIVE Interview with Lindy Hop Legend Debra Youngblood," *YouTube*, April 22, 2021, retrieved from https://www.youtube.com/watch?v=MU85-7KKCwo.

67 White, "The 1951 Harvest Moon Ball."

68 Heinilä, "A Great Weekend in Harlem."

69 "Willie Ray—James Brown Tribute," The Plate Bar & Grill, *Facebook*, retrieved March 14, 2024, https://www.facebook.com/events/the-plate-bar-grill/willie-ray-james-brown-tribute/298181430646905/.

70 "Behind the Scenes," *Ballroom Dancemagazine* 1, no 10 (November 1960).

71 "James Brown," *Bubby Gram*, retrieved March 14, 2024, http://www.bubbygram.com/jamesbrownwrlv.htm.

72 "March 3, 2010—Las Vegas, Nevada, USA—ILLIE RAY performs as James Brown during the 10th Annual Celebrity Impersonators Convention at the Stratosphere Hotel and Casino," *alamy*, retrieved from https://www.alamy.com/stock-photo-march-3-2010-las-vegas-nevada-usa-willie-ray-performs-as-james-brown-42402930.html.

73 Photo of Willie Ray, Swing Dance Vegas, *Facebook*, retrieved March 14, 2024, https://www.facebook.com/SwingDanceVegas/photos/a.1848920725161336/1884789868241088/?type=3.

74 "Hip Hop Culture and Voice," *The Kennedy Center*, retrieved January 2024, https://www.kennedy-center.org/education/resources-for-educators/classroom-resources/media-and-interactives/media/hip-hop/hip-hop-a-culture-of-vision-and-voice; Thomas DeFrantz, "Hip Hop Habitus v2.0," in *Black Performance Theory* (Durham, NC: Duke University Press, 2014), 225.

75 Julie Fraad (director of The Force), in personal communication with the author, March 2024.

76 "Breaking Away!" *The Learning Annex Newsletter*, July 1985, 89.

77 Sally Banes, *Writing in the Age of Postmodernism* (Middletown, CT: Wesleyan University Press, 1983), 131.

78 Harry Chalfont and Tony Silver, dir., *Style Wars* [Film] (New York: Public Art Films, 1983).
79 Richard Lee Sisco, dir., *Beat Street* [Film] (Los Angeles, CA: Orion Pictures, 1984).
80 Julie Fraad, "Fresh Faust: A Rap Opera in Progress," *New York Magazine* 20, no. 16 (1987), 105.
81 Julie Fraad, "Dancing Hands 1988," MGZIC 9-2106, Jerome Robbins Dance Division, New York Public Library for the Performing Arts.
82 Fraad (director of The Force).
83 "MrWigglesHipHop," *WIGZEE.BIZ*, retrieved March 21, 2024, http://www.wigzee.biz/bio.
84 Mr. Wiggles, "What Does a Legendary Hiphop Dance OG Wanna Say to YOU?" *YouTube*, retrieved January 2024, https://www.youtube.com/watch?v=3F-rixHNdPA.
85 Ibid.
86 Kory Grow, "Road to Recovery: A Hip-hop Pioneer Was Left for Dead," *Rolling Stone*, December 22, 2023.
87 "Inside the Mind of Hip Hop Legend Mr. Wiggles—the Future of Dancers, Technology, and Social Media," *YouTube*, retrieved March 28, 24, https://www.youtube.com/watch?v=3F-rixHNdPA.
88 Ibid.
89 Ibid.
90 PopMaster Fabel, "Physical Graffiti: The History of Hip Hop Dance," *Davey D's Hip Hop Corner*, retrieved March 12, 2024, http://www.daveyd.com/historyphysicalgrafittifabel.html?fbclid=IwAr1JUipwV0ObTMQWGnAqpLBqutE9olZLMYnLg1n93yfgvcYeifAsjBiIjE_aem.
91 Grow, "Road to Recovery."
92 "Jorge Pabon," *NYU TISCH*, retrieved March 12, 2024, https://tisch.nyu.edu/about/directory/drama/101283448.
93 "Breaking in the Olympics 2024—ABC News (unedited) interview with Jorge 'POPMASTER FABEL' Pabon," *YouTube*, retrieved September 28, 2024, https://www.youtube.com/watch?v=do-hFzDoWJA.
94 "The Original Magnificent Force," *YouTube*, retrieved March 12, 2024, https://www.youtube.com/watch?v=DHsrWu8An-Q.
95 "Rennie Harris," *RHPM*, retrieved March 1, 2024, https://www.rhpm.org/founder/.
96 Jeff Chang, "Profile 7: Dancing on the Through-line: Rennie Harris and the Past and Future of Hip-hop Dance," *Digital Commons @ Columbia College Chicago*, retrieved from http://digitalcommons.colum.edu/cap_vistas/7.
97 Rennie Harris, Guest Artist, *DanceNJ Annual Festival*, February 3, 2024, Rutgers University, New Brunswick, NJ.
98 Chang, "Profile 7."

99 Dehn, Clippings, MGZR.
100 "Importance to the Field," *Rennie Harris University*, retrieved March 1, 2024, https://www.rennieharrisuniversity.org/importance-to-the-field.
101 Dehn, Notebooks.
102 "Importance to the Field."
103 Ibid.
104 "Rennie Harris," *AILEY*, retrieved March 2, 2024, https://www.alvinailey.org/rennie-harris.
105 Chang, "Profile 7.
106 Mark Hikara, "Mura Dehn and Spirit Moves," *Swing It Seattle*, December 2021, https://www.swingitseattle.com/blog/mura-dehn-and-spirit-moves.

Chapter 7

1 Mura Dehn, Vitae, MGZMD-72, Box 20, Folders 213–15, Jerome Robbins Dance Division, New York Public Library for the Performing Arts.
2 Afro-American Folklore," *The Village Voice*, February 23, 1967.
3 Mura Dehn, Contracts, MGZMD-72, Box 23, Folder 300, Jerome Robbins Dance Division, New York Public Library for the Performing Arts.
4 Allen Blitz (Dehn's Company Manager), in personal communication with author, March 15, 2022.
5 Blitz, in personal communication with author, May 19, 2023.
6 Dehn, Clippings.
7 Blitz.
8 Dehn, Contracts, Folder 245.
9 Dehn, Clippings.
10 Dehn, Scrapbooks.
11 Dehn Papers, MGZMD-72, Box 17, Folder 158.
12 Charles Reinhart Management, Inc., "Summary," Duke University Archives and Manuscripts, North Carolina, USA.
13 United States Bureau of Educational and Cultural Affairs, Jazz Dance Theatre, MC 468 21, Box 67, Folder 15, 25, Special Collections, University of Arkansas, USA, Cultural Presentations Program, 1935–80.
14 Danielle Fosler-Lussier, *Music in America's Cold War Diplomacy* (Berkeley, CA: University of California Press, 2015), 4, 41.
15 United States Bureau of Educational and Cultural Affairs, Folders 15, 25.
16 Ibid., 23.
17 Ibid., Folders 15, 21, 126.
18 Fosler-Lussier, *Music in America's Cold War Diplomacy*, 41.

19 Ibid., 10.
20 United States Bureau of Educational and Cultural Affairs, Folder 14, 1-23.
21 Pepsi Bethel, in personal communication with author, March 1996.
22 Brian and Joy Pape, "Characters of The Village: Chenault Spence, a Southern Accent in The Village," *Village View*, August 4, 2023, https://villageview.nyc/2023/08/04/chenault-spence-a-southern-accent-in-the-village.
23 Chenault Spence (lighting designer), in personal communication with author, January 4, 2024.
24 Ibid.
25 United States Bureau of Educational and Cultural Affairs, Folder 14, 102.
26 Ibid., 104.
27 Ibid., 12, 7–8.
28 "Dick Vance," *AllMusic*, retrieved April 5, 2024, https://www.allmusic.com/artist/dick-vance-mn0000359702#biography.
29 Dehn, Programs, MGZB, Jerome Robbins Dance Division, New York Public Library for the Performing Arts.
30 "Dick Vance," *Wikipedia*, retrieved April 5, 2024, https://en.wikipedia.org/wiki/Dick_Vance.
31 "Eddie Barefield," *Wikipedia*, retrieved April 5, 2024, https://en.wikipedia.org/wiki/Eddie_Barefield.
32 *The Baltimore Afro American*, Eddie Barefield, October 20, 1942, p. 10.
33 Eddie Barefield, *Discography of American Historical Recordings*, retrieved April 5. https://adp.library.ucsb.edu/index.php/mastertalent/detail/108186/Barefield_Eddie.
34 Ibid.
35 Eugene Chadbourne, "Joe Marshall," *AllMusic*, https://www.allmusic.com/artist/joseph-marshall-mn0001757823.
36 "Joe Marshall," *Wikipedia*, retrieved March 18, 2024, https://en.wikipedia.org/wiki/Joe_Marshall_(musician).
37 Dehn, Programs.
38 "Milton Sealey," *jazzleadsheets.com*, retrieved March 13, 2024, https://jazzleadsheets.com/composers/milton-sealey.html.
39 "About," *Vera's Lament: A Jazz Opera by Jeri Brown*, retrieved March 13, 2024, https://someonewhollwatchoverme.wordpress.com/about.
40 "Andrew Bernard 'Bernie' Upson, 11/30/1937–07/17/2014," *TCPALM*, retrieved February 20, 2024, https://www.legacy.com/us/obituaries/tcpalm/name/andrew-upson-obituary?id=22886397.
41 Bernie Upson, *Facebook*, retrieved February 20, 2024, https://www.facebook.com/BernieUpson.

42 Meeker, David, Author. *Jazz on the Screen: A Jazz and Blues Filmography*. Washington, D.C.: Library of Congress, 2019, 131. Pdf. https://www.loc.gov/item/2023871300/.

43 Bernie Upson, "Bernie Upson, Beloved Ithaca Jazz Musician, Dies; Tribute Scheduled," *The Ithaca Voice*, retrieved February 20, 2024, https://ithacavoice.org/2014/07/beloved-jazz-musician-dies-thursday/.

44 Brenda Bufalino, dir., *Great Feats of Feet* [Film] (New York: NY: Alexander Street, 1977).

45 "New Show at Plantation Club," *New York Times*, November 6, 1938.

46 "Avon Long," *Broadway World*, retrieved January 15, 2024, https://www.broadwayworld.com/people/Avon-Long.

47 "Avon Long," *Wikipedia*, retrieved January 15, 2024, https://en.wikipedia.org/wiki/Avon_Long.

48 Dehn, Clippings.

49 "Charles Cook (Dancer)," *Wikipedia*, retrieved April 1, 2024, https://en.wikipedia.org/wiki/Charles_Cook_(dancer).

50 Terry Monaghan, "Ernest 'Brownie' Brown: He Was the 'Funny Guy' in Cook and Brown," *The Guardian*, October 28, 2009.

51 Constance Valis Hill, A Twentieth-Century Chronology of Tap Performance on Stage, Film, and Media by Constance Valis Hill searchable database presentation formerly available at https://memory.loc.gov/diglib/ihas/html/tda/tda-home.html and web archived at https://webarchive.loc.gov/all/20220120151149/http://memory.loc.gov/diglib/ihas/html/tda/tda-home.html Is now a downloadable database found at https://www.loc.gov/item/2024562029. Charles 'Cookie' Cook's biography is number 58.

52 Dehn, Clippings.

53 Valis Hill, "Charles 'Cookie' Cook Biography," https://www.loc.gov/item/2024562029. Charles 'Cookie' Cook's biography is number 58.

54 Ibid.

55 "Ernest Brown (Dancer)," *Wikipedia*, retrieved May 4, 2023, https://en.wikipedia.org/wiki/Ernest_Brown_(dancer).

56 Monaghan, "Ernest 'Brownie' Brown."

57 Constance Valis Hill, A Twentieth-Century Chronology of Tap Performance on Stage, Film, and Media by Constance Valis Hill searchable database presentation formerly available at https://memory.loc.gov/diglib/ihas/html/tda/tda-home.html and web archived at https://webarchive.loc.gov/all/20220120151149/http://memory.loc.gov/diglib/ihas/html/tda/tda-home.html Is now a downloadable database found at https://www.loc.gov/item/2024562029. Ernest Brown's biography is number 31.

58 Dehn, Clippings.

59 Ibid.

60. Marv Goldberg, "3 Chocolateers," *Unca Marvy*, retrieved May 4, 2023, https://www.uncamarvy.com/3Chocolateers/3chocolateers.html.
61. Constance Valis Hill, A Twentieth-Century Chronology of Tap Performance on Stage, Film, and Media by Constance Valis Hill searchable database presentation formerly available at https://memory.loc.gov/diglib/ihas/html/tda/tda-home.html and web archived at https://webarchive.loc.gov/all/20220120151149/http://memory.loc.gov/diglib/ihas/html/tda/tda-home.html Is now a downloadable database found at https://www.loc.gov/item/2024562029. Albert Gibson's is mentioned with the Chocolateers number 52.
62. Goldberg, "3 Chocolateers.
63. "By Word of Foot II: Teaching Tap Festival, Tribute to Albert Gibson," NYPL Digital Collections, MGZIDF 7589, retrieved from https://www.nypl.org/research/research-catalog/bib/b13873433?originalUrl=https%3A%2F%2Fcatalog.nypl.org%2Frecord%3Db13873433.
64. Constance Valis Hill, details on Buster Brown, in "About the International Tap Dance Hall of Fame," *American Tap Dance Foundation*, retrieved January 10, 2024, https://www.atdf.org/hall-of-fame-bios. The State Department record of Brown's passport differs from the birthdate in his obituary and Hall of Fame speech by Valis Hill; the claim that he gave a "command performance" is a stretch, as it was a scheduled stop on the embassy tour, and *everyone* was gifted a coin.
65. Mura Dehn, "Press and Promotional Materials," MGZMD-72, Box 21, Folder 251, Jerome Robbins Dance Division, New York Public Library for the Performing Arts.
66. *Dr. James "Buster" Brown*, retrieved January 10, 2024, https://www.drbusterbrown.com; Dehn, "Press and Promotional Materials."
67. Valis-Hill, details on Buster Brown.
68. "Buster Brown, Tap Master," *New York Times*, May 9, 2002, retrieved from https://www.nytimes.com/2002/05/09/arts/buster-brown-tap-master-and-charmer-is-dead-at-88.html.
69. Dehn, "Press and Promotional Materials.
70. "Buster Brown, Tap Master."
71. Dehn, "Press and Promotional Materials."
72. "James Cross, the Stump of Vaudeville Dance Act," *New York Times*, January 29, 1981, retrieved January 10, 2024, https://www.nytimes.com/1981/01/29/obituaries/james-cross-the-stump-of-vaudeville-dance-act.html.
73. Constance Valis Hill, *Tap Dancing America: A Cultural History* (New York: Oxford University Press, 2010).
74. Ibid.
75. Dehn, "Press and Promotional Materials.
76. Constance Valis Hill, A Twentieth-Century Chronology of Tap Performance on Stage, Film, and Media by Constance Valis Hill searchable database presentation

77. Bufalino, *Great Feats of Feet, 1977*.
78. "Newsletter by Dickie Harris," Valerie Rochon papers, 1973–2000, MGZMD 142, Box 7, Folder 26, Jerome Robbins Dance Division, New York Public Library for the Performing Arts.
79. Terry Monaghan, "Mama Lou Parks by Terry," *authenticjazzdance*, March 25, 2015, https://authenticjazzdance.wordpress.com/2015/04/25/mama-lou-parks-by-terry-monaghan/; "Mama Lu Parks, 61; Actress and Dancer Headed Jazz Troupe," *New York Times*, September 26, 1990, retrieved from https://www.nytimes.com/1990/09/26/obituaries/mama-lu-parks-61-actress-and-dancer-headed-jazz-troupe.html.
80. Vernon Gibbs, "Mama Lu and the Bugaloo," *Essence Magazine*, October 1973, 30, 96.
81. Harri Heinilä, "The Beginning of Louise 'Mama Lou' Parks' Parkettes," *authenticjazzdance*, December 14, 2022, retrieved from https://authenticjazzdance.wordpress.com/2022/12/14/the-beginning-of-louise-mama-lou-parks-parkettes/.
82. Robert White, "Mama Lu," December 21, 2023, *Swungover*, retrieved from https://swungover.wordpress.com/2023/12/21/mama-lu/.
83. "Mama Lu Parks, 61; Actress and Dancer Headed Jazz Troupe."
84. Monaghan, "Mama Lou Parks by Terry Monaghan."
85. White, "Mama Lu."
86. Dehn, "Press and Promotional Materials," 252.
87. Gibbs, "Mama Lu and the Bugaloo."
88. Monaghan, "Mama Lou Parks by Terry Monaghan.
89. "Special Guests," *Flying Home*, July 7, 2023, retrieved from https://www.flyinghomenc.com/news/special-guests.
90. Ibid.
91. Rochon Papers, 1973–2000.
92. White, "Mama Lu."
93. Terry Monaghan, "'Dickie' Harris, Director of Mama Lu Parks Dancers," Dance Forums, August 22, 2003, retrieved from https://www.dance-forums.com/threads/dickie-harris-director-of-mama-lu-parks-dancers.480/.
94. Mikey Perdoza, "Mama Lu Parks & Her Parkets," *YouTube*, March 19, 2008, retrieved from https://www.youtube.com/watch?v=v2oioVB8Mkc.
95. Monaghan, "'Dickie' Harris, Director of Mama Lu Parks Dancers.
96. Monaghan, "Mama Lou Parks by Terry Monaghan."
97. Rochon Papers, 1973–2000.

98 David Cairns (Lou Parks dancer), in personal communication with author, April 7, 2023.
99 Peter Strom, "Interview with Gloria Caldwell and David Cairns 2006," retrieved April 2023, https://ilhc.com/legacy-series/. This video is available on the ILHC.com website under About/Legacy Series/Interview with Gloria Caldwell and David Butts.
100 Cairns.
101 Ibid.
102 United States Bureau of Educational and Cultural Affairs, Folder 15, 133.
103 "Harvest Moon Ball," *New York Daily News*, September 9, 1961, 10.
104 United States Bureau of Educational and Cultural Affairs, Folder 14, 1–23.
105 Ibid., Folder 16, 67.
106 Dehn, Clippings.
107 United States Bureau of Educational and Cultural Affairs, Folder 14, 1–23.
108 Dehn, Papers, Box 21, Folder 246.
109 Peter Strom, "Mama Lu Parks Dancers and Harvest Moon Ball Champs with JL Hooker," The Harlem Swing Dance Society, *Facebook*, October 15, 2017, retrieved from https://www.facebook.com/watch/?v=1686852174681311.
110 Harlem Swing Dance Society, retrieved January 2024, https://www.facebook.com/HarlemSwingDance.
111 Blitz.
112 Heinilä, "The Beginning of Louise 'Mama Lou' Parks' Parkettes."
113 White, "Mama Lu."
114 Dehn, Programs.
115 "February 27 Harlem Swing: Black History Month Family Day," *The Ph.D. Program in History at the Graduate Center of the City University of New York*, retrieved January 2024, https://historyprogram.commons.gc.cuny.edu/february-27-harlem-swing-black-history-month-family-day/.
116 Harri Heinilä, comment on "Harlem Swing Dance," Authentic Jazz Dance History, *Facebook*, retrieved January 20, 2024, https://www.facebook.com/AuthenticJazzDanceHistory?comment_id=Y29tbWVudDoxMTYxOTk1MDQ3MjA3MDIyXzExNjIwMTE2MjM4NzIwMzE%253D.
117 Strom, "Mama Lu Parks Dancers and Harvest Moon Ball Champs with JL Hooker."
118 Ibid.
119 Mike McDermott, "Interview with Gloria Thompson Caldwell May 2021," https://youtu.be/cnlpcNTz-ic?si=af3CNPGHZLFU2d9u can be found on the Jazz Attack website.
120 Strom, "Mama Lu Parks Dancers and Harvest Moon Ball Champs with JL Hooker."
121 Ibid.

122 McDermott, "Interview with Gloria Thompson Caldwell May 2021."
123 Ibid.
124 Strom, "Mama Lu Parks Dancers and Harvest Moon Ball Champs with JL Hooker."
125 Ibid.

Chapter 7

1 Tsung-Hsin Lee, "Taiwanese Eyes on the Modern: Cold War Dance Diplomacy and American Modern Dances in Taiwan 1950–1980" (Ed.D. diss., Ohio State University, 2020), 142; Naima Prevots, *Dance for Export: Cultural Diplomacy and the Cold War* (Middletown, CT: Wesleyan University Press, 1998), 8.
2 Bethel, *Authentic Jazz Dance*, 40; United States Bureau of Educational and Cultural Affairs, "Jazz Dance Theatre," MC 468 21, Box 67, Folder 16, 177, Special Collections, University of Arkansas Cultural Presentations Program, 1935–80.
3 Ibid., Folder 14, 16.
4 Ibid., Folder 16, 140.
5 Ibid., Folder 14, 166.
6 Ibid., Folder 13, 25.
7 Spence, January 4, 2024.
8 United States Bureau of Educational and Cultural Affairs, Folder 14, 125.
9 Ibid., 166.
10 Ibid., 52.
11 Ibid., 61.
12 Ibid., 55.
13 Ibid.
14 Ibid., 169.
15 Ibid., 123.
16 Ibid., Folder 13, 52.
17 Ibid., Folder 14, 176.
18 Blitz.
19 Dehn, Scrapbooks.
20 United States Bureau of Educational and Cultural Affairs, Folder 13, 21.
21 Ibid., Folder 15, 55.
22 Bob Boross and Moncell Durden, in *Uprooted: The Journey of Jazz Dance* [Film], dir. Khadifa Wong (London: On the Rocks Films, 2020).
23 Larry Neal, "The Black Arts Movement," *Drama Review* (Summer 1968), 1.
24 Gibbs, "Mama Lu and the Bugaloo."
25 Neal, "The Black Arts Movement."
26 Hazzard-Gordon, *Jookin'*, 46.

27 United States Bureau of Educational and Cultural Affairs, Folder 16, 172.
28 Ibid., Folder 14, 116.
29 Ibid., Folder 13, 47.
30 Ibid., 3.
31 Ibid., 16.
32 Ibid., Folder 16, 173; Bethel, *Authentic Jazz Dance*, 33.
33 Ibid., 3.
34 Blitz.
35 Dehn Papers, 1902–87, 80.
36 United States Bureau of Educational and Cultural Affairs, Folder 13, 1.
37 Ibid., Folder 14, 159.
38 Ibid., 110.
39 Dehn Papers, 1902–1987, 78.
40 Ibid., Folder 14, 108.
41 Bethel, *Authentic Jazz Dance*, 38.
42 United States Bureau of Educational and Cultural Affairs, Folder 14, 159; ibid., Folder 13, 41.
43 Ibid., 40.
44 Ibid., Folder 14, 148.
45 Blitz.
46 Ibid.
47 United States Bureau of Educational and Cultural Affairs, Folder 14, 149.
48 Ibid., 150.
49 Ibid., Folder 13, 38.
50 Ibid., Folder 16, 176.
51 Ibid., Folder 13, 38.
52 Ibid., Folder 14, 1–23.
53 Ibid., Folder 14, 151.
54 Ibid.
55 Dehn Papers, 1902–87, 75.
56 United States Bureau of Educational and Cultural Affairs, Folder 14, 1–23.
57 Ibid., Folder 16, 109.
58 Ibid., 107.
59 Ibid.
60 Blitz; Spence.
61 United States Bureau of Educational and Cultural Affairs, Folder 14, 67.
62 Ibid., Folder 16, 107.
63 Ibid., 110.
64 Blitz.
65 United States Bureau of Educational and Cultural Affairs, Folder 14, 99.

66 Ibid., Folder 13, 80.
67 Ibid., Folder 14, 152–5.
68 Ibid., 105.
69 Blitz.
70 Spence.
71 United States Bureau of Educational and Cultural Affairs, Folder 16, 174.
72 Blitz; Spence.
73 United States Bureau of Educational and Cultural Affairs, Folder 14, 128.
74 Blitz, April 4, 2024.
75 United States Bureau of Educational and Cultural Affairs, Folder 14, 127.
76 Blitz.
77 United States Bureau of Educational and Cultural Affairs, Folder 13, 80.
78 Ibid., Folder 14, 1–23.
79 Ibid.
80 Ibid., Folder 14, 128.
81 Ibid., Folder 13, 33.
82 Ibid., Folder 14, 138.
83 Ibid., Folder 16, 107.
84 Ibid., Folder 14, 138.
85 Ibid., Folder 16, 67.
86 Ibid., 175.
87 Ibid., 66.
88 Ibid., Folder 13, 7.
89 Ibid., Folder 16, 174.
90 Ibid., Folder 15, 144.
91 United States Bureau of Educational and Cultural Affairs, Folder 14, 1–23.

Chapter 8

1 Dehn Papers, 1902–87, 63.
2 Lyena Dodge (Friend of Mura).
3 Dehn Collection, Box 1, Folder 7.
4 Dehn Papers on Afro-American Social Dance, Box 18, Folders 181–3.
5 Ibid.
6 Ibid.
7 Ibid., Box 23, Folder 300.
8 Ibid., Box 20, Folder 242.
9 Dehn, Programs.
10 Dehn, Clippings.

11 Dehn Papers on Afro-American Social Dance, Box 20, Folder 242.
12 Blitz.
13 Blitz, September 23, 2023.
14 Dehn Papers on Afro-American Social Dance, Box 20, Folder 242.
15 Dehn, Programs.
16 Dehn, Clippings.
17 Ibid.
18 Anna Kisselgoff, "Show Recalls Era of Black Dancers," *New York Times*, March 15, 1973.
19 Dehn, Clippings.
20 Dehn, Programs.
21 "How Much Can You Learn in Three Weeks?" *The Village Voice*, August 2, 1973.
22 "Baby Franklin Seals," *Wikipedia*, retrieved April 20, 2024, https://en.wikipedia.org/wiki/Baby_Franklin_Seals.
23 Stearns and Stearns, *Jazz Dance*.
24 Jacqui Malone, *Stepping on the Blues: The Visible Rhythms Of African American Dance* (Champaign, IL: University of Illinois Press, 1996), 81.
25 "Stage Music," *The Afro American* (Baltimore), November 7, 1942, 10.
26 "Stage Music," *The Afro American* (Baltimore), October 31, November 7, and November 14, 1942.
27 Baby Seals, "Brownskin Models," *The Indianapolis Recorder*, February 24, 1938.
28 Bernard Peterson, *Century of Musicals in Black and White: An Encyclopedia of Musical Stage Works*, (Santa Barbara, CA: ABC-CLIO), 1993.
29 *The Afro-American* (Baltimore), 1941, 13.
30 Ibid., 15.
31 *The Afro-American* (Baltimore), September 5, 1942.
32 Ibid., October 20, 1942.
33 Ibid., August 28, 1943, 10.
34 Ibid., 1945, July 21, 1945; ibid., March 31, 1945, 8.
35 *The Leader-Post* (Regina, Saskatchewan, Canada), July 4, July 28, 1953.
36 *The Afro-American* (Baltimore), March 28, 1949; ibid., May 7, 1960.
37 *The Montreal Gazette*, November 2, 1960, 17.
38 "Pigmeat Markham," *Wikipedia*, retrieved May 1, 2024, https://en.wikipedia.org/wiki/Pigmeat_Markham.
39 Kliph Nesteroff, "Last Man in Blackface: The World of Pigmeat Markham," *WFMU's Beware of the Blog*, November 11, 2010, retrieved from https://blog.wfmu.org/freeform/2010/11/the-forgotten-pigmeat-markham.html.
40 Dodge, *Hot Jazz and Jazz Dance*.
41 Nesteroff, "Last Man in Blackface."
42 Dixon Gottschild, *Waltzing in the Dark*, 4; Nesteroff, "Last Man in Blackface."

43 Ibid.
44 "Why Have Negro Comedians Failed to Make the Big Time?" *Ebony Magazine*, October 1960, in Nesteroff, "Last Man in Blackface."
45 Ibid.
46 "Artists: Pigmeat Markham," *Last.fm*, retrieved May 1, 2024, https://www.last.fm/search?q=Pigmeat+Markham.
47 Nesteroff, "Last Man in Blackface."
48 Last.fm, "Artists."
49 Nesteroff, "Last Man in Blackface."
50 Ibid.
51 Last.fm, "Artists."
52 Harris, "Workshop on Hip Hop."
53 C. Gerald Fraser, "Groping for a New Level of Struggle," *New York Times*, May 13, 1973, 193.
54 Jon Nordheimer, "The Dream: Blacks Move Painfully Toward Full Equality," *New York Times*, August 26, 1973m 1, 44.
55 Dehn, Clippings.
56 Ibid.
57 Dehn Papers on Afro-American Social Dance, Box 20, Folder 216.
58 Dehn, Clippings.
59 Ellen Shaw, "Vaudevillians Give Money's Worth," *The Evening Bulletin* (Philadelphia), March 23, 1974.
60 Dehn Papers, 1902–87, 89.
61 Dehn Papers on Afro-American Social Dance, Box 5, Folder 120.
62 Ibid.

Chapter 9

1 Mura Dehn, "The ABC's of Jazz Dance," Mura Dehn Papers on Afro-American Social Dance, c. 1969–87, (S) *MGZMD 72, Jerome Robbins Dance Division, New York Public Library for the Performing Arts, Box 1, Folder 2.
2 Laurent Goddet, "Harlem Jazz Dance," *Le Jazz Hot*, 355, 36–9.
3 Mura Dehn, A Few Words about Jazz Dancing," *Jazz Record* 52 (1947), 22–3, 39.
4 Dehn, "The ABC's of Jazz Dance," 5.
5 Lillian Morrison (friend of Mura), personal communication with author, March 1996.
6 Stella Snead (friend of Mura), personal communication with author, March 1995.
7 Eiko (friend of Mura), personal communication with author, January 1995.
8 Ibid.

9 Mura Dehn Papers on Afro-American Social Dance, Box 18, Folder 186.
10 Dehn, Clippings.
11 Mura Dehn Papers on Afro-American Social Dance, Box 18, Folder 168.
12 Ibid., Box 5, Folder 146.
13 "Artist Biography and Facts: Benjamin Benno," *askART*, retrieved May 9, 2024, https://www.askart.com/artist/Benjamin_Greenstein_Benno/100784/Benjamin_Greenstein_Benno.asp.
14 Mura Dehn Papers on Afro-American Social Dance, Box 18, Folder 187.
15 Mark Scherzer (Mura's lawyer), personal communication with author, September 15, 2023.
16 Ibid.
17 Ibid.
18 "Dunham Dancers to Honored," *New York Times*, March 5, 1981, 18.
19 Mura Dehn Papers on Afro-American Social Dance, Box 18, Folder 187.
20 Ibid., Box 17, Folder 176.
21 Celia Epiotis, "Glances of the Past: Documentation of Jazz Dance," *Eye on Dance* [television series], MGZIC 9-2846 (New York: ARC Videodance, June 1982).
22 Mura Dehn Papers on Afro-American Social Dance, Box 21, Folder 255.
23 "The Spirit Moves," Dehn, Clippings.
24 Mura Dehn Papers on Afro-American Social Dance, Box 18, Folder 187. Note that it is difficult to know from the handwriting whether it is "Meyer" or "Meger."
25 Blitz, in personal communication with author, May 19, 2023; Scherzer; Lillian Morrison (friend of Mura), Eiko.
26 Charlie Dorkins (friend of Mura), personal communication with author, December 1995.
27 Mura Dehn Papers on Afro-American Social Dance, Box 5, Folder 145.
28 Ibid., Box 18, Folder 176.
29 Lillian Morrison, personal communication with author, 1996; Sally Sommer, personal communication with author, May 2023; Eiko, personal communication with author, April 2023.
30 Mura Dehn, *Lion Tamer, and Other Poems* (Sunnyside, NY: Waterford Press, c. 1987).
31 Mura Dehn Papers on Afro-American Social Dance, Box 5, Folders 144–5; Sandra Martz, ed., *When I Am an Old Woman I Shall Wear Purple* (Watsonville, CA: Papier-Mache Press, 1987).
32 Mura Dehn Papers on Afro-American Social Dance, Box 5, Folders 144–5.
33 Louise Ghertler and Pamela Katz, dir., *In a Jazz Way: A Portrait of Mura Dehn* [Film] (New York: Filmakers Library, 1986).
34 Jack Anderson, "Films Show History of Black Social Dancing," *New York Times*, November 6, 1986, C21.

35 Lillian Morrison.
36 Dehn, *Lion Tamer, and Other Poems*.
37 Eiko, personal communication with author, January 2024.
38 "Mura Dehn, a Choreographer and Specialist In Black Dance," *New York Times*, February 14, 1987, Section 1, 15.
39 Emma Cohn, "Mura Dehn: The Preservation of Black Jazz Dance on Film," *Sightlines* (Spring 1987), 11.
40 Jennifer Eberhardt (New York Public Library librarian), personal communication with author, May 30, 2023.
41 Lillian Morrison.
42 Eiko.
43 Lillian Morrison.
44 Eiko, personal communication with author, 1995.

Chapter 10

1 Dehn Papers on Afro-American Social Dance, Box 5, Folder 123.
2 Dehn Papers, 1902–87, 26.
3 Dehn Papers on Afro-American Social Dance, Box 5, Folder 123. Diaghilev is sometimes transliterated as "Diaghileff" in French and Russian.
4 Dehn Papers on Afro-American Social Dance, Box 4, Folder 77; ibid., Box 20, Folders 230–231; Dehn, Clippings, MGZR; Dehn, Scrapbooks, MGZR 90-9612.
5 Ibid.
6 Robert Sylwester, *A Celebration of Neurons: An Educator's Guide to the Human Brain*, (Alexandria, VA: Association for Supervision and Curriculum Development, 1995).
7 Wynton Marsalis, "What Iazz Is–and Isn't," *New York Times*, July 31, 1988, 21, 24, 26.
8 Karen Hubbard, "Valuing Cultural Context and Style Strategies for Teaching Traditional Jazz Dance from the Inside Out," *Journal of Dance Education* 8, no. 4, (2008): 110–16.
9 Susan R. Koff, *Dance Education: A Redefinition* (London: Methuen Drama, Bloomsbury Collections, 2021).
10 Marsalis, "What Jazz Is–and Isn't."
11 Joanne Kealiinohomoku, "The Non-art of the Dance: An Essay," *Journal of the Anthropological Study of Human Movement* 1, no. 1 (1980): 40.
12 Jamake Highwater, *The Primal Mind: Vision and Reality in Indian America* (New York: Harper & Row, 1983), 74.
13 Mura Dehn, quoted in J. Dunning, "Film: Mura Dehn, Dancer, as Subject and Chronicler," *New York Times*, December 16, 1987.

14 V.H. yaTande Whitney, "The Ring Shout: A Corporeal Conjuring in Black Togetherness," *Dance Research Journal* 55, no. 2 (August 2023): 55.
15 Michael Polyani, in Mari Sorri, "The Body Has Reasons: Tacit Knowing in Thinking and Making" *Journal of Aesthetic Education* 28, no. 2 (January 1994): 15–27.
16 Dehn Papers, 1902–87, The Spirit Moves Manuscript, 11.

Bibliography

1st National Dance Congress and Festival Proceedings, New York. 793.04 N213. Jerome Robbins Dance Division, The New York Public Library for the Performing Arts, 1936.
Abdoulaev, Alexandre. "Savoy: Reassessing The Role of the 'World's Finest Ballroom' in Music and Culture, 1926-1958." Theses & Dissertations, Boston University, 2023.
Academy of Swing. MGZ. Jerome Robbins Dance Division, The New York Public Library for the Performing Arts.
Adams, Henry. "Adolf Dehn, American Watercolorist and Printmaker, 1895-1968." Accessed January 25, 2024. www.thomasfrenchfineart.com.
Adams, Henry. *Adolf Dehn Biograph*. Accessed December 1, 2023. http://www.adolfdehnart.com/DrHenryAdams.
Adams, Henry. *The Sensuous Life of Adolf Dehn*. Columbia, MO: University of Missouri Press, 2021.
Admin. June 6, 2006. Accessed March 10, 2023. https://Www.Swingpatrol.Co.Uk/Frankie-Manning-Melbourne-1939/.
Afro American Baltimore. Eddie Barefield. October 20, 1942.
Afro American Baltimore. March 28, 1959. May 7, 1960.
Afro American Baltimore. Stage Music. November 7, 1942, 10. https://books.google.com/books?id=kBAmAAAAIBAJ&printsec=frontcover&source=gbs_all_issues_r&cad=1#v=onepage&q&f=false.
Afro American Baltimore. "Tharpes-Roberts Affair." Saturday, July 5, 1930.
Alamy.com. "Willie Ray." March 3, 2010. https://www.alamy.com/stock-photo-march-3-2010-las-vegas-nevada-usa-willie-ray-performs-as-james-brown-42402930.html.
Aldrich-Moodie, Mary Jane. "Savoy Ballroom Style: Harlem Entertainment And Creative Black Resistance." MGW 92-2685. Independent Study, Jerome Robbins Dance Division, The New York Public Library for the Performing Arts, Barnard College, New York, NY, 1990.
All Music.com. "Dick Vance Biography." Accessed April 5, 2024. https://www.allmusic.com/artist/dick-vance-mn0000359702#biography.
Anderson, Jack. "Films Show History of Black Social Dancing." *The New York Times*, November 6, 1986, C21.
Archives of Early Lindy Hop. "The Call of the Jitterbug 1988." Accessed March 1, 2024. http://www.savoystyle.com/call_of_jitterbug.html.
Asante, Kariamu. "Commonalities in African Dance: An Aesthetic Foundation." In *African Culture: The Rhythms of Unity*, edited by M. Asante and K. W. Asante. Trenton, NJ: Africa World Press, 1990, 144–159.

Ask Art.com. "Benno Greenstein Benjamin, Artist Biography and Facts." https://www.askart.com/artist/Benjamin_Greenstein_Benno/100784/Benjamin_Greenstein_Benno.asp.

Backstein, Karen. "Dancing Images: Choreography, Cinema and Culture." PhD Dissertation, Department of Cinema Studies, New York University, 1996.

Ballroom Dancemagazine. "Behind the Scenes." 1, no. 10, November 1960.

Banes, Sally. *Writing dancing in the Age of Postmodernism.* Hanover, NH: Wesleyan University Press, 1994.

Beantown Camp. "Special Guests Sugar Sullivan." Accessed May 30, 2024. https://www.beantowncamp.com/team/special-guests/sugar-sullivan.

Berendt, Joaquim. *The Jazz Book: From Ragtime to Fusion and Beyond.* Chicago, IL: Lawrence Hills Books, 1975.

Bethel, Pepsi. *Authentic Jazz Dance: A Retrospective.* New York: The American Authentic Jazz Dance Company, 1990.

Boross, Bob. "The Legacy of Jazz Dance Historian Mura Dehn, With Kim Chandler Vaccaro of Rider University." Jazz and Tap Dance Life. https://www.youtube.com/watch?v=u4tMjnv8bao, July 31, 2020.

Broadway World. "Credits, Bio, News & More." Accessed January 15, 2024. https://www.broadwayworld.com›people›Avon-Long.

Brown, Ernest. Accessed January 10, 2024. https://www.drbusterbrown.com.

Brown, Jeri. Accessed March 13, 2024. https://someonewhollwatchoverme.wordpress.com/about.

Brown, LaTasha. "Interview with Sugar Sullivan." Herrang Dance Camp, 2019. https://www.youtube.com/watch?v=wLraVWqEvy8.

Bubbygram.com. "James Brown." Accessed March 14, 2024. http://www.bubbygram.com/jamesbrownwrlv.htm.

Bufalino, Brenda. *Great Feats of Feet.* New York: Alexander Street, 1977, film.

Buzynski, Isabella. "Café Culture in the 'Jewish City.'" Accessed December 4, 2023. https://scalar.usc.edu/works/odessa/a-brief-history-of-odessa.

Carolina Time. "An Evening of Jazz and Dance." June 20, 1981. https://newspapers.digitalnc.org/lccn/sn83045120/1981-06-20/ed-1/seq-19/.

Carter, Sandy. "Civil Rights and Southern Soul." *Z Magazine,* January 1994.

Chadbourne, Eugene. "Joe Marshall." https://www.allmusic.com/artist/joseph-marshall-mn0001757823.

Chalfont, Harry, and Tony Silver, directors. "Style Wars." New York: Public Art Films, Inc., 1983.

Chang, Jeff. "Profile 7: Dancing on the Through-Line: Rennie Harris and the Past and Future of Hip-Hop Dance." 2002. https://digitalcommons.colum.edu/cgi/viewcontent.cgi?article=1006&context=cap_vistas.

Cohn, Emma. "Mura Dehn, the Preservation of Black Jazz Dance on Film." *Sightlines,* Spring 1987, 8.

Corporation for Public Broadcasting. "Blackface Minstrelsy The American Experience." Accessed January 25, 2024. https://www.pbs.org/wgbh/americanexperience/features/foster-blackface-minstrelsy/.

Cox, Richard. "Adolf Dehn: Satirist of the Jazz Age Author." *Archives of American Art Journal* 18, no. 2 (1978): 11–18. https://www.jstor.org/stable/1557409.

Crease, Robert. "Profiles of Original Lindy Hoppers: Al Leagins." *New York Swing Dance Society Footnotes A Quarterly Newsletter* 1, no. 4 (1986). https://www.frankiemanningfoundation.org/profiles-of-original-lindy-hoppers.

Crease, Robert. "Profiles of Original Lindy Hoppers: Sandra Gibson." *New York Swing Dance Society Footnotes A Quarterly Newsletter* 2, no. 2 (1987).

Crease, Robert. "The Savoy Ballroom Remembered." *New York Swing Dance Society Footnotes A Quarterly Newsletter* 5, no. 2 (1990).

Dance, Stanley. *World of Swing*. New York: Charles Scribner's Sons, 1974.

Davey D's Hip-Hop Corner. "PopMaster Fabel." Accessed March 12, 2024. http://www.daveyd.com/historyphysicalgrafittifabel.html?fbclid=IwAR1JUipwV0ObTMQWGnAqpLBqutE9olZLMYnLg1n93yfgvcYeifAsjBiIjE_aemA.

Dehn, Adolf. Letter to Editor of *Arts Weekly*, May 1932. Mura Dehn Clippings. MGZR. Jerome Robbins Dance Division, The New York Public Library for the Performing Arts.

Dehn, Adolf Papers, 1912-1987. Archives of American Art, Smithsonian Institution. Box 1, Folder 6.

Dehn, Mura. "A Few Words About Jazz Dancing." *Jazz Record* no. 52 (1947): 22–23, 39.

Dehn, Mura. "A Few Words About Jazz Dancing." Proceedings of the 1st National Dance Congress and Festival, The National Dance Congress, New York, 1936, 43–46.

Dehn, Mura. "Georgia Peach: 'Spiritual+émotion=Gospel,' interview par Mura Dehn." *Jazz Hot* no. 173 (February 1962).

Dehn, Mura. "Introduction au 'Gospel Singing' par Mura Dehn." *Jazz Hot* no. 70 (October 1952).

Dehn, Mura. "Is Jazz Choreographic?" *Dance Magazine* 18, no. 2 (1948): 24–25.

Dehn, Mura. "Jazz a Folk Dance." *Dance Magazine* 19, no. 11 (1945).

Dehn, Mura. "Jazz Dance." *Sound & Fury* 2, no. 3 (1966): 14–18.

Dehn, Mura. "Jazz Musique/Jazz Danse par Mura Dehn." *Jazz Hot* no. 60 (1952). https://www.jazzhot.net/PBSCProduct.asp?ItmID=3659662.

Dehn, Mura. *Lion Tamer* (Published Posthumously). New York: The Waterford Press, 1987.

Dehn, Mura. "More Respect for the Clown." *Dance Magazine* 17, no. 2 (1946): 34.

Dehn, Mura. "Negro Dance and Puritanism." *Jazz Monthly: The Magazine of Intelligent Jazz Appreciation* 2, no. 4 (1956): 2–4.

Dehn, Mura. "New Spirit in an Ancient Dance: World's Fair Indonesian Dancers Are Eager to Learn, Eager to Share." *Dance Magazine* 35, no. 9 (1964): 16, 18–19, 68–69.

Dehn, Mura. "Summing Up 1975," Mura Dehn 1902-1987, (S) MGZMB-Res.+ 87-205, The Spirit Moves Manuscript, 89.

Dehn, Mura. "The ABC's of Jazz Dance." *The Dance Notation Record* 8, no. 2 (1957): 3–5.

Dehn, Mura. "The Thugs." In *When I'm Old I Shall Wear Purple*, edited by Sandra Martz, 176. Watsonville, CA: Papier Mache Press, 1987.

Dehn, Mura, Herbert Matter, and Leo Hurwitz, directors. *Dancing James Berry*. Rochester, NY: Eastman Museum, 1958, film. https://www.eastman.org/dancing-james-berry-us-1958.

Deitch, Mark. "Pepsi Bethel – Master of Jazz Dance." *The New York Times*, August 6, 1978, Section D, 12.

Delaunay, Charles. "Introduction, Les Noirs et la danse par Mura Dehn." *Jazz Hot* no. 59 (1952). https://www.jazzhot.net/PBSCProduct.asp?ItmID=3659662.

Delgado, Jimmy. "Millie Donay Passed Away." https://www.salsaforums.com/threads/millie-donay-passed-away.4738/#google_vignette.

Dixon Gottschild, Brenda. *Black Dancing Body: A Geography from Coon to Cool*. New York: Palgrave Macmillan, 2003, 223.

Dixon Gottschild, Brenda. *Digging the Africanist Presence in American Performance: Dance and Other Contexts*. Westport, CT: Greenwood Press, 1996.

Dixon Gottschild, Brenda. "Stripping the Emperor." In *Looking Out: Perspectives on Dance and Criticism in a Multicultural World*, edited by David Gere. New York: Schirmer Books, 1995, 95–121.

Dixon Gottschild, Brenda. "The 'Swingin' Lindy: Origins of a Legacy." Accessed February 2024. https://artsandculture.google.com/story/the-swingin-lindy-origins-of-a-legacy-by-brenda-dixon-gottschild-lincoln-center/JwWxl1IJ7CwnJQ?hl=en.

Dodge, Pryor, ed. *Hot Jazz and Jazz Dance*. New York: Oxford University Press 1995, 246.

Dodge, Roger P. Accessed May 24, 2024. https://en.wikipedia.org/wiki/Roger_Pryor_Dodge.

Dodge, Roger P. "East St Louis Toodle -oo." Accessed February 2023. https://www.youtube.com/watch?v=oVSm_dX8Jqs&t=46s, 1937, film.

Dodge, Roger P. "Jazz Dance, Mambo Dance, Part 1." *Jazz Review* 2, no. 10 (1959): 59, 63.

Dodge, Roger P. "Negro Jazz." *The Dancing Times*, October 1929.

Dodge, Roger P. "Negro Jazz as Folk Material for Our Modern Dance." 1st National Dance Congress and Festival Proceedings, (1936) 48. New York: The National Dance Congress.

Dodge, Roger P. "The Dance-basis of Jazz." *The Record Changer* 4, no. 1 (1945): 15.

Douglas, Ann. *Unspeakable Honesty*. New York: Farrar, Straus and Giroux, 1995.

Down Beat. "Authentic Jazz Dance." 31, no. 8 (March 26, 1964): 193.

Duke University Archives and Manuscripts. "Charles Reinhart Management, Inc., Summary." North Carolina, USA.

Duncan, Isadora. "I See America Dancing, 1927." In *The Art of The Dance*, edited by Sheldon Cheney, 47–50. New York: Theatre Arts, Inc., 1928.

Dunning, Jennifer. "Pepsi Bethel, 83, A Champion of American Popular Dance." *The New York Times*, September 6, 2002, Section A, 21.

Dunning, Jennifer. "The Spirit Moves: A History of Black Social Dance on Film." *The New York Times*, December 16, 1987, Section C, 22.

Ebony Magazine. "Why Have Negro Comedians Failed to Make the Big Time." October 1960.

Englebrecht, Barbara. "The Savoy Ballroom Harlem, New York, 1930." *Harlem World Magazine*. Accessed October 27, 2023. https://www.harlemworldmagazine.com/the-savoy-ballroom-harlem-new-york-1930/.

Ellington, Duke. *Music is My Mistress*. New York: Doubleday & Co, 1973, 100.

Emery, Lynne Fauley. *Black Dance: From 1619 to Today*. Princeton, NJ: Princeton Book Company, 1988, 91.

Epiotis, Celia, and Jeff Bush, directors. *Glances at the Past: Documentation of Jazz Dance*. New York: ARC Videodance, 1982, Video recording.

Everything Explained Today. Adolf Dehn. Accessed February 2023. https://everything.explained.today/Adolf_Dehn/.

"Exploration of Jazz Dance Forum: What is Jazz Dance?" Dance Notation Bureau. Accessed December 5, 2023. http://dancenotation.org/news/Library_News/library_v10_n3.pdf.

Facebook.com. "Bernie Upson." Accessed February 20, 2024. https://www.facebook.com/BernieUpson.

Feather, Leonard. "The Encyclopedia of Jazz." New York: Horizons Press, 1960.

Felipe. "Air Mail Special, 1941." June 8, 2021. https://estiloswing.es/air-mail-special-1941/.

Feuerstein, Alan. "Mambo Legends Cuban Pete and Millie Architects of Excitement." Accessed May 28, 2024. http://www.justsalsa.com/culture/mambo/history/articles/alanfeuerstein/mambolegendscubanpeteandmille/.

Flaherty, Caedra Scott. "Melanie George Presents Jazz at the Joyce and More." *The Observer*. January 8, 2024. https://observer.com/2024/01/melanie-george-presents-jazz-at-the-joyce-and-more/.

Flying Home. "Special Guests." Accessed January 20, 2024. https://www.flyinghomenc.com/news/special-guests.

Fortunato, Joanne. *Major Influences Affecting The Development Of Jazz Dance, 1950-1971*. Marietta, GA: Dance Press, 1974.

Fosler-Lussier, Danielle. *Music in America's Cold War Diplomacy*. Berkeley, CA: University of California Press, 2015.

Fraad, Julie. "Dancing Hands, 1988." MGZIC 9-2106. Jerome Robbins Dance Division, The New York Public Library for the Performing Arts.

Fraad, Julie. "Fresh Faust, a Rap Opera in Progress." *New York Magazine* 20, no. 16 (1987): 105.

Frankie Manning Foundation. Accessed March 10, 2023. https://www.frankiemanningfoundation.org/profiles-of-original-lindy-hoppers?pgid=leo97hvo3-420f4d05-d186-452c-94b2-fa13e814ab9b.

Frankie Manning Foundation. "Willa Mae Ricker." Accessed March 2024. https://www.frankiemanningfoundation.org/willa-mae-ricker.

Fraser, C. Gerald. "Groping for A New Level of Struggle." *New York Times*, May 13, 1973, 193.

Gates, Henry Louis. *This is Our Story; This is Our Song*. London: Penguin Press, 2021.

Gibbs, Vernon. "Mama Lu and the Bugaloo." *Essence Magazine*, October 1973, 30, 96.

Gibson, Albert. "Biography." Accessed May 4, 2023. http://memory.loc.gov/diglib/ihas/loc.music.tdabio.52/default.html.

Gibson, Albert. "Word of Foot Tribute to Albert Gibson." https://www.nypl.org/research/research-catalog/bib/b13873433?originalUrl=https%3A%2F%2Fcatalog.nypl.org%2Frecord%3Db13873433.

Ghertler, Louise, and Pamela Katz, directors. *In a Jazz Way: A Portrait of Mura Dehn*. New York: Filmakers Library, 1986, film.

Gillespie, Dizzy. "To be, or not . . . to bop." Garden City, NY: Doubleday & Company, 1979.

Goddet, Lauren. "Harlem Jazz Dance." *Jazz Hot* no. 355 (1975): 36–39.

Goldberg, Marv. "3 Chocolateers." Schooltime Publications. 2014. https://www.uncamarvy.com/3Chocolateers/3chocolateers.html.

Graff, Ellen. "Federal Dance Project (1936–1938)." In *The Routledge Encyclopedia of Modernism*. doi:10.4324/9781135000356-REM64-1.

Gridley, Mark. *Jazz Styles: History and Analysis*, 5th ed. Englewood Cliffs, NJ: Prentice Hall, 1994.

Grow, Kory. "Road to Recovery: A Hip-Hop Pioneer was Left for Dead." *Rollingstone Magazine*, December 22, 2023. https://www.rollingstone.com/music/music-features/popmaster-fabel-hip-hop-pioneer-recovery-1234933123/.

Hanna, Judith Lynne. "Dance and Ritual." *Journal of Physical Education, Recreation and Dance* 59, no. 6 (1988): 40–43.

Hannel, Susan. "The Influence of Jazz on Fashion." Bloomsbury Fashion Central, University of North Texas, 2019, 57–78. https://libproxy.library.unt.edu:2823/products/berg-fashion-library/bo...eth-century-american-fashion/the-influence-of-american-jazz-on-fashion.

"Harlem Swing Black History Month Family Day." Accessed January 2024. https://historyprogram.commons.gc.cuny.edu/february-27-harlem-swing-black-history-month-family-day/.

Harris, Denise. "The Pivotal Role of Al Minns in Modern Day Lindy Hop." Lincoln Center's Midsummer Night Swing. Accessed March 10, 2023. https://www.youtube.com/watch?v=jbuWlXZnBTY&t=10s.

Harris, R. G. "Adolf's Dehn's Humanity." *The New York Times*, Sunday, April 13 1930, 133. Accessed March 1, 2024. https://www.rhpm.org/founder/.

Harris, Rennie. Accessed March 2, 2024. https://www.alvinailey.org/rennie-harris.

Harris, Rennie. "Dr Lorenzo 'Rennie' Harris on Street Dance." Accessed March 2, 2024. https://www.youtube.com/watch?v=uOPlcpFJVxY.

Harris, Rennie. "Hip-Hop Workshop." DanceNJ Annual Festival, Rutgers University, New Brunswick, NJ, February 3, 2024.

Harris, Rennie. "Importance to the Field." Accessed March 1, 2024. https://www.rennieharrisuniversity.org/importance-to-the-field.

Harris, Richard. *Jazz*. Westport, CT: Greenwood Press, 1955.

Hazzard-Gordon, Katrina. "Afro-American Core Culture Social Dance: An examination of Four Aspects of Meaning." *Dance Research Journal* 15, no. 2 (1983): 24.

Head, Giltrecia. Quoting Karen Backstein in "Unmasking the Blues: Gẹlẹdẹ and the Creation of Blues Alchemy." Master's Thesis, Florida State University College of the Arts 2021, 19.

Heard, Marcia Ethel. "Asadata Dafora Biographical Essay." Free To Dance Biographies. Accessed February 17, 2024. https://www.thirteen.org/freetodance/biographies/dafora.html.

Heinila, Harri. "An Endeavor by Harlem Dancers to Achieve Equality – The Recognition of the Harlem-Based African American Jazz Dance Between 1921 and 1943." EdD Dissertation, University of Helsinki, 2016.

Heinila, Harri. "Debra Youngblood, a Great Weekend in Harlem." May 19, 2013. https://authenticjazzdance.wordpress.com/2013/05/19/a-great-weekend-in-harlem/.

Heinila, Harri. "The Beginning of Louise 'Mama Lou' Parks' Parkettes." December 14, 2022. https://authenticjazzdance.wordpress.com/2022/12/14/the-beginning-of-louise-mama-lou-parks-parkettes/.

Heinila, Harri. "The Creators of the Lindy Hop." Accessed February 2023. https://authenticjazzdance.wordpress.com/2012/07/04/the-creators-of-the-lindy-hop-george-shorty-snowden-and-mattie-purnell/.

Heinila, Harri. "Harlem Swing Dance." Accessed January 20, 2024. https://www.facebook.com/AuthenticJazzDanceHistory?comment_id=Y29tbWVudDoxMTYxOTk1MDQ3MjA3MDIyXzExNjIwMTE2MjM4NzIwMzE%253D.

Highwater, Jamake. *The Primal Mind: Vision and Reality in Indian America*. New York: Harper and Row, 1983.

Hikara, Mark. "Mura Dehn and the Spirit Moves." December 2021. https://www.swingitseattle.com/blog/mura-dehn-and-spirit-moves.

Hill, Constance Valis. "Buster Brown." Accessed January 10, 2024. https://www.atdf.org/hall-of-fame-bios.

Hill, Constance Valis. "Charles 'Cookie' Cook [Biography]." Library of Congress. Accessed May 4, 2022. http://memory.loc.gov/diglib/ihas/loc.music.tdabio.58/default.html.

Hill, Constance Valis. "James Stump Cross." Accessed January 10, 2023. http://memory.loc.gov/diglib/ihas/loc.music.tdabio.65/.

Hill, Constance Valis. "Tap Dancing America, a Cultural History 2010." Accessed January 10, 2024. https://www.atdf.org/hall-of-fame-bios.

Hodeir, André. *Jazz: It's Evolution and Essence*. New York: Grove Press, 1956.

Holley, Joe. *Washington Post*, January 23, 2002.

Hubbard, Karen. "The Authentic Jazz Dance Legacy of Pepsi Bethel." In *Jazz Dance: A History of Roots and Branches,* edited by Guarino and Oliver. Gainesville, FL: University of Florida Press, 2014, 75–81.

Hubbard, Karen. "Valuing Cultural Context and Style Strategies for Teaching Traditional Jazz Dance from the Inside Out." *Journal of Dance Education* 8, no. 4 (2008).

Hubbard, Karen, and Terry Monaghan. "Negotiating Compromise on a Burnished Wood Floor: Social Dancing at the Savoy." In *Ballroom, Boogie, Shimmy Sham, Shake: A Social And Popular Dance Reader*. University of Illinois, 2009, 126–145.

Hurston, Zora Neale. *Folklore, Memoirs, & Other Writings*. New York: The Library of America, 1995.

Hurston, Zora Neale. *The Sanctified Church*. Berkeley, CA: Turtle Island, 1981.

IMDb. "James Berry." Accessed March 12, 2024. https://www.imdb.com/name/nm0077569/.

Indianapolis Recorder. "Brownskin Models," Marion County, Indiana, 24 February 1938.

Interview of Terry Monaghan, International Lindy Hope Championships Legacy Series, Part I.

Ithaca Voice.com. "Bernie Upson, Beloved Ithaca Musician." July 2017. https://ithacavoice.org/2014/07/beloved-jazz-musician-dies-thursday/.

Jackson, Jamin. "Why Was the Savoy Ballroom Important?" Street Smart Swing. Accessed May 2024. https://jaminjackson.com/the-savoy-ballroom/.

Jazz Lead Sheets. "Milton Sealey." Accessed March 13, 2024. https://jazzleadsheets.com/composers/milton-sealey.html.

Jenkins, Chris. "Is Classical Music Racist? An Aesthetic Approach." Aesthetics for Birds. February 2,2021. https://aestheticsforbirds.com/2021/02/26/is-classical-music-racist-an-aesthetic-approach.

Jerome Robbins Dance Division, New York Public Library Digital Collections. "Dance and Immigration." Accessed May 30, 2024. https://digitalcollections.nypl.org/items/dad0b85c-d568-47dd-9fdc-8d5fc40eefa1.

Jerome Robbins Dance Division, The New York Public Library for the Performing Arts. Mura Dehn 1902-1987. Scrapbooks. MGZRS 90-9612, Vol. 1.

Jerome Robbins Dance Division, The New York Public Library for the Performing Arts. Mura Dehn Clippings, MGZR.

Jerome Robbins Dance Division, The New York Public Library for the Performing Arts. Mura Dehn Collection, Administrative Information, MGZMD 483.

Jerome Robbins Dance Division, The New York Public Library for the Performing Arts. Mura Dehn Collection, MGZMD 483, Box 3, Folder 6.

Jerome Robbins Dance Division, The New York Public Library for the Performing Arts. Mura Dehn Notebooks. MGZMD 72.

Jerome Robbins Dance Division, The New York Public Library for the Performing Arts. Mura Dehn Papers on Afro-American Social Dance, ca. 1869-1987, MGZMD 72, , Box 21, Folder 254.

Jerome Robbins Dance Division, The New York Public Library for the Performing Arts. Mura Dehn Programs, MGZB.

Jerome Robbins Dance Division, The New York Public Library for the Performing Arts. Mura Dehn *Roger Dodge- A Jazz Dancer*. (S) *MGZM-Res. Dod R.

Jerome Robbins Dance Division, The New York Public Library for the Performing Arts. Mura Dehn Traditional Jazz Dance Company, Programs. MGZB.

Jerome Robbins Dance Division, The New York Public Library for the Performing Arts. "Newsletter by Dickie Harris." Valerie Rochon papers, 1973-2000. *MGZMD 142, Box 7, Folder 26.

Jerome Robbins Dance Division, The New York Public Library for the Performing Arts. Strohman, Clarence. "Social Dancing: At the Cotton Club and the Savoy." MGZIC 9-2942.

Jerome Robbins Dance Division, The New York Public Library for the Performing Arts. "The Spirit Moves Manuscript." Mura Dehn 1902-1987. MGZMB-Res.+ 87-20, 217.

Kealiinohomoku, Joanne. "An Anthropologist Looks at Ballet as an Ethnic Form of Dance." *Impulse Magazine*, 1970, 24–33.

Kealiinohomoku, Joanne. "Ethical Considerations for Choreographers, Ethnologists and White Knights." *Journal of the Association of Graduate Dance Ethnologists* 5 (1981): 10–23.

Kealiinohomoku, Joanne. "The Non-Art of the Dance: An Essay." *Journal of The Anthropological Study of Human Movement* 1, no. 1 (1980): 40–41.

Kelley, Robin. *Africa Speaks, America Answers: Modern Jazz in Revolutionary Times*. Cambridge, MA: Harvard University Press, 2012, 13.

Kennedy Center. "Herbert 'Whitey' White." Accessed February 2023. https://www.kennedy-center.org/education/resources-for-educators/classroom-resources/media-and-interactives/artists/white-herbert/.

Kennedy Center. "Hip Hop Culture and Voice." Accessed January 2024. https://www.kennedy-center.org/education/resources-for-educators/classroom-resources/media-and-interactives/media/hip-hop/hip-hop-a-culture-of-vision-and-voice.

Kisselgoff, Anna. "Show Recalls Era of Black Dancers." *The New York Times*, March 15, 1973.

Koff, Susan R. *Dance Education: A Redefinition*. London: Methuen Drama, Bloomsbury Collections, 2021.

Kraus, Richard, Sarah Hilsendager, and Brenda Dixon. *History of the Dance in Art and Education*, 3rd ed. Englewood Cliffs, NJ: Prentice Hall, 1991.

Kraut, Anthea. *Choreographing the Folk: The Dance Stagings of Zora Neale Hurston*. Minneapolis, MN: University of Minnesota Press, 2008.

Kraut, Anthea. "Re-Framing the Vernacular: The Dance Praxis of Zora Neale Hurston." EdD Dissertation, Northwestern University, 2002.

Kriegel, Loraine P. "Engendering Jazz (or . . . Read My Hips)." Unpublished Manuscript, 1994.

La Rocco, Claudia. "Entertainment Review." *New York Times*, March 2, 2010.

Lally, Kathleen Ann. "A History of the Federal Dance Theatre of the Works Progress Administration, 1935-1939." PhD Dissertation, Texas Woman's University, 1978.

Last.fm. "Artists: Pigmeat Markham." Accessed May 1, 2024. https://www.last.fm/search?q=Pigmeat+Markham.

Leader-Post. Regina Saskatchewan, July 4–28, 1953.

Learning Annex Newsletter. "Breaking Away!" New York, July 1985, 89.

Lee, Tsung-Hsin. "Taiwanese Eyes on the Modern: Cold War Dance Diplomacy and American Modern Dances in Taiwan 1950-1980." PhD Dissertation, The Ohio State University, 2020.

Legacy.com. "Bernie Upson." Accessed February 20, 2024. https://www.legacy.com/us/obituaries/tcpalm/name/andrew-upson-obituary?id=22886397.

Leohurwitz.com. "Leo Hurwitz Biography." Accessed March 14, 2024. https://leohurwitz.com/why/.

Library of Congress. "Bernie Upson, Jazz on Screen." Accessed February 20, 2024. https://www.loc.gov/item/jots.200013560.

Library of Congress. "Berry Brothers [Biography]." Accessed March 12, 2024. http://memory.loc.gov/diglib/ihas/loc.music.tdabio.

Library of Congress. "Ernest Brown Biography." Accessed May 4, 2023. http://memory.loc.gov/diglib/ihas/loc.music.tdabio.

Library of Congress. "Interviews Dehn-Thomas, Mura, 1960," Sigmund Freud Papers: Interviews and Recollections, -1998, Set A, -1998. https://www.loc.gov/item/mss3999001450/.

Library of Congress. "New Dance Group Collection." Accessed February 13, 2023. http://memory.loc.gov/diglib/ihas/loc.natlib.scdb.200033868/.

Loggins, Peter. "So You Wanna Dance Fast?" February 8, 2010. https://Jassdancer.Blogspot.Com/Search?Q=Sugar+Sullivan.

Lumsdaine, Joycelyn Pang, and Thomas O'Sullivan. "The Prints of Adolf Dehn: A Catalogue Raisonné." St. Paul, MN: Minnesota Historical Society, 1987.

Malone, Jacqui. *Stepping on the Blues: The Visible Rhythms of African American Dance*. Champaign, IL: University of Illinois Press, 1996.

Marsalis, Wynton. "What Jazz Is – And Isn't." *The New York Times*, July 31, 1988, 21, 24, 26.

Martin, John. "Dance: A Congress." May 31, 1936. https://timesmachine.nytimes.com/timesmachine/1936/05/31/88669393.html?pageNumber=156.

Martin, John. "Dances in Jazz Form Given by Mura Dehn." March 16, 1945. https://timesmachine.nytimes.com/timesmachine/1945/03/16/84628698.html?pageNumber=20.

Martin, John. "Native Cast Gives an African Opera: Kyunkor Produced in an East Side Playhouse Appraised as Exciting Theater Art." *The New York Times*, May 9, 1934.

Martin, John. "The Dance: A Convention." May 17, 1936. https://timesmachine.nytimes.com/timesmachine/1936/05/17/110048926.html?pageNumber=186.

Martin, John. "Two Dance Recitals Full of Contrasts." March 4, 1932. https://timesmachine.nytimes.com/timesmachine/1932/04/11/100824642.pdf?pdf_redirect=true&ip=0.

McCormack, Alexandre. Accessed February 2024. https://www.instagram.com/reel/C0QtVCZo9Ze/.

McCormack, Karen Campos. Accessed March 10, 2023. https://atlanticlindyhopper.wordpress.com.

McDermott, Mike. "Interview with Gloria Thompson Caldwell May 2021." Accessed January 20, 2024. https://www.youtube.com/channel/UCgDSY4KveMxA6TDWyoP4mHQ/videos.

McDermott, Mike. "Interview with Lindy Hop Legend Debra Youngblood." Accessed March 13, 2024. https://www.youtube.com/watch?v=MU85-7KKCwo.

Meek, William, ed. "Adolf Dehn: American Artist Retrospective Series." Naples, FL: Harmon Meek Gallery, 1984.

McPherson, Elizabeth. "The New Dance Group: Transforming Individuals and Community." September 1, 2016. https://dancetimepublications.com/dance-culture-editorial/the-new-dance-group-transforming-individuals-and-community/.

Miller, Norma, and Evette Jensen. *Swingin' at the Savoy: The Memoir of a Jazz Dancer*. Philadelphia, PA: Temple University Press, 1996.

Mills, Biz. "Savoy Gives Happy Feet a Chance to Dance." Savoy Ballroom Archives Wayback Machine-Internet Archives.

Monaghan, Terry. "Al Minns: The Incorrigible Lindy Hopper, 1920-1985." https://authenticjazzdance.wordpress.com/2020/01/01/al-minns-the-incorrigible-lindy-hopper-1920-1985-by-terry-monaghan/.

Monaghan, Terry. "Crashing Cars & Keeping The Savoy's Memory Alive." https://authenticjazzdance.wordpress.com/2015/04/25/mama-lou-parks-by-terry-monaghan/.

Monaghan, Terry. "Dickie Harris." Accessed August 22, 2003. https://www.dance-forums.com/threads/dickie-harris-director-of-mama-lu-parks-dancers.480/.

Monaghan, Terry. "Ernest 'Brownie' Brown: He was the 'Funny Guy' in Cook and Brown." *The Guardian*, October 28, 2009.

Monaghan, Terry. "Obituary, Pepsi Bethel." *The Guardian*, September 27, 2002. https://www.theguardian.com/news/2002/sep/28/guardianobituaries.arts.

Monaghan, Terry. "Remembering Shorty." *The Dancing Times*, July 2004, 49, 51. http://jassdancer.blogspot.fi/2012/10/shorty-george-snowden.html.

Monaghan, Terry. "Savoy Ballroom," July 2011–February 2012. Internet Archive Wayback Machine. http://www.savoyballroom.com/introduction/welcome.htm.

Monaghan, Terry. "The Legacy of Jazz Dance." *Annual Review of Jazz Studies*, 1997/1998, The Institute of Jazz Studies, Rutgers University, Newark, NJ.

Monaghan, Terry. "The Third Generation." https://authenticjazzdance.wordpress.com/2017/03/11/the-third-generation-by-terry-monaghan/.

Montreal Gazette. "All Star Show at Rockheads." Advertisement, Montreal, November 2, 1962, 17.

Moon, Clay. "The Savoy Ballroom: Rejecting Black Exoticism Through Community-Driven Design." Accessed June 10, 2023. https://www.mcgill.ca/race-space/article/arch-355/savoy-ballroom-rejecting-black-exoticism-through-community-driven-design.

Ndiaye, Marie. "Interview with Sugar Sullivan & Denise Minns Harris." International Swing Dance Championships in Houston, TX. December 2023. https://www.youtube.com/watch?v=ftftdc4uWA4.

Neal, Larry. "The Black Arts Movement." *Drama Review,* Summer 1968, 1.

Nesteroff, Kliph. "Last Man in Blackface: The World of Pigmeat Markham." *WFMU's Beware of the Blog Radio Station That Bites Back Home*, November 14, 2010. https://blog.wfmu.org/freeform/2010/11/the-forgotten-pigmeat-markham.

New York Daily News. "Harvest Moon Ball." September 9, 1961, 10.

New York Times. "Buster Brown, Tap Master." May 9, 2002. https://www.nytimes.com/2002/05/09/arts/buster-brown-tap-master-and-charmer-is-dead-at-88.html.

New York Times. "Dehn's Splendid Drawings." Friday, April 4, 1931, 20.

New York Times. James Cross. January 29, 1981. https://www.nytimes.com/1981/01/29/obituaries/james-cross-the-stump-of-vaudeville-dance-act.html.

New York Times. "Mama Lu Parks, 61; Actress and Dancer Headed Jazz Troupe." September 26, 1990. https://www.nytimes.com/1990/09/26/obituaries/mama-lu-parks-61-actress-and-dancer-headed-jazz-troupe.html.

New York Times. "Mura Dehn, a Choreographer and Specialist in Black Dance." February 14, 1987.

New York Times. "New Show at Plantation Club." November 6, 1938.

New York Times. "Red Scare Protest Issued by Liberals." May 19, 1930, 18. https://timesmachine.nytimes.com/timesmachine/1930/05/19/issue.html.

Nordheimer, Jon. "'The Dream,' 1973: Blacks Move Painfully Toward Full Equality." Special to *The New York Times*, August 26, 1973, 1, 44.

Oliver, Wendy, and Lindsay Guarino. *Jazz Dance: A History of Its Roots and Branches*. Gainesville, FL: University of Florida Press, 2014.

Ostransky, Leroy. *The Anatomy of Jazz*. Seattle, WA: The University of Washington Press, 1960.

Otake, Eiko. *I Invited Myself, vol. III: Duets*. Philadelphia, PA: Fashion Workshop and Museum, February 2024.

Otto, Pamela. "African American Social Dance Forms of the Harlem Renaissance: Embracing a Deeper Understanding of Jazz Dance and Aesthetic Principles." *Impulse*, 3 no. 3 (1995): 160.

Panganiban, Riki. July 22, 2022. http://www.yehoodi.com/blog/2022/7/22/happy-85th-birthday-harvest-moon-ball-champion-sugar-sullivan.

Pape, Brian and Joy. "Characters of the Village: Chenault Spence, a Southern Accent in the Village." August 4, 2023. https://villageview.nyc/2023/08/04/chenault-spence-a-southern-accent-in-the-village.

Perdoza, Mikey. "Mama Lu Parks & Her Parkets." Accessed May 31, 2024. https://www.youtube.com/watch?v=v2oioVB8Mkc.

Perpener, III, John. "Asadata Dafora." 2017. https://danceinteractive.jacobspillow.org/themes-essays/african-diaspora/asadata-dafora/.

Perron, Wendy. "Dance in the Harlem Renaissance: Sowing Seeds." In *EmBODYing Liberation – The Black Body in American Dance*, edited by Dorothea Fischer-Hornung and Alison D. Goeller. Hamburg: LIT, Transaction Publishers, 2001, 23–40.

Peterson, Bernard. *Century of Musicals in Black and White: an Encyclopedia of Musical Stage Works*. Santa Barbara, CA: ABC-CLIO, 1993.

Plate Bar and Grill. Accessed March 14, 2024. https://www.facebook.com/events/the-plate-bar-grill/willie-ray-james-brown-tribute/298181430646905/.

Prevots, Naima. *Dance for Export: Cultural Diplomacy and the Cold War*. Middletown, CT: Wesleyan University Press, 1998.

Prichett, Judy. "Billy Ricker." January 16, 2006. http://savoystyle.com/billy-ricker.html.

Randall, Pamela Renee. "Exploring Black Social Dance from the Viewpoint of Mura Dehn: Psychological, Sociological, and Spiritual Purposes, Functions, and Meanings." Master's Thesis, University of California, Los Angeles, 1999.

Roman, Gene. "Latin Music Museum Honors Cuban Pete in NYC." Accessed May 28, 2024. https://puertoricoherald.com/issues/2002/vol6n27/LatMuseumCubanPt-en.html.

Rothfield, Philipa. "Philosophies of Motion." *Writings on Dance* 11, no. 12 (1994): 77–86.

Savoy Hop. "The Berry Brothers." Accessed March 12, 2024. https://www.youtube.com/watch?v=bghET2QjVxA._https://www.youtube.com/watch?v=bghET2QjVxA.

Savoy Style. "Whitey's Lindy Hoppers." Accessed February 2023. http://www.savoystyle.com/wlh.html.

Schomburg Center for Research in Black Culture. Asadata Dafora Papers. The New York Public Library. https://digitalcollections.nypl.org/collections/f76a9680-10ca-0135-e410-43962e862982#/?tab=about.

Schuller, Gunther. *The Swing Era: The Development of Jazz, 1930-1945*. Oxford: Oxford University Press, 1991.

Shaw, Ellen. "Vaudevillians Give Money's Worth." *The Evening Bulletin*, March 23, 1974.

Sisco, Richard Lee, director. "Beat Street." Stan Lathan, Los Angeles: Orion Pictures, 1984, film.

Smith, Jason Samuel, "History of Tap Dance." DanceNJ Professional Development Day, Ocean County Technical and Vocational School, Tom's River, NJ, November 16, 2023.

Sylwester, Robert. *A Celebration of Neurons: An Educator's Guide to the Human Brain.* Alexandria, VA: Association for Supervision and Curriculum Development, 1995.

Sommer, Sally. "Mura Dehn 1903-1987." In *Routledge Encyclopedia of Modernism.* Informa UK, 2018. doi:10.4324/9781135000356-REM1904-1.

Sommer, Sally. "The Spirit Moves: A History of Black Social Dance on Film." *Village Voice,* December 2, 1986.

Sorri, Mari. "The Body has Reasons: Tacit Knowing in Thinking and Making." *The Journal of Aesthetic Education* 28, no. 2 (January 1994).

Spalding, Susan. "Aesthetic Standards in Old Time Dancing in Southwest Virginia: African American and European-American Threads." EdD diss., Temple University, 1993.

Stearns, Marshall W. *The Story of Jazz.* New York: Oxford University Press, 1967.

Stearns, Marshall W. and Jean Stearns. *Jazz Dance: The Story of American Vernacular Dance.* New York: Da Capo Press, 1968.

Stevens, Tamara and Erin Stevens. *Swing Dancing.* New York: Bloomsbury Publishing, 2011.

Stovall, Tyler. *Paris Noir: African Americans in the City of Light.* Boston, MA: Houghton Mifflin Company, 1996.

Strom, Peter. "Interview with David Cairns and Gloria Thompson Caldwell." 2006. https://www.youtube.com/watch?v=kzRLNaSmY8U.

Swing Dance Vegas. "Willie Ray." Accessed March 14, 2024. https://www.facebook.com/SwingDanceVegas/photos/a.1848920725161336/1884789868241088/?type=3.

Swingin at the Savoy. "Sugar Sullivan." Accessed March 1, 2024. https://swinginatthesavoy.com/staff/sugar-sullivan/.

Syncopated City. Accessed March 10, 2023. https://syncopatedcity.com/the-jazz-dancers-a-brief-survey-of-the-lives-of-al-minns-leon-james/.

Thompson, Aniya. "Harlem Renaissance Project." January 13, 2021. https://prezi.com/p/5egoaemvyhkl/harlem-renaissance-project/#:~:text=Herbert%20Whitey%20White%20worked%20as,kids%20who%20have%20all%20passed.

Tolzmann, Don Heinrich. *Adolf Dehn: Life and Work of a German American Artist on Both Sides of the Atlantic.* Loyola Notre Dame Library. Accessed December 1, 2023. https://Loyolanotredamelib.Org/Php/Report05/Articles/Pdfs/Report47-10-Adolf-Dehn-Tolzmann.Pdf.

UCSB Library. "Barefield, Eddie." Accessed April 5, 2024. https://adp.library.ucsb.edu/index.php/mastertalent/detail/108186/Barefield_Eddie.

United States Bureau of Educational and Cultural Affairs, Jazz Dance Theatre. Cultural Presentations Program, 1935-1980, Box 67, Folders 13-16. MC 468 21. Special Collections, University of Arkansas, USA.

Vaccaro, Kim Chandler. "Moved by the Spirit: Illuminating the Voice of Mura Dehn and Her Efforts to Promote and Document Jazz Dance." EdD Dissertation, Temple University, 1997.

Van Manen, Martin. *Researching Lived Experience*. Albany, NY: State University of New York Press, 1990, 181.

Ventura, Michael, "Hear That Long Snake Moan." In *Shadow Dancing in the U.S.A.* Los Angeles, CA: Jeremy Torcher, Inc., 1985, 103–162.

Village Voice. "Afro-American Folklore." February 23, 1967.

Village Voice. "Dance Workshops." January 14, 1965.

Village Voice. "How Much Can You Learn in Three Weeks?" August 2, 1973.

Village Voice. "In Harlem They're Still Dancing the Original Swing." Accessed March 10, 2023. https://www.villagevoice.com/iWillie-Posey-and-n-harlem-they're-still-dancing-the-original-swing/.

Warren, Richard. "Empathetic Embodiment: The Dance of Roger Pryor Dodge." October 31, 2020. https://richardawarren.wordpress.com/2020/10/31/empathetic-embodiment-the-dance-of-roger-pryor-dodge/.

Watkins, Mary F. "Paul Haakon Seen at Cort in Dance Recital, Mura Dehn at the Guild." *New York Herald Tribune*, April 11, 1932.

Watkins, Mary F. "The Dance." *Arts Weekly*, n.d., in Mura Dehn, Clippings, MGZR, Jerome Robbins Dance Division, The New York Public Library for the Performing Arts.

Wells, Christopher J. "'And I Make My Own': Class Performance, Black Urban Identity, and Depression-Era Harlem's Physical Culture." In *The Oxford Handbook of Dance and Ethnicity*, edited by Anthony Shay and Barbara SellarsYoung, 17–40. New York: Oxford University Press, 2016.

Wells, Christi Jay. "Counter-Bopaganda and Torn Riffs: Bebop as Popular Dance Music." In *Between Beats: The Jazz Tradition and Black Vernacular Dance*. doi:10.1093/oso/9780197559277.003.0004.

White, Robert. "Mama Lu." *Swungover*, December 12, 2023. https://swungover.wordpress.com/2023/12/21/mama-lu/.

White, Robert. "Sandra Gibson." *Swungover*, February 1, 2011. https://swungover.wordpress.com/2011/02/01/mildred-boogie-pollard-and-sandra-gibson-isdfnka-1/.

White, Robert. *Swungover*, April 6, 2023. https://swungover.wordpress.com/2023/04/06/the-1952-harvest-moon-ball/.

White, Robert. "The 1948 Harvest Moon Ball." *Swungover*, March 16, 2022. https://swungover.wordpress.com/2022/03/16/the-1948-harvest-moon-ball/.

White, Robert. "The 1951 Harvest Moon Ball." *Swungover*, October 19, 2022. https://swungover.wordpress.com/2022/10/19/the-1951-harvest-moon-ball/.

White, Robert. "The 1953 Harvest Moon Ball." *Swungover*, August 8, 2023. https://swungover.wordpress.com/2023/08/08/the-1953-harvest-moon-ball/.

White, Robert. "The 1955 Harvest Moon Ball." Accessed May 30, 2024. https://swungover.wordpress.com/?s=Sugar+Sullivan.

White, Robert. "Theresa Mason." Accessed March 10, 2023. https://swungover.wordpress.com/?s=Theresa+Mason.

White, Robert. "Willa Mae." Accessed February 2024. https://swungover.wordpress.com/?s=Willa+Mae+Ricker.

Wickre, Karen. "Interview with Mura Dehn, April 20, 1978." Voices of the WPA: Oral Histories of the Works Progress Administration. The Research Center for the Federal Theatre Project. Fairfax, VA: George Mason University.

Wiggles, Mr. Accessed March 21, 2024. http://www.wigzee.biz/bio.

Wiggles, Mr. "What Does a Legendary Hiphop Dance OG Wanna Say to YOU?" Accessed January 2024. https://www.youtube.com/watch?v=3F-rixHNdPA.

Wikipedia. "Avon Long." Accessed January 15, 2024. https://en.wikipedia.org/wiki/Avon_Long.

Wikipedia. "Charles Cook." Accessed April 1, 2024. https://en.wikipedia.org/wiki/Charles_Cook.

Wikipedia. "Cuban Pete." Accessed March 2024. https://en.wikipedia.org/wiki/Pedro_Aguilar.

Wikipedia. "Dick Vance." Accessed April 5, 2024. https://en.wikipedia.org/wiki/Dick Vance.

Wikipedia. "Eddie Barefield." Accessed April 5, 2024. https://en.wikipedia.org/wiki/Eddie_Barefield.

Wikipedia. "Ernest Brown, Dancer." Accessed May 4, 2023. https://en.wikipedia.org/wiki/Ernest_Brown_(dancer).

Wikipedia. "Ergy Landau, Biography." Accessed January 20, 2024. https://en.wikipedia.org/wiki/Ergy_Landau.

Wikipedia. "Franklin Baby Seals." Accessed April 20, 2024. https://en.wikipedia.org/wiki/Baby_Franklin_Seals.

Wikipedia. "Joe Marshall." Accessed March 18, 2024. https://en.wikipedia.org/wiki/Joe_Marshall_(musician).

Wikipedia. "Lindy Hoppers." Accessed February 2023. https:/en.wikipedia.org/wiki/Whitey%27s Lindy Hoppers.

Wikipedia. "Pigmeat Markham, Biography." Accessed May 1, 2024. https://en.wikipedia.org/wiki/Pigmeat_Markham.

Williams, Joe. "The Delsarte Project." Accessed February 2023. https://www.delsarteproject.com/joe-williams-bio.

Williamson, Liz, and Mike Moore. "That Eclectic, Elusive Dance Called Jazz." *Dance Magazine* 49, no. 2 (1978): 63–75.

Wilson, John S. "Jazz Dancing Gets New Support." *The New York Times*, May 22, 1962, 30.

Wilson, John S. "Lecture on Dance Steals Jazz Fete." *New York Times*, July 6, 1958, 50.

Wilson, John S. "Scoby Stohman Drummer-Dancer." *New York Times*, April 7. https://timesmachine.nytimes.com/timesmachine/1996/04/07/issue.html.

Wilson, John S. "Two Jazz Dancers Recreate the Past." *The New York Times,* January 20, 1969.

Wilson, Olly. "Black Music as an Art Form." *Black Music Research Journal* 3 (1983).

Wintz, Carl D. "The Harlem Renaissance: What was it and Wy Does it Matter?" 2015. https://www.humanitiestexas.org/news/articles/harlem-renaissance-what-was-it-and-why-does-it-matter.

Wong, Khadifa, director. "Uprooted." 2020, film. https://uprootedfilm.com.

You Tube. "Al Minns Dancing in New York." Accessed March 10, 2023. https://www.youtube.com/watch?v=dvegobsHOVE.

You Tube. "Inside the Mind of Hip Hop Legend Mr. Wiggles – The Future of Dancers, Technology, and Social Media." Accessed March 28, 2024. https://www.youtube.com/watch?v=3F-rixHNdPA.

You Tube." The Original Magnificent Force." Accessed March 12, 2024. https://www.youtube.com/watch?v=DHsrWu8An-Q.

Index of Mini-Bios

Arnold, Gregory "Waco" 97, 121, 133–4, 152, 163, 167

Barefield, Eddie 120, 122–3, 133, 163–4
Berry, James 6, 70, 77, 84–9, 92, 96–7, 103, 106, 113, 116, 128–9, 158, 160, 176–7
  Berry Brothers, the 65, 84–6, 88, 90, 97
Bethel, Alfred "Pepsi" 2, 10, 63, 68–71, 82, 87, 93, 96–7, 118, 120–1, 146, 159, 163–4
Blitz, Allen 113–16, 118–21, 129, 133, 137–8, 140–1, 143–6, 148–52, 154, 159–61, 163–4, 175–6, 178
Brown, Buster 88, 114, 120–1, 127–8, 161, 162, 164
Brown, Ernest "Brownie" 126, 131, 161, 163–4. *See also* Cook and Brown
Brown, Mary Jesse "Gigi" 97, 121, 124, 133, 161–3, 167
Brown, Theophilus "Teddy" 65, 87, 92, 96–8

Cairns, David Butts 97, 105, 121, 129, 131–2, 161–3, 167–8
Clemente, Steffan "Mr. Wiggles" 98, 107–9
Cook, Charles "Cookie" 71, 125–6, 151, 161, 163–4
  Cook and Brown 114, 120, 125–6, 159, 167
Cross, James "Stump" 87, 120–1, 128, 162
Cuban Pete 97, 104–5

Dafora, Asadata 56–61, 73, 159, 182
Dodge, Roger Pryor 7–9, 19, 46, 48, 53, 55, 77, 88, 93, 164, 177
Donay, Millie 97, 98, 104–5

Fraad, Julia 98, 107, 110

Gibson, Albert 65–6, 88, 114, 120–1, 126–7, 154, 159, 162, 168
Gibson, Sandra (Sandra Givens, née Mildred Pollack) 61, 63, 65–6, 69, 96, 97, 106, 127, 159

Harris, Lorenzo Rennie "Prince" 98, 107, 110–11, 166
Harris, Richard "Dickie" 97, 121, 130–1, 133, 161, 163, 167

James, Leon 41, 44, 60, 61, 63, 65–70, 82, 96, 97, 99, 159, 171
Johnson, Edward "Roe" 97, 105, 167, 168

Leagins, Al (Alfred) 11, 46, 58, 60, 82, 94, 178
Long, Avon 70, 120–1, 125, 147, 153–4, 164

Manning, Frankie 42, 69, 95, 97–101
Markham, Dewey "Pigmeat" 97, 106, 162, 164–8
Marshall, Joe 120, 123, 164
Minns, Al (Albert) 65–6, 70, 96, 97, 99, 102, 159

Pabon, George "Popmaster Fabel" 98, 107, 109
Parks, Mama Lou 69, 97, 105, 129, 131–2, 134, 169

Raynor, Willie "Ray" 95, 106
Ricker, Willamae 66, 67, 96, 98–9

Sealey, Milton 120, 123–4, 155, 162–4
Seals, Ernest "Baby" 97, 106, 162–4, 167
Snowden, "Shorty George" 44–46, 54, 58, 94

Spence, Chenault   118, 121, 137, 139, 148, 151–2, 163
Strohman, Clarence "Scoby"   97, 103
Sullivan, Sugar   64, 69, 97–9, 102–3

Upson, Bernie   120, 124, 162

Vance, Dick   120–123, 133, 154, 159, 164, 168

Wall, Micky   97, 133, 151, 154
Washington, Esther   61, 63–5, 68, 82, 96, 159
White, Herbert "Whitey"   43–46, 58, 63, 65–7, 99, 100

Youngblood, Debra (Deborah)   97, 105, 129, 131, 161

Index of Subjects

Academy of Swing   3, 45, 56–60, 64, 111, 182, 185
Africa, the continent   30, 75, 78–9, 81, 89, 95, 103, 111, 118–19, 123–4, 167, 182
   art, gifts, aesthetics, culture of Africa   3, 19, 46, 56, 75, 78
   tour of Africa   3, 6, 71, 89, 113–55, 158
African
   African American(s)   2–4, 6, 8, 13, 17, 23, 29, 40, 43, 49–50, 53, 81–2, 103, 110, 121, 155, 163, 165, 184
   African American community   18, 43
   Africanist   12, 17, 71
   Black American   41, 96, 101, 140, 150, 155, 159
   culture, folk traits   30, 46, 78, 145
   dance   55–59, 78, 110, 168–9
   drumming   56, 59, 78
   retentions, memory   59, 76, 78, 96
African and European aesthetics, art, culture   2, 7, 8, 11, 13, 14, 18, 20, 30
African American, vernacular, folk dance   86, 112, 143, 159, 167, 173, 182, 184
African American aesthetics, culture   10, 12, 14, 15, 18, 29, 47, 71, 75, 183
African American folk artists, folklore   49, 54
Apollo Theater   65–6, 85, 102, 104, 106, 108, 124–5, 127–8, 130, 131, 133–4, 163–5
Asante, Kariamu   3

Baby Laurence   20, 87, 88
Baker, Josephine   9, 28, 30–1

ballet   2, 11, 12, 18, 19, 24–5, 34, 41, 48, 50, 70, 72, 83, 91, 102, 143, 182
   ballet master   44
   Diagheleff's (Diaghilev) Ballet Russe   181
   jazz ballet   73
   Negro Ballet   54
Bauhaus, Dada   26, 28, 48
Beat Street   107–9
bebop   4, 17, 20, 81–2, 97, 99, 103, 107, 182, 184
Berlin   26–8, 33, 37, 39
Berry, Nyas   84–5
Berry, Warren   84–6, 90, 96
blackface   115, 163, 165, 166
Black folk forms, artists, folklore   23, 49, 140, 167
Black narrative   4, 30, 31, 40, 142, 161
Black social dance   1, 3, 20, 47, 74, 79, 88, 95–6, 113, 143, 179, 185
blues   4, 8, 9, 20, 59, 62, 75, 81, 96, 123, 133
   Pierrot in Blues   31
   The Harlem Blues and Jazz Band   105, 130, 132
bohemian   21, 26–7, 29, 30, 37, 94
Boross, Bob   81, 114, 142
Brown, James   95, 105–6, 109, 131–2, 134
Buchanan, Charles   40, 97, 129

cakewalk   1, 2, 143, 162, 181
Calloway, Cab   65, 87, 100, 105, 122–3, 125, 127, 132
Carnegie Hall   18, 77, 82, 104, 124, 130
   Carnegie Recital Hall   70, 86, 99, 129
Chalfant, Henry   96, 98–9, 107, 109
Charleston   9, 15, 29, 31, 33, 40, 45, 61, 65–6, 73–4, 92, 97, 120, 129, 171
church   20, 22, 42, 65, 66, 75–9, 84
   African American   77
   African American Folklore and the Church   92

Baptist Church 77
Black, Negro 77, 78, 182
  church artists 159
  church songs 8
  Methodist Church 75
  Metropolitan Baptist 46
  Riverside Church 69
Civil Rights 107, 113–14, 137, 142, 169
Coburg Opera 34
  Rudolph Bing 34
Coles, Honi 126, 127, 159, 161
commedia dell'arte 21–23, 88
Cooper Union 62, 63, 89, 92, 113, 127
Copasetics, The 126–128, 130, 152
Cotton Club 41, 44–5, 47, 65, 66, 85, 125, 128, 162
Count Basie 16, 47, 70, 100, 128
  Count Basie Centennial Ball 130
Crease, Robert 41–2, 66, 68, 69, 94, 101
creative resistance 11, 14, 40, 77, 81, 107, 166, 169, 183
  Black awareness through art 77, 79, 169
culture 5, 11, 13, 26, 52, 58, 78, 117, 183
  American Folk 10, 29, 114, 139, 144, 179
  Black culture 41, 80, 101, 114, 140, 141
  Caucasian dance culture 95
  euro-American 78, 81
  Eurocentric 31, 81
  hip-hop 108, 109
  jazz culture 40
  Jewish 21
  of Lindy Hop, swing 15, 101
  rock 140
  secular, freedom 111
  twentieth century 13
  urban popular, street 98, 108
  Western 28
  white culture 13, 42, 58, 79
  world culture 91, 93

Dalcroze, Émile-Jacques 21–4, 28, 31, 48
Dance Magazine 1, 60, 68, 88, 91, 172
DeFrantz, Thomas 4, 9
Dehn, Adolf 25–28, 32, 33, 50, 157
Delaunay, Charles 83, 159
DelSarte, François 21, 22, 24

Dodge, Anne 54, 55, 59
Dodge, Lyena 32, 36
Dorkins, Charles 96, 97, 172, 176
Duncan, Isadora 24, 25, 28, 31, 51
Dunning, Jennifer 1

Eiko Yamada Otake 3, 6, 36, 94, 172, 177, 179
Ellington, Duke 1, 9, 14, 16, 34, 48, 67, 85, 100, 122, 123, 125, 127, 128
Eurocentric 3, 4, 11, 13, 25, 140
European Americans 2, 8, 18, 78
expatriate intellectuals 26
  avant-garde 21, 28, 31, 35, 51, 95, 114, 173, 182
  progressive 28, 52, 62, 87, 137, 166
  socialist 26, 28, 35, 55, 150

Federal Theater Project, (FTP) 52–55, 57, 60
Fitzgerald, Ella 85, 100, 122, 128
folk 1, 11, 19, 28, 73, 74, 77, 94
  Black folk 75
  dance 13, 14, 20, 47, 54, 74, 78, 83, 84, 92, 168, 174
  dancers 59
  European folk dance 182
  folk art 3, 13, 14, 37, 49, 53, 73, 77, 79, 80, 84, 150, 182, 183
  folklore 20, 50, 56, 57, 59, 78, 80, 86, 92, 96, 113, 141, 161
  humor 23
  music 8, 13, 114, 161
  rituals 55
  urban, street dance 110, 111

Gillespie, Dizzy 16, 20, 159
Golden Era 3, 7, 97, 168, 182, 183
  Georgia Peach 70, 77, 87
  gospel 46, 72, 77, 79, 84
Goodman, Benny 13, 14, 18, 122, 123, 127
Gottschild, Brenda Dixon 3, 6, 9–11, 15, 17, 77, 165
Great Feats of Feet: A Portrait of the Jazz and Tap Dancer 125, 127, 128

Harlem 1, 15, 16, 34, 39–46, 49, 54, 56, 66, 70, 77, 83, 97–8, 103, 105,

109, 116, 124, 129–31, 168, 171, 181
artists   79, 80
Cotton Club   129, 162
The Harlem Blues and Jazz Band   132
Harlem Renaissance   42, 80
Harlem Swing Dance Society   133
Heights   115
Plaza   88–89
Spanish Harlem   98, 104, 107–9
tradition(s)   101, 102
Whitey's Harlem Congaroos   66, 100
Harvest Moon Ball (HMB)   61, 64–5, 67, 70, 71, 99, 101, 105, 129–32, 134
champions   6, 61–2, 66, 82, 97, 102, 105, 111, 113, 166
Hellzapoppin'   44, 65–6, 69, 99, 100, 102
Henderson, Fletcher   43, 123
hip-hop   81, 98, 108–11, 166
breakdancing   98, 107, 166, 184
street dance(s)   110, 111, 141
Hirsch, Harry   140, 142, 143, 148, 149
Home of Happy Feet   134, 181
Hubbard, Karen   41, 43, 71
Hughes, Langston   3, 42, 49, 75, 85, 103
Hurston, Zora Neale   3, 49–51, 54

improvisation   7–9, 12, 15, 17–19, 23–4, 35, 43, 49, 58, 63, 84, 88, 90, 97, 111, 114, 163, 183
In a Jazz Way   46, 47, 93, 178, 180
individuality   7, 12, 16, 18, 19, 24, 25, 71, 84, 88, 95, 111, 125, 166, 185

jazz dance
authentic   68–71
Golden Era   3, 7, 97, 168, 182, 183, 185
Jazz Dance Theatre   115–17, 119, 133, 137, 138, 140, 149, 150, 154
jazz tap dancing   19, 20
meaning, ingredients   7, 10, 12, 13, 16, 18, 24, 78
research   19, 58, 60, 73, 75
Traditional Jazz Dance Company   3, 6, 66, 88, 123, 140, 157–70, 172
vernacular, folk, popular, social   19, 47, 53, 59, 92, 179, 183
jazz musicians   9, 29, 30, 60, 63, 103

Jazz Record   16, 60
Johnson, James Weldon   7, 80, 88
Johnson, Momodu   54, 55, 57

Kriegel, Lorraine   9, 16

Landau, Ergy   33, 52
Le Jazz Hot   76, 77, 82, 83, 171
Lindy, Lindy hop   4, 15, 17, 24, 42, 44–7, 54, 58, 61, 66, 68–71, 73–4, 82, 92, 101–2, 105–6, 111–12, 120–1, 128, 130, 132, 134–5, 143
International Lindy Hop Championship   94, 101
jitterbug   58, 60, 70, 74, 94, 106, 132, 162
Lindy Hoppers   19, 42–5, 63–5, 67, 70–1, 85, 92, 99–101, 105, 130–1
Lion Tamer   36, 89, 177–8
Lomax, Alan   4, 74, 93, 114, 173, 175, 179
London   2, 24, 25, 27, 35–6, 71, 100, 157, 173, 175

mambo   82, 97–9, 103–5, 109, 111, 182
Martin, John   7, 43, 50–1, 54, 57, 59
masters   6, 61, 63–4, 111, 113, 129, 162, 173
Masters of Jazz concerts   64–66, 69, 70
Matter, Herbert   82, 85, 87, 95–7, 160, 161
Miller, Norma   42, 69, 95, 99, 102
minstrelsy   2, 19, 28–9, 42, 87, 143
modern dance   3, 11, 12, 18, 19, 33, 48, 70, 73, 93, 118, 182
Monaghan, Terry   4, 45, 94, 95, 130
Morrison, Lillian   1, 36, 49, 94, 107, 171, 173, 176–9

National Dance Congress   53–54
National Endowment for the Arts, (NEA)   96, 100, 115–16, 133, 158–9, 161, 168, 172–3
New Orleans   8, 9, 72, 84, 120, 135, 145, 160–1, 163–4, 182
New York
City College of New York   113
debut   49–50
New York Daily News   66

Index of Subjects

New York Times 43, 50, 62, 81, 86, 95, 125, 159, 162, 178-9
   Public Library (NYPL) 3, 21, 25, 33, 48, 79, 93, 94, 96, 103, 107, 173-5, 178-9
   State Council on the Arts (NYSCA) 159, 162, 167
   State University 116, 158, 161, 175

Odessa 20-2, 24, 157
Olympic Games 115-6, 126, 128
   Olympic Games Festival 122, 126, 130

Palladium 71, 97, 98, 103-5, 126
   Palladium champions 98
Paris 7, 25-39, 44, 48, 51-2, 62, 76, 82-3, 91, 126, 157, 172-3, 175, 181
   bohemian 21, 27, 30
   Conservatory 22, 123
   Latin Quarter 28, 33, 34
   Left Bank 32, 33, 51
Paris, Carl 3, 77
Parkettes 105, 106, 129-31
primitive, noble savage 30-1, 39, 42, 51, 55, 58, 142

Radio City Music Hall 40, 85, 122, 126, 131
ragtime 2, 6, 8, 9, 32, 96, 120, 182
Rag to Rock 6, 113-16, 120, 133, 140, 159
rhythm 3, 6, 12, 16, 19, 23-5, 28-9, 44, 47, 51, 89-90, 104, 109, 123, 143, 185
   African 20, 78-9, 99, 152
   African American 8, 9
   be-bop 81
   counter rhythms 10
   dancer 103
   definition 14-15, 17, 25, 182
   embodied 10, 20, 22, 31, 71, 171, 183
   impetus 10, 16, 60
   jazz 53, 58, 171
   in motion 10, 22, 176
   motivation of 88, 171
   organic 16, 17, 93
   polycentrism 11
   polyrhythm 10

syncopation 8, 17, 31, 58, 97
   the Prince of 46
   withheld, pause 58, 83, 110
   of words 177, 180
rhythmic 1, 8, 14, 71, 78, 148
   awareness 22, 24
   creations, originalities 15, 29
   gymnastics 22-3
   imperative, pull 12, 15, 183
   patterns 10, 15, 20, 90
   rhythmically 77, 78, 86
   rhythmic puzzle 12
   withheld 58, 171
      pause 58, 83, 90, 98
rock 'n' roll 6, 18, 20, 88, 97, 106, 113, 114, 121, 129, 157, 168, 169, 185
Roseland Ballroom 45, 71, 102, 172

Savoy Ballroom 1, 6, 9, 16, 24, 39-48, 62-6, 68-72, 79, 82, 88, 94, 96, 97, 99-103, 106, 122, 129, 134, 180
   aficionado, habitue, originators 1, 60, 181
   dancers 45, 62, 64, 67, 69, 75, 87, 97, 99, 102, 113
   King of 45
   Manor 97, 102, 134
   routines, dances 73, 96
   style 102, 162
   Swingsters 6, 60, 61, 92, 114
   The Track 4, 11, 47, 97
Scherzer, Mark 94, 172, 173, 175
Shuffle Along 9, 85, 88, 125
Sissle, Noble 88, 159
Smithsonian Institution 21, 26, 89, 104, 110, 113, 115, 117
Snead, Stella 5, 173
Sommer, Sally 4, 39, 91, 97, 174, 177
spirit 14, 17, 20, 31, 75-6, 80, 81, 86, 93, 101, 111, 120, 125, 142, 171, 174, 180, 185
   getting the spirit, got the spirit, embodying the spirit 77, 148
The Spirit Moves 1, 3, 4, 6, 64-5, 68, 82-3, 86, 91-6, 105, 111-12, 129-30, 132, 133, 162, 172, 178-80

spirit of Africa   76, 157
spiritual   9, 10, 13, 75, 91, 145, 168
spirituality   13, 110
spiritually   16
spirituals   50, 79
Stearns, Marshall   3, 16, 41, 67–8, 72–4, 82
  Newport Jazz Festival   68, 126
Sullivan, Ed   66, 71, 99, 102, 106, 165
swing   11, 14–15, 39, 47, 88, 113–14, 120
  dance   3, 4, 6, 12, 18, 19, 24, 94, 101
  dancer   44, 66, 94
  dance revival   18, 19, 69
  dance websites   64, 94
    Swing it Seattle, Mark Hikara   112
    Yehoodi, Riki Panganiban   99, 101
    Jassdancer, Peter Loggins   101, 102
    Swungover, Robert White   95, 98, 101, 133
  enthusiasts, revivalists   100, 111, 128–9
  era   14, 15, 81, 113–14, 120
  swing music   7, 15–16, 18, 55
Switzerland   37, 91, 116, 131, 157

Tels, Ellen   24, 25, 27, 31
Thomas, Herman "Dutch"   60, 172, 175–7, 179
Tsiperovitsch, Maria Mura   5, 21, 33, 34
  Boris   24, 35, 36

David   24, 36, 37
Fanny (Chaprik)   22, 24, 32, 35–7, 157, 177

Uncle Tom   115, 119, 162, 165
University of Arkansas (UArk)   117
US Information Agency (USIA)   117, 121, 137, 139, 153
  Service (USIS)   118, 137, 139, 140, 146–7, 149–50
US State Department Bureau of Educational and Cultural Affairs (CU)   115–17, 133, 137, 138, 140, 149, 152
  Cultural Presentations (CP)   116, 129, 137, 140

Vienna   21–7, 29, 31–3, 35, 157

Washington, DC   6, 28, 115, 116, 140
Webb, Chick   16, 122, 128
Wickre, Karen   29, 42, 57
Wilson, John   68, 86, 103
Wilson, Olly   9, 10

YMHA Dance Center   49, 68, 73, 89
  92nd Street   53, 126
Yurchenco, Henrietta   113, 114, 137, 161, 178